Belize: A Concise History

Belize: A Concise History

P. A. B. Thomson

MACMILLAN
CARIBBEAN

Macmillan Education
Between Towns Road, Oxford OX4 3PP
A division of Macmillan Publishers Limited
Companies and representatives throughout the world

www.macmillan-caribbean.com

ISBN 0 333 77925 8

First published 2004

Designed by Jeffrey Tabberner
Typeset by EXPO Holdings, Malaysia
Illustrated by Tek-Art
Cover design by Gary Fielder at AC Design
Cover illustration shows Belize Harbour in 1888.

Printed and bound in Thailand

2007   2006   2005   2004
10   9   8   7   6   5   4   3   2   1

Contents

List of Illustrations   vi
List of Maps   vii
Preface   ix
Introduction   xiii

 1 The Original Inhabitants   1
 2 Spanish Conquerors and British Adventurers   10
 3 External Rivalry and Internal Dissent: The Eighteenth
     Century   21
 4 The Settlement at the Beginning of the Nineteenth Century   37
 5 Slavery and Emancipation   53
 6 Land   65
 7 Constitutional Development   75
 8 Mexico and the Maya   88
 9 Disputes between Britain and Guatemala   98
10 Development of the Economy in the Nineteenth Century   108
11 The Colony at the Beginning of the Twentieth Century   117
12 Wars, a Hurricane and a Global Slump: The First Half of the
     Twentieth Century   127
13 The Economy after the Second World War   139
14 The Road towards Independence   153
15 The Dispute with Guatemala in the Twentieth Century   165
16 The Nation State at the Beginning of the Twenty-first
     Century   179

Index   187

List of Illustrations

1 A late classic (c.600–900) vase from Buenavista, Cayo District. Courtesy of the Belize Historical Society.
2 A Maya site, Altun Ha. Courtesy of the Belize Archives Department.
3 The Belize River settlement in 1787.
4 The first bridge over the Belize River, built in the early nineteenth century. Courtesy of the Craig family Collection.
5 St John's Cathederal, work on which started in 1812. Courtesy of Nicholas Gilliard.
6 The former Government House, built in 1815. Courtesy of the Belize Archives Department.
7 The Belize River mouth, from Fort George, 1842. Courtesy of the Craig Family Collection.
8 Woodcutters about to fell a mahogany tree. Courtesy of the Craig Family Collection.
9 Mahogany tree cut in lengths for transport to the river bank. Courtesy of the Craig Family Collection.
10 A cattle team loaded up with mahogany trunks. Courtesy of the Craig Family Collection.
11 Transporting logs by cattle team. Courtesy of the Craig Family Collection.
12 Mahogany logs in the lower reaches of the Belize River. Courtesy of the Craig Family Collection.
13 Squaring up logs for export. Courtesy of the Craig Family Collection.
14 Harvesting bananas. Courtesy of the Belize Archives Department.
15 Harvesting chicle. Courtesy of the Belize Archives Department.
16 A Maya woman. Courtesy of the Belize Archives Department.
17 The Stann Creek Railway. Courtesy of the Belize Archives Department.
18 The Court House. Courtesy of the Belize Archives Department.
19 The market. Courtesy of the Belize Archives Department.
20 The hospital. Courtesy of the Belize Archives Department.
21 North Front Street. Courtesy of the Belize Archives Department.
22 The harbour entrance. Courtesy of the Belize Archives Department.
23 The Parade Ground. Courtesy of the Belize Archives Department.

24 The aftermath of the 1931 hurricane. Courtesy of the Belize Archives Department.
25 San Pedro town on Ambergris Cay. Courtesy of the Belize Archives Department.
26 Independence Plaza, Belmopan. Courtesy of the Belize Archives Department.
27 The Princess Hotel, Belize city. Courtesy of the Belize Archives Department.
28 Lobster smacks at the entrance to Haulover Creek, Belize city. Courtesy of the Belize Archives Department.
29 The lighthouse at Fort George, Belize City. Courtesy of the Belize Archives Department.

List of Maps

A Modern Caribbean   viii

B Modern Belize   xi

C The Maya world   2

D Maya sites in Belize   6

E Early British settlements in Mexico and Central America   14

F Battle of St George's Cay   34

G British Honduras in the mid-nineteenth century   84

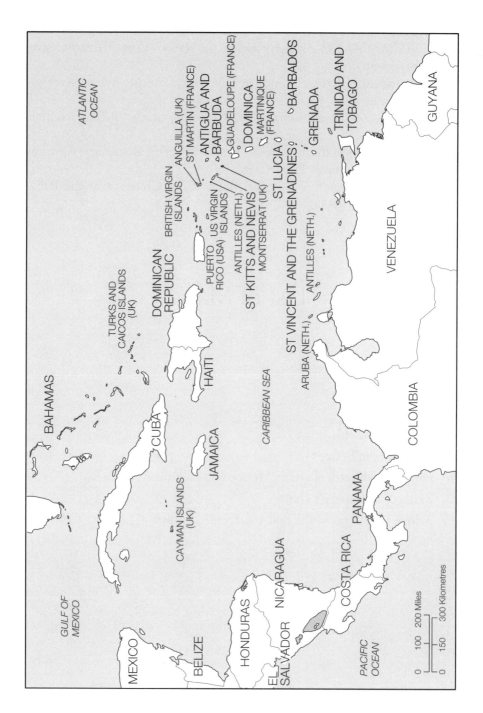

Map A Modern Caribbean

Preface

This book does not pretend to be a comprehensive textbook like Narda Dobson's *History of Belize*, published in 1973, or a re-interpretation of Belizean history like Assad Shoman's *Thirteen Chapters of the History of Belize*, which came out twenty years later. Nor is it primarily a social study, which would have involved recourse to oral history and the somewhat special skills that calls for. It rather aims simply to set out a concise and, as far as possible, factual framework of political, administrative and economic history, to introduce the student, or the curious visitor, to the subject. It takes the unfashionable form of an overall narrative, but each chapter is designed to be free-standing, so that the reader who wants to tackle a single aspect or period of the country's history can do so.

Much of the book was written in London. That was because England is where I live, and because financial constraints have limited my time in Belize since retirement to two visits totalling just over two months. Living in England on the other hand did have the advantage that I was able to study at leisure the Colonial Office records at the Public Record Office in London. These remain the principal source of our information on the political and economic development of Belize during the eighteenth and nineteenth centuries, arguably the formative period in its modern history. That does not mean that what follows has evolved as a justification of British policy. I have avoided judgements of that kind beyond the self-evident one that British policy was less than generous. Otherwise I have tried to allow the recorded facts of what was decided and what happened to speak for themselves.

For two chapters where the topics have been exhaustively investigated by specialists, the text is drawn entirely from the secondary sources listed. The other fourteen chapters are annotated with references to a broad range of both primary and secondary sources. The former are mostly, but by no means entirely, drawn from Colonial Office files. In the latter case there are multiple references to information dug up by Nigel Bolland, if not to the conclusions in his three books. Another debt is to R.A. Humphries, whose pioneering work on cross-border relations in the nineteenth century identified for re-examination, for Chapters 8 and 9, the appropriate Foreign Office files in the Public Record Office.

More personal gratitude is due for the unstinting help of staff at the Archives Department in Belize, and the Public Record Office, Foreign Office and Canning House Libraries, and Foreign Office Research Department in London; and for the generosity of the Craig family in lending a wide selection of photographs and engravings from their collection. Last, but by no means least, I owe sincere thanks for their advice to Dr Joseph Palacio, Bobby Leslie, David Gibson, Derek Courtenay, Henry Canton, Said Flores and Keith Arnold in Belize; and Dr Norman Hammond, Jeremy Hobbs and Sir Roger Hervey in Britain. Interpretation of that advice was mine, and they bear no responsibility for what appears in print. But without their help there would have been more errors than there may still be.

Peter Thomson
Sherborne, Dorset

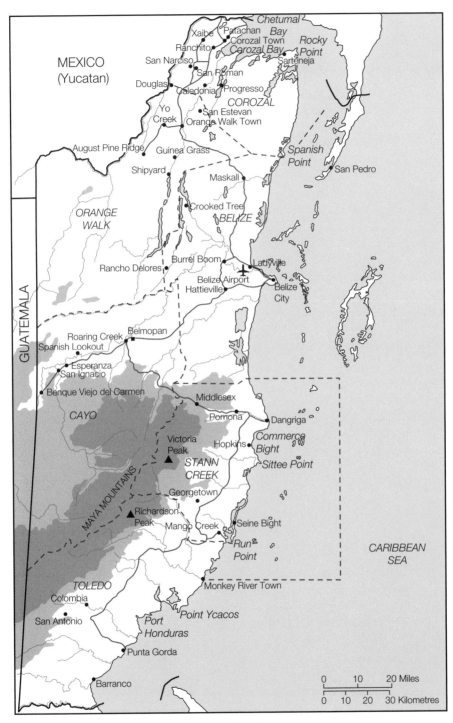

Map B Modern Belize

Introduction

Belize is on the eastern coast of Central America. It is a country with a singular history and therefore identity. In early history, an important part of the civilisation of the Maya; in the seventeenth, eighteenth and early nineteenth centuries, a British settlement under Spanish sovereignty. In due course it became a British Crown Colony claimed by a neighbouring country, Guatemala. Today, it is an independent English-speaking United Nations member state in an otherwise Spanish-speaking region. A country which still acknowledges the British monarch as Head of State even though surrounded by others with a strong republican tradition, it forms an enclave which has grown up under the rule of English common law in a part of the world where the legal tradition is Roman. These differences are lodged in the consciousness of Belizeans as is awareness of the long history of territorial dispute to which they gave rise.

Lying between the latitudes of 16 and 18½ degrees north, Belize is a tropical but not an equatorial country: the temperature during the months of the European winter is slightly cooler than during the rest of the year. The climate is, however, different from that of the eastern Caribbean islands on the same latitude: whereas the Leeward Islands broadly enjoy seven months a year of dry weather and five of wet, in Belize the case is the reverse. On the other hand, Belize is much less frequently hit by hurricanes. Most vulnerable to these storms when they do come are the small islands, or cays, scattered along the barrier reef 10–20 miles offshore. This is one of Belize's most striking features. Co-terminous with the length of the mainland coastline, it is second only in extent to the Great Barrier Reef of northeastern Australia. Inside it, the waters off the northern half of Belize are shallow. Access for deep-sea shipping to this, ashore, more penetrable part of the country is limited to a narrow and tortuous channel from the reef to the port of Belize City. This difficulty of access to the main settlement was to prove a vital defence when external attack was threatened during the eighteenth century.

As to the topography of the mainland, the northern half of Belize divides into three belts as the traveller moves inland and slowly upwards from the coast towards the western and northwestern borders with, respectively, Guatemala and Mexico. First there is a quite narrow strip of mangrove swamp generally suitable for neither habitation nor farming. Then there is a broader belt of savannah country, dominated by stunted pine, some of which has proved more exploitable. Lastly there is a wide swathe of denser hardwood forest only cleared in comparatively small patches where there has been a particular incentive to do so. This was the source of most of the timber that Europeans came to extract, on which the country's economy rested for so long.

The southern half of the country, also bounded by Guatemala and largely taken up with the Maya mountains, is wetter, steeper, and even less penetrable than the northern half. With rainfall three times that of the north, this is where the true rain forest lies. Not quite so dense on the narrow lowland belt between the mountains and the sea, where a system of shifting (milpa) cultivation continues, it is more so in the mountains themselves except for an area (the Bald Hills) which, for geological reasons, is completely open.

Until the last century, access to this difficult interior was for the north largely by means of three longish rivers (Hondo, New and Belize) and for the south via a number of shorter rivers running down from the Maya mountains. The fourth longer river, the Sarstoon, forms the territory's southern boundary with Guatemala. Apart from San Pedro on Ambergris Cay, the main towns of Belize lie either at the mouths of these rivers (Corozal in the north, Belize City itself, and, in the south, Dangriga – formerly Stann Creek – and Punta Gorda); or further up the northern rivers (Orange Walk in the north and Belmopan and San Ignacio in the west). The inland towns now also lie either on the main road leading north to the Yucatan peninsula of Mexico or on the one road which leads west to Guatemala.

The building of these two roads, and a third connecting the western district to the southern coastline, has enabled the development in the last fifty years of a diverse and sustainable commercial agriculture to replace timber extraction as forest resources were depleted. These newer industries – sugar, citrus fruit and bananas – are the mainstay of the contemporary economy, although tourism is now catching up.

Although Belize is larger in area than Jamaica, El Salvador, or even pre-1967 Israel, it has a much smaller population. But its people are as diverse as the landscape. The two main groups are the Creoles, most of whom speak at home a dialect variant of English, and the mestizos, whose first language is Spanish. The principal minorities are the Maya Indians, of the same stock as the original inhabitants and divided between two sub-groups, the Ketchi of the south and the Mopan of the northwest; the Garifuna, descendants of Africans, with an admixture of Carib blood, exiled to the Bay of Honduras from the eastern Caribbean by the British in the late eighteenth century; and the Mennonites, who sought escape from the advanced material civilisation of North America during the second half of the last century. Each of these groups is culturally and linguistically, as well as ethnically, distinct. There are, too, small Chinese, (Asian) Indian, and middle-eastern communities who also, to a varying extent, maintain their own languages and customs. But enough unity in this considerable diversity comes from acceptance across the society of common institutions, based largely on English models, and a lingua franca, again English, with which to sustain the functioning of a nation state. Since independence in 1981, this has been characterised by a striking degree of internal political stability even if relations with the country's principal neighbour have been much more difficult.

This then is mainly the story of the formation and evolution of an unusually heterogeneous society over the last three centuries. It is a story that may explain two characteristics that strike an outsider today: tolerance and individualism, not a natural combination, but one which sits easily enough in Belize. Not only very different political views but also fundamental cultural differences are accepted in this society where migration has been and is still the norm. But at the same time each Belizean has his own opinions about most things and does not hesitate to express them. The explanation may lie in the primitive egalitarianism of the early logging camps; the compromises that had to be made at a later stage between masters and slaves when working in the bush; and the struggles first to retain the Public Meeting, then to secure a local majority in the legislature, and finally to achieve an all-elected assembly, in each case so that individual voices could be heard or represented. Of course these voices were for most of Belize's history the voices of a minority; and internal struggles between those who were represented and those who were not also loom large, as the following chapters show. But in a broader sense what distinguishes the political history of Belize is surely the steady assimilation of outsiders coming in and an equally steady resistance to externally imposed structures. For the economy there is another recurrent theme: the constant effort to establish new industries as existing resources run down or become less competitive. That continues.

Such are the hallmarks of the story that follows, and arguably what makes this small nation distinct today. But before exploring those themes it is necessary first to describe a much earlier society, traces of which remain, then to summarise the circumstances which first brought Europeans to this part of the western Caribbean as that earlier society declined.

1

The Original Inhabitants

The cultural identity of Belize was not always as mixed as it is now. Indeed for much of the fifteen centuries before the irruption of the Spaniards into the western hemisphere it was broadly homogeneous. For Belize then was a part of that accomplished civilisation known generically as Mesoamerica. For the Maya, who inhabited the eastern portion of the Mesoamerican region, the golden age passed with the advent of the tenth century. By the sixteenth they were living not only in much smaller communities than before, but also at a much simpler level. But the organisational, intellectual, artistic and architectural achievements of the Classic period of Maya civilisation, from CE 250 to 900, are nonetheless a part of Belize's heritage, and visible remains are there for all to see.

The common cultural denominators in the constituent parts of Mesoamerica, where a late flowering produced the highly unified Aztec empire of central and southern Mexico, were large-scale social organisation, imposing and highly decorated tombs and associated monuments, hieroglyphic writing, documents made of bark or skin, an elaborate calendar based on detailed astronomical knowledge, human sacrifice, and a complex pantheon of divinities. All of these features characterised the Maya polities which evolved in the highlands of central Guatemala and the Chiapas region on the Pacific side of southern Mexico; lowland Tabasco and the Yucatan Peninsula on the Atlantic side; and, again a lowland region, all of Belize, western Honduras, and, perhaps most significantly, the Peten region of northern Guatemala.

It has been argued that the origins of the two most important of these characteristics, public architecture and a system of writing, were, respectively, the Olmec culture of the Gulf of Mexico coast, which flourished for eight hundred years from 1200 BC, and the broadly contemporaneous Zapotec culture of the Oaxaca region of southwestern Mexico. To the Olmec the Maya have also been said, with less evidence, to have owed the complex calendar which in its final development enabled them to date events with precision. In this case more remote influences have been suggested too, including the possibility that Maya astronomy and cosmology might be ultimately traceable to comparable systems in China and

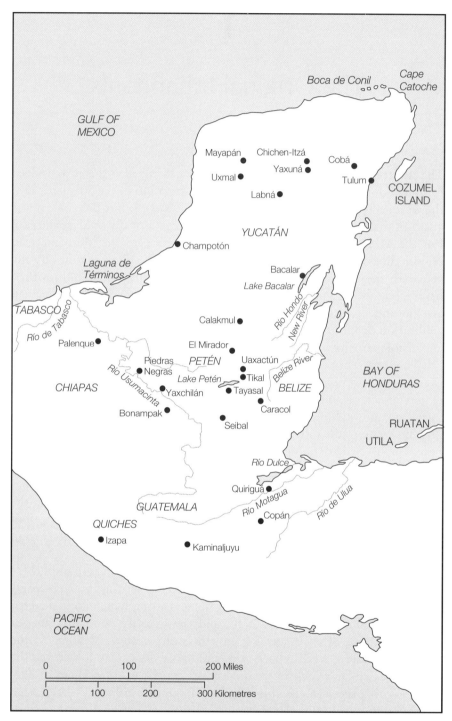

Map C The Maya world

southeast Asia. But the more general modern conclusion is that to a large extent the Maya civilisation evolved independently, as one school of thought has always held. Although it latterly influenced societies further north, and was itself then subject to heavy influence from that direction, in its early years it is less likely to have absorbed from elsewhere the greater part of the cultural basis on which its people built.

Before the Classic era of the Maya civilisation, there was a 1500 year period, from about 1250 BC to CE 250, during which that process took place. Already farmers, with a staple diet of maize, the Maya established themselves in progressively larger settlements as, from about 600 BC, they developed their agriculture with drained wetland field systems. Shortly afterwards they also started to build stepped platform monuments. This led to the emergence of some large cities such as El Mirador and Izapa, where the monuments were inscribed with motifs from Mayan mythology and were more diverse in design. Much of the style and iconography of this evolving Maya art appeared in later centres after the end of these early polities in the first century CE.

The Maya who led the way in taking this development forward were those of the southern part of their homeland, the Chiapas and Guatemalan highlands and the low-lying Pacific coast of Guatemala. The most important of the Maya cities towards the end of the Preclassic period, significant for both its size and the quality of its remains, is Kaminaljuyu, on the edge of Guatemala City. Sadly, much of this site has been buried under the urban sprawl that now blights Guatemala's capital. But enough has been recovered to show that its people were capable not only of constructing elaborate monuments, but also of executing large-scale and complex carving in stone, and fashioning pottery utensils of a high aesthetic quality. Unlike Maya people in other regions at that time, they also adopted a hieroglyphic system of writing, and developed an ideal of dynastic kingship.

Curiously, Kaminaljuyu, like El Mirador and Izapan before it, was abandoned around the beginning of the third century CE, and the city was not brought to life again until the whole of the southern Maya area came under the influence of the central Mexican Teotihuacan culture somewhat later. But enough of the imagination and ideas of the people there and nearby had spread northwards for the development of the new Maya civil-isation to continue, energised also by native inspiration, in those central and northern areas. Particularly in the Peten region of northern Guatemala, massive and highly decorated temple monuments had been rising around ceremonial plazas from about 300 BC onwards, as already noted in the case of El Mirador. These were highly decorated, and towards the end of the Preclassic period began to embody the corbelling that was to be the hallmark of Maya architecture. These developments, together with advances in the design and decoration of Maya ceramics, retained a striking vigour as they continued into the Classic period. Although writing was transmitted from the south more slowly than architecture, stone sculpture and pottery, essentially the only major characteristic that was missing from Classic Maya culture by CE 250 was the fully developed Long Count calendar, which was to enable precise dating of events in Maya inscriptions.

Belize, together with the Tabasco region (on the southern edge of the Gulf of Mexico) and the Peten, was at the epicentre of this culture in its full flowering. This lowland area saw a growth in population to perhaps 8–10 million at its height, compared with an overall total of 2 million for the number of Maya in Central America today. Some estimates put the population of the pre-eminent lowland site of Tikal in the Peten, founded in the late Preclassic period (BC 300–CE 250) and traditionally taken as the largest of the Maya cities, at close to 70,000 at the height of its influence in the eighth century. Excavations in recent years suggest that Caracol, on the Belize side of the border, might possibly have grown at some point in the Late Classic period (CE 600–900) to an even larger size. Although it seems never to have become the supreme regional centre, Caracol's weight in the shifting pattern of alliances that marked that period was probably crucial. The other city in the central Maya area that was at least comparable in size was Calakmul, seventy miles north of Tikal which it actually, indeed decisively, eclipsed in the sixth and seventh centuries. In the Yucatan, where this high culture also quite quickly took hold, the major Classic centre was Uxmal, founded about CE 600, in the middle of the period. It lasted as such until the ascendancy of the central Mexican Toltecs in the northern area of the Maya homeland, which brought about a significant if not complete change in cultural life there.

Besides the massive site of Caracol near the Guatemalan border, there are other important remains in Belize of centres that were active in this era. At Cerros, near the border with Mexico and already a flourishing centre in the Preclassic age, there is an interesting group of plaster representations of masks forming an elaborate cosmological diagram like those on some of the buildings at Tikal. At the comparatively small site of Xunantunich, in the west, there is a magnificent Late Classic (CE 600–900) main pyramid 127 feet high. In the far south, on a high ridge near Punta Gorda, is the even later (CE 730) site of Lubaantun, large (five main and thirteen secondary plazas), but curiously lacking in stone carving and only occupied for 150 years. At the upper New River site of Lamanai on the other hand, where there is a group of large late Preclassic (BC 300–CE 250) temple-pyramids, construction continued throughout the Classic period, and the site seems to have been one of the last to be abandoned. Altun Ha, between the New and the Belize rivers and where the population has been estimated at 8–10,000, also continued to function as a city at least into the tenth century, although construction had stopped before the beginning of the Classic age. That all these sites are within a hundred-mile swathe of countryside shows the extent to which Belize, possibly with a population of as much as a million, was a part of this extraordinary cultural phenomenon.

As already indicated, the Classic period is conventionally divided by archaeologists into two halves, early and late. The break, in 600, was preceded by two centuries of cultural influence from Teotihuacan, then the dominant central Mexican metropolis. This particularly affected the southern area, which became Mexican-controlled and where Maya cultural evolution had in any case been less energetic following the demise of Kaminaljuyu. It led to the emergence of a hybrid culture there which saw no further development in technical or artistic terms, and indeed the disappearance of some established forms. A degree of the same influence, though less than in the south, penetrated the Maya culture of the central and northern areas. But following the fall of Teotihuacan around 600, these lowland Maya polities flourished as city states, albeit competitively with each other, largely free of external pressure. Under its quasi-divine ruler, each state was run by an hereditary elite, who provided the senior administrators, military officers and, as important, clergy. From the city that was his seat of power, the ruler and his nobility governed, via a complex system of ritual, a society of commoners, who worked the land, and slave menials.

In the central area of the Maya civilisation (which included Belize), these cities were usually sited on low ridges, in the drier northern area (the Yucatan) close to well systems known as *cenotes*. Despite evidence of recurrent warfare between states, defensive earthworks were the exception rather than the rule. The cities were not laid out according to any fixed plan. The temple monuments at the heart of each site were generally pyramids built on high stepped platforms and surmounted with the characteristic elongated stone crown of the Classic Maya known as the roof comb. There was much rebuilding, so that earlier monuments were buried inside later ones. Decoration consisted of beautifully painted stucco murals and highly wrought carved stone *stelae* (vertical slabs) and altars. Both painting and sculpture were narrative in theme and baroque in style. In both cases there was what has been called 'order in complexity'. Gods and individual human beings were portrayed, in the case of stone sculpture in both low relief, where the Maya excelled, and in three dimensions. A typical theme was a victory scene, either depicting the battle itself, the subsequent celebration or a parade of prisoners. Other public buildings around the central plaza or plazas were one-storey stone palaces mounted

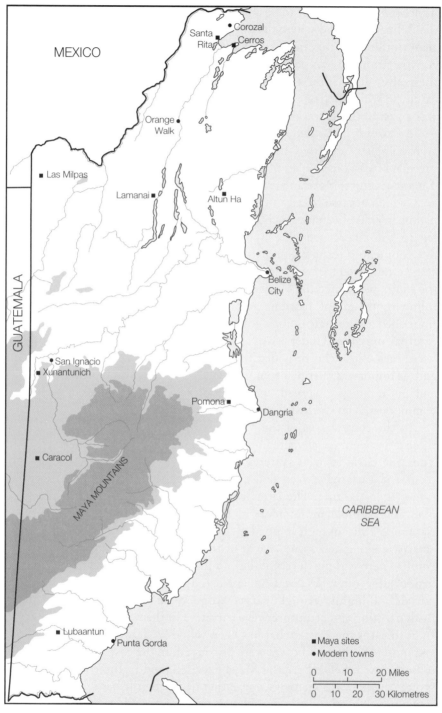

Map D Maya sites in Belize

on lower platforms. Another feature to have survived at most sites is the ceremonial ball-court, also situated close to the centre, where some kind of rubber-ball game of religious and political significance was played.

The cultural achievements of the Maya Classic period were not limited to architecture and associated ornamentation. The Maya of the period also produced a wide range of pottery, some of it finely sculpted. It was highly decorated by means of techniques which included incising, ribbing and fluting, and the use of polychrome. They were also expert at working jade, marble and shell. Some of these things, together with the salt that they produced in the Yucatan and the cacao that was cultivated more widely, they traded as far afield as central Mexico. But perhaps their greatest achievements other than buildings and art lay in the field of astronomy. Not only were they able to measure the precise length of the solar and lunar years, they also mastered the calculations necessary to predict the occurrence of eclipses. As to planetary observation, the Maya certainly measured, and could predict, the movement of Venus, which had a particular importance for them. They were probably also familiar with the movements of Mars and Jupiter, and there is some evidence to suggest that they may have developed a stellar zodiac.

Their knowledge of astronomy enabled the Maya during the Classic period to exploit the sophisticated Long Count calendar referred to earlier. This may not have been a Maya invention, but it seems to have been a system that the Maya were the first to take into widespread use. Unlike earlier 'round' calendars, it provided an absolute basis for dating events in that dates were measured from a fixed time point in the remote past. This in turn, together with the hieroglyphic writing which defied scholars until the 1950s, enabled the Maya to record something of their history. Naturally that history focuses on the rise and fall of dynasties: the accession of kings, their marriages, the births of offspring, alliances, victories over neighbouring states, and kings' deaths. There is thus emerging, as work proceeds on deciphering hieroglyphics on lintels and stelae, at least a shadowy framework within which to explore other evidence of the history of these hitherto mysterious people.

The overall picture that emerges, then, is of a people whose administrative, artistic, and intellectual achievements were unrivalled in the western hemisphere and unusual in the rest of the world; of a collection of city states relations between which were as often hostile as peaceful; of a way of life that nonetheless, partly through extensive trade, brought enough stability and prosperity to support a surprisingly large settled population throughout the northern half of Central America.

What caused this accomplished civilisation to disintegrate in the early ninth century? In the south the Maya never recovered from first the overlordship of Teotihuacan during the fifth and sixth centuries, then the later domination of a linguistically Mayan but culturally Mexican people from the Vera Cruz region. In the north, the Yucatan peninsula, they were also subjected to strong influence from elsewhere, particularly from the highland warrior Toltecs who then dominated central Mexico. Although the classic Maya culture did not wither as rapidly as in the south, and indeed Uxmal continued to flourish for nearly another century, some of the impressive remains of the partly Toltec city at Chichen, which overtook it, show a martial spirit characteristic of these formidable people. By that time the local rulers of the Classic period had in any case been supplanted by a Maya group from the Tabasco region, the Itza. They in turn were displaced by another dynasty, the Kokoom, whose rule was centred on a new city at Mayapan and lasted until only fifty years before the arrival of the conquistadores. Their fall marked the final disappearance of such elite cultural energy as remained in the area.

But the strangest collapse of the Maya kingdoms came in the central area, principally modern Belize and the Peten. There the destructive force seems to have been internal. Various theories have been put forward. The three most widely held seem to be overpopulation, economic degradation, and social revolution, or indeed the three together. The decline may have started in the second half of the eighth century, as the cities began to outgrow the capacity of the rural economy to sustain them. Certainly it was steep throughout the ninth, with a falling population and a halt to construction. The cities were not all abandoned at the same time. Some, including Lamanai in Belize, lasted long after collapse elsewhere. But most were deserted by the great bulk of their populations, and all traces of kingship and sophisticated cultural activity disappeared. As that was lost, so were the knowledge, the techniques, the intellectual drive, and the creative spirit of the elite who had lived in these centres of civilisation. What the Spaniards found in their initial exploration in the sixteenth century were small communities of subsistence farmers who were neither settled nor organised beyond the most primitive level. The glory of the classic Maya age had long departed.

On their arrival the Spaniards discovered three main groups of Maya living in the territory now known as Belize. The total population has been estimated variously at between 50,000 and 400,000, mostly living on the rivers and lagoons that lace the countryside. The group with which the newcomers had most contact was that living around modern Chetumal and Corozal. Controlling the mouths of the Hondo and New Rivers, and the coastline either side, this group played an important part in the coastal trade. The other group with which the Spaniards had significant dealings, if only in the form of missionary activity and occasional punitive expeditions, was the Chan, also known as the Muzul and (from the Maya name for the New River) the Dzuluinicob. They inhabited an area extending to the west from a line between modern Orange Walk and the Sitee River. Their main centre was at Tipu a little south of modern San Ignacio. The third group, the Manche Chol of southern Belize, seems to have been largely left alone by the Spaniards until the end of the seventeenth century. All three groups became from time to time a focus of resistance to the rule of the European invaders further north and west. But they are said to have been severely weakened by disease caught from the newcomers; and by the time the latter began to occupy the Yucatan peninsula in the 1520s, the European invaders were in any case already well on the way to domination of the whole region.

Sources

Michael Coe, *The Maya*, fourth edition, New York (1987).
Norman Hammond, *Ancient Maya Civilisation*, Cambridge (1982).
Grant D. Jones (ed.), *Anthropology and History in Yucatan*, Austin, Texas and London (1977).
Simon Martin and Nikolai Grube, *Chronicle of the Maya Kings and Queens*, London (2000).
J. Eric Thompson, *The Maya of Belize*, 1970 manuscript, published Belize (1988).

2

Spanish Conquerors and British Adventurers

Spain

Christopher Columbus established the first Spanish settlement in the western hemisphere, on the island of Hispaniola, during his initial voyage of exploration in 1492 and 1493. This was consolidated in 1494 during his second voyage. Hispaniola, now divided between the modern states of Haiti and the Dominican Republic, remained the base of Spanish activity and influence for the next thirty years. But the Spaniards became aware of the existence of the long Caribbean shore of Central America early on in that period with Columbus' fourth exploratory voyage, from 1502 to 1504. While searching for a strait or channel leading to India, he discovered and followed the coastline of what is now Honduras and Nicaragua. It is not known whether he sighted the cays of Belize then. What is more likely is that two slightly later explorers, Vicente Pinzon, one of Columbus' captains in 1492, and Juan de Solis, did so when they entered the Gulf of Honduras together on a voyage of more detailed discovery, in 1508 and 1509.

The energy behind Spanish ambitions became apparent with the appointment in 1509 of Columbus' son, Don Diego Colon, as Governor of the Indies residing in the main settlement in Hispaniola, Santo Domingo. Within two years they had occupied Cuba and Jamaica, and established a colony at Darien on the Caribbean shore of what is now Panama. By 1517, following Balboa's dramatic crossing to the Pacific coast four years earlier, they had conquered the isthmus and begun to occupy modern Costa Rica and Nicaragua. The year 1517 also saw, further north, the first of a series of expeditions leading to the astonishing conquest of the Aztecs of central Mexico; and it was from there that the Spaniards came quite quickly to occupy the territory which surrounds Belize: the Yucatan peninsula of Mexico, Guatemala, and Honduras.

That first expedition inside the Gulf of Mexico was led by Hernandez de Cordoba. Having rounded Cape Catoche, which encloses the Gulf of Mexico from the south, Cordoba explored the western shore of the

Yucatan peninsula, landing at various points as he did so, as far south as modern-day Champoton, just beyond Campeche. He was followed the next year by Juan de Grijalva, who, having taken possession of the island of Cozumel just outside the Gulf, extended Cordoba's exploration to the area of Tampico, halfway along its western side. These two voyages laid the ground for a third expedition the stated aim of which was further discovery, but which for the leader and for most of those who signed up with him was intended from the start as a voyage of colonisation. The leader was of course Hernan Cortes, matched as a 'conquistador' only by Francisco Pizarro, who, five years later, embarked on his discovery and, later, conquest of the Incas of Peru.[1]

Setting off from Cuba in February 1519 with a force of five hundred soldiers and a hundred sailors in eleven ships, Cortes landed near the site of present-day Vera Cruz at Easter to begin a campaign which, within two and a half years, made him master of central Mexico. Because that involved the total defeat of the one organised military power in the region, it also created the conditions for a rapid southwards expansion of Spanish power soon after the Aztec capital had been secured. In 1523 Pedro de Alvarado, one of Cortes' subordinate commanders, set out to conquer what is now Guatemala, a process which was broadly accomplished within four years; while concurrently Cristobal de Olid, another of Cortes' generals, led an invasion by sea of the northern coast of modern Honduras, founding the city of Trujillo. In 1524, because Olid was claiming the government of the Honduran coast in his own right, Cortes sent another expedition there under Francisco de las Casas. At the end of that year Cortes then decided to assert his personal supremacy in the region. To that end he himself led a remarkable southwards march overland from Tabasco in southern Mexico to Trujillo, a march which, topographical descriptions suggest, may have taken him through southwestern Belize.[2]

The achievement of a Spanish presence throughout the region was completed by yet another expedition, launched in 1527, to occupy the Yucatan peninsula. This was undertaken, under a quite separate commission from the Spanish crown, by Francisco de Montejo, who was duly appointed 'adelantado' (governor) of the area. In this case the campaign of pacification was a long one. It was not until twenty years later that resistance was sufficiently overcome for the Spaniards to establish a civil administration based at Merida.[3] This was because, unlike in central Mexico, the Spaniards were not fighting against a centrally organised kingdom, but rather against a collection of Maya tribes whose mode of warfare was mobile. It was in the Yucatan that Maya resistance to Spanish, and indeed Mexican, rule continued longer than anywhere else.

Meanwhile in 1531 Montejo's second-in-command Alonso Davila, with a force of fifty men, established a settlement in the far south of the province near present-day Chetumal. But a year later they had to evacuate it, the tiny garrison undertaking a difficult withdrawal in small boats to Honduras. It was then not until 1544 that a more serious Spanish expedition under Gaspar Pacheco, with a base at Bacalar where the Spanish fort still stands, began to pacify both the Chetumal and the Chan (or Dzuluinicob) Maya, and, in so doing, to penetrate northern Belize. Pacheco subdued the Chetumal Maya quite quickly, though Spanish power was challenged only two years later by Chetumal participation in a wider Maya revolt. It is likely, but not certain, that the Spaniards then also brought the Chan and their centre of Tipu under a degree of control, for a punitive expedition against them in 1568 has the appearance of attempted re-conquest rather than initial suppression. A 1582 list of nine religious missions established in what is now Belize certainly includes some in Chan territory. In 1608, however, the Spaniards had to launch a further expedition against Tipu; and subsequent harsh treatment as they attempted to consolidate their grip in the area led to yet another major rebellion in 1637–8 which seems to have dislodged them from present-day Belize altogether until the end of the seventeenth century.[4] Even then they chose not to stay.

These expeditions were essentially local initiatives undertaken overland, as lesser Spanish commanders tried to make their foothold around Bacalar more secure against the Maya of northern Belize. But Montejo's ambitions went beyond conquest of the Yucatan, where he left his son to complete the process, and the area immediately to the south of it. He himself aspired to a further-reaching southern horizon, where chaos had developed following Cortes' return from Honduras to Mexico in 1526. It was this that will have brought him into contact with the full extent of the Belize coastline. Seven years before a long campaign, from 1535, in northern Honduras, Montejo undertook a more detailed exploration than that of Pinzon-Solis of the coast south of Yucatan. This took him as far south and then east as the present-day Honduran port of Puerto Cortes.[5] Although he must have observed the cays of Belize and the Maya Mountains, there is no record of his landing on those shores south of Bacalar. That seems to have been left to British adventurers with a much more specific purpose over a hundred years later. By that time the Spanish grip on southern Mexico, Guatemala and Honduras had been consolidated.

Why the Spaniards did not make more effort to assert and retain control of wider Belize is not clear. The small settler community at Chetumal experienced considerable hardship when withdrawing southwards along the coastline of modern Belize in 1532.[6] They may have reported the terrain as both less hospitable and likely to be less productive than that of the Yucatan or of Honduras. A simpler explanation might be administrative. In 1544 Montejo lost the position he had secured as governor of Honduras (as well as of Yucatan), which was joined in a new 'audiencia' (jurisdiction) with Nicaragua and Panama.[7] In 1549 authority in the area inland from the head of the Gulf of Honduras, subdued by another expedition sent by Montejo in 1546–7, passed to the Dominican order whose priority was conversion rather than conquest.[8] Belize then fell between three Spanish jurisdictions. It seems likely that for reasons of communications the Spaniards would have established some kind of at least military presence within the territory of modern Belize if Honduras and the Golfo Dulce area had been governed from Merida as Montejo intended. But, whatever the reason, the fact that they did not do so opened the way for others. These later arrivals then proved less easy to dislodge than other British settlers who established themselves at much the same time on different parts of the coast, both north of Belize, where the administrative writ of Spain did run, and much further south, where the Spaniards were unable to subdue the local Indians for a further century.

Britain

It was in somewhat different circumstances from those of the Spaniards that the British, or more correctly at that stage the English, had first entered the Caribbean around 1560. They had followed French raiders who had been active there during a series of wars between France and Spain over the previous thirty years. The English purpose was initially to break the Spanish embargo on foreign trade in the region and then, slightly later, to seize treasure that the Spaniards were beginning to ship home to finance pursuit of their European ambitions. Although no state of general war existed until 1585, Protestant England saw these shipments as an increasing threat. Queen Elizabeth therefore condoned aggressive behaviour by individual seamen if there was a shred of justification. This, and, later, open warfare, was the political context in which the slaving and buccaneering expeditions of John Hawkins and Francis Drake took place in the last forty years of the sixteenth century.[9]

This was followed by British occupation of Barbados and Antigua in the first thirty years of the next century. But because Spain already dominated Central America and the western Caribbean, British settlement in that part of the region was slower, small-scale, and very sporadic. The first documented colonisation was that of Providence Island off the coast

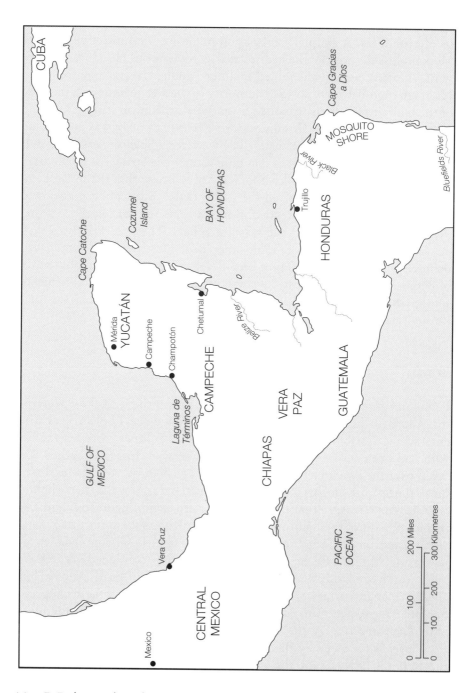

Map E Early British settlements in Mexico and Central America, shown in italics

of what is now Nicaragua, in 1631. A company, headed by the Earl of Warwick, had been formed to finance the venture, which was to be a tobacco plantation. The colonists themselves were Puritans inspired by a religious as well as a commercial ideal. Perhaps for that reason they were even less welcome to the Spaniards than the roving traders led by Hawkins seventy years before. By 1641 they had been evicted.[10] But during the previous twelve years British traders based on Providence had established themselves also not only on Ruatan, the largest of the Bay Islands from which they were expelled in 1642, but also around Cape Gracias a Dios on the Mosquito Coast of modern Honduras and Nicaragua. Curiously, and presumably because the native Indians of the Coast were better disposed towards English traders than towards Spanish rulers, these southern mainland settlements were never entirely suppressed: they came to an end much later by treaty agreement.

One writer, E. O. Winzerling, himself a twentieth-century settler, has speculated that traders from Providence also set up in modern Belize during the brief life of Warwick's colony.[11] His hypothesis is based on a connection he saw between some Belize place names and names associated with the Providence venture. The theory, which is self-evidently tenuous, has not been taken up by others. But the notion does persist that a British settlement was established on the Belize River at about the same time by a former pirate called Peter Wallace or Wallis. He is said to have been active in the central Caribbean during that decade until driven out of his base at Tortuga, off the north coast of modern Haiti, around 1640. But his appearance in Belize is suggested rather than borne out by such circumstantial evidence as there is, and again the case is based on a possible connection between Spanish renderings of his name and the name given to the territory. This theory has appealed in the past to more historians than has Winzerling's. But more recently it has been held that the name Belize derives from one of a number of appropriately descriptive Maya words, such as one meaning muddy waters. The truth of the matter seems unlikely to be resolved.

What is more certain is that around 1660 some twenty years after the end of the Providence Island experiment, British adventurers arrived on the Central American mainland to cut logwood(Haematoxylon campechianum). There was a considerable market in Europe for this tropical softwood because of the utility of its heart as a dyestuff for woollen goods. Spanish traders in the Yucatan had entered the business in the second half of the previous century. But a hundred years later demand exceeded supply by a sufficient margin to allow, despite Spanish objections, opportunities for others.

Britain's involvement in this trade seems to have developed soon after the end of her war with Spain between 1654 and 1659, during which much of the fighting took place in the Caribbean. That war, and especially the capture of Jamaica in 1655, led for the first time to a significant British presence close to the Spanish Main. At that stage such further interest as the British had in the region was focused principally on the Yucatan peninsula, in particular Cape Catoche, the northeast tip of the peninsula, and the stretch of coastline below Campeche, inside the southern arm of the Gulf of Mexico. Here logwood grew close to the sea. As Cuba had been the base for the opening up of Mexico by the Spaniards, so it was from Jamaica that the British in turn gained their foothold on the mainland. By 1669 a substantial number of British woodcutters were active in the region, especially around the Laguna de Terminos south of Campeche. Although motivated by trade rather than conquest, this intrusion represented a challenge to the complete supremacy hitherto enjoyed by Spain. Moreover many of those who gravitated to the primitive logging camps had been involved in the recent fighting against Spain as buccaneers, a status somewhere between that of the free-booting pirate who continued to infest the Caribbean and the more formally licensed privateer of later wars. The Treaty of Madrid of 1667, dealing with trade relations, formally banned buccaneering. This had the effect of reinforcing that element in the camps. Altogether it was not a situation to make for stability. Nor did a further treaty negotiated in 1670 by Lord Godolphin, the British Minister in Madrid, help: dealing with arrangements in the Americas, it acknowledged British sovereignty over territories the British occupied ('now hold and possess'); but the Spaniards interpreted that to mean places where there was a settled administration.[12] In this sense the treaty begged the question of the legitimacy of the logging communities which the British insisted had been established before the conclusion of both treaties. This lacuna was to bedevil international relations in the region for a long time to come.

For the late seventeenth century we are fortunate to have in the navigator William Dampier an acute observer of the life led by these adventurers and of the atmosphere in their settlements. Frustrated in his position as a salaried employee on a plantation in Jamaica, and before his adventures on the isthmus of Panama and his later voyage around the world, Dampier took his chances as a logwood cutter in the Campeche area between 1676 and 1678. He recorded particularly well the wildlife of the swamps where he worked. There is also a vivid description of a hurricane which destroyed the camp where he lived. But he describes too the harsh living conditions, the fluctuating relations between members of the group with which he worked, the arduous nature of cutting and carrying logwood, the excitement of hunting wild boar, and the *modus vivendi* reached with some if not all of the neighbouring Spanish settlers. The impression is of a hard life led by a rough crew.[13]

Successive governors of Jamaica tried to regulate the logwood trade and to obtain guidance on the status of the camps in both the Yucatan and what they called, when referring to modern Belize, the Bay of Honduras.[14] They also tried to restrain their more enterprising countrymen, with one governor, in 1682, even proposing withdrawal.[15] But while declining to declare these primitive settlements to be within the King's dominions,[16] the British government upheld the right of the woodcutters to work there. Although apparently not a bone of contention at the time of the 1670 Treaty, this foreign presence emerged as such the year after as the Spaniards sought to reassert their commercial monopoly. The character of the logwood cutters, and the attitude towards Spain engendered by their background, would have made matters worse. In 1672 the Spanish position hardened, with a royal decree that interlopers on the Mexican and Central American mainland were to be treated as pirates.[17] The same year the British Minister in Madrid referred to tension when he observed in a despatch that 'if the cutters would restrain themselves to that alone in places remote from towns and avoiding depredations, the Spaniards may not authorise (their activity) but they may connive'.[18] In the Yucatan, unlike on the Mosquito Coast of Nicaragua or on the Belize River, the Spaniards had established enough local control to take action. Attacks on British logwood cutters and associated shipping began with the royal decree of 1672, two years after the Godolphin Treaty. By 1675 the settlements at Cozumel, an island off the east coast of the peninsula, and Cape Catoche on the northern coast had been abandoned, leaving Laguna de Terminos, forty miles south of Campeche, as the focus of activity.[19] The woodcutters were dislodged from there for two or three months in 1680, but then reoccupied it.[20] Continuing Spanish pressure, including further attacks in 1702 and 1716,[21] steadily reduced its importance in the early eighteenth century. But as late as 1728, the British presence there was still the subject of Spanish diplomatic protest.[22]

It was as a result of that Spanish determination to clear the Yucatan of British loggers, finally achieved in 1735,[23] that the settlement on the Belize River came into its own. The diary of a Spanish priest travelling from Guatemala to Bacalar records a British presence, including the well-known pirate Bartholomew Sharpe, on the cays of what is now Belize in 1677.[24] A settlement as such was first explicitly documented in 1682.[25] By 1705 it was already described as the place 'where the English for the most part load their logwood'.[26] Belize in turn only became rivalled in importance for logwood by the Mosquito Coast settlements, which actually predated the others, in the middle of the century. This happened partly because the latter were less vulnerable to attack as the Spaniards extended their grip on the Yucatan peninsula. But the British presence in Belize was to last far longer than that in Honduras and Nicaragua, and indeed far longer than the importance of logwood itself.

Throughout the eighteenth century such evidence as there is suggests a very rough and ready society in what developed as the Belize settlement. An association with piracy continued: William Teach, better known as Blackbeard, is said to have refitted his ship on Turneffe Island, off the barrier reef, in 1717. A ship's captain wrecked nearby in 1719 described the logwood cutters as 'a rude drunken crew', most former sailors, some former pirates, who 'do most work when they have no strong drink, for while the liquor is moving they don't care to leave it'.[27] Their numbers fluctuated, partly with the pressure put upon the settlement by the Spaniards. Whereas a naval surgeon who visited the settlement in 1735 put the total population at 500, an appeal for military assistance ten years later indicates that at that time the total population was less than two hundred.[28]

Small and disorderly though the community was, and complicated though their trade was by arguments about the applicability of the shipment rules of the Navigation Acts, logwood was nonetheless a profitable business for those involved. The trade had become firmly established after the repeal in 1662 of an act banning its importation into England. As early as 1672 the Governor of Jamaica reported that 2000 tons of logwood had been cut on the mainland coast the previous year; while his predecessor had stated that the price the cutters could command per ton was £25–30.[29] A Board of Trade report of 1717, when the British declared their right to maintain the trade, indicates that by then annual production had more or less doubled, although the price was subject to wider fluctuations.[30] By 1756 the annual figure had, with the development of industrial activity in Europe, leapt to 18,000 tons.[31] But the price fetched, only £11 per ton, perhaps foreshadowed the rapid decline in demand that occurred in the next two decades. For by 1765 the tonnage loaded had fallen to 7449 tons, with a further fall in price per ton to £7.10. For 1770 the figure was between 5000 and 6000 tons at £5–6 per ton.[32] During the next decade annual exports from the Bay, as the Belize settlement was still called, were down to 2–3000 tons; and by the last years of the century that figure had halved again.[33]

The reason for this dramatic decline, in what had been an important and prosperous industry, was largely technological, although competition from supplies of logwood from areas under Spanish control played a part. Logwood was being replaced as a source of dyestuff for general use by chemical dyes which were both cheaper and more readily available. To meet the residual demand for vegetable dye, exports of Belize logwood continued during the first half of the nineteenth century at about the same level as in the 1790s. But the trade never regained its former significance.

Fortunately for Belize, as demand for logwood fell steadily, the market for another Central American timber product, mahogany, soared. Between 1765, when mahogany accounted for a quarter of exports by value, and 1787, the volume of the new trade increased more than tenfold.[34] This development was driven partly by shortage of the main English hardwoods, oak and walnut, and partly by fashion, rather than by technology. Due to a significant increase in shipbuilding in the late eighteenth century, oak was becoming scarce at a time when walnut resources were already in decline for natural reasons; while late eighteenth century prosperity allowed the great cabinet makers of the day, such as Chippendale and Sheraton, to adopt imported mahogany, which can be very highly polished, for their exquisite furniture creations.

They had many imitators. The Bay of Honduras quickly became the leading source of supply and its economy became almost entirely based on mahogany for over a century and a half. Because mahogany cutting and transportation was more labour intensive than the extraction of logwood, it was with this development that African slaves arrived in the territory in larger numbers than before, with a consequent change in the settlement's ethnic balance. Mahogany cutting was also more capital intensive. The larger scale of enterprise that resulted marked a trend to a less transient population and to the emergence of the small, powerful elite that dominated the settlement's affairs from the 1780s. It was moreover at the beginning of this period that the British presence in Belize was at last granted some sort of recognition by the Spanish authorities.

Notes

1. F. A. Kirkpatrick, *The Spanish Conquistadores*, London (1934), 62–9 and 146.
2. ibid., 104–5.
3. Narda Dobson, *A History of Belize*, London (1973), 45–6.
4. See Grant D. Jones, 'Maya-Spanish Relations in Sixteenth Century Belize', *Belcast Journal of Belizean Affairs*, Vol. 1 No. 1, December (1984); and G. Jones, R. Kautz and E. Graham, 'Tipu: a Maya Town on the Spanish Colonial Frontier', *Archaeology*, January/February (1986).
5. Dobson, 45.
6. D. A. G. Waddell, *British Honduras: a Historical and Contemporary Survey*, London (1961), 5.
7. ibid. and Linda Newson, *The Cost of Conquest: Indian Decline in Honduras under Spanish Rule*, Boulder, Colorado (1986), 96–9.
8. Dobson, 46.
9. Kris E. Lane, *Blood and Silver*, Oxford (1999), 31–51.
10. Waddell, 7.
11. E. O. Winterzling, *The Beginning of British Honduras 1506–1765*, New York (1946), 37–45.
12. R. A. Humphries, *The Diplomatic History of British Honduras 1638–1901*, London (1961), 1–2.

13. See Dampier's *New Voyage Round the World* as quoted in A. Gill, *The Devil's Mariner: William Dampier, Pirate and Explorer*, London (1997), 52–61.
14. Gilbert Joseph, *John Coxon and the Role of Buccaneering in the Settlement of the Yucatan Colonial Frontier* , Belizean Studies, Vol. 17 No. 3 (1989), 9–10.
15. Gilbert Joseph, *The Logwood Trade and its Settlements (Part 2)*, Belizean Studies, Vol. 5 No. 3 (May 1977), 2.
16. This emerged with a series of test cases in the late seventeenth and early eighteenth centuries about the applicability of the Navigation Acts to the logwood trade – see James McLeish, *British Activities in Yucatan and on the Mosquito Shore in the Eighteenth Century*, unpublished MA thesis for the University of London (1926), 29–35.
17. McLeish, 24.
18. Godolphin/Secretary of State, 20 May 1672, CO 123/3.
19. Gilbert Joseph, *The Logwood Trade and its Settlements (Part 1)*, Belizean Studies, Vol. 5 No. 2, March (1977), 6.
20. ABH Vol. 1, 65.
21. Joseph, *The Logwood Trade and its Settlements (Part 2)*, 8.
22. ABH Vol. 1, 66.
23. Dobson, 64.
24. See J. Eric Thompson, *The Maya of Belize*, 1970 manuscript, published Belize (1988), 35–42. Bartholomew Sharp, who was active in the Caribbean during most of the 1670s, made his name as the leader of a pirate expedition to the Pacific coast of South America from 1680 to 1682.
25. Humphries, 2, and McLeish, 16.
26. ABH Vol. 1, 60.
27. Alfred Dewar (ed.), *The Voyages and Travels of Captain Nathaniel Uring*, London (1928), 241–2.
28. Inhabitants/Caulfield, 8 June 1745, enclosed with Trelawny/Board of Trade, 24 November 1745, CO 137/48. The appeal stated that the numbers available for defence were 'not exceeding above 50 white men and about 120 negroes'. Caulfield was the officer commanding the garrison at Ruatan. The reason for the appeal was a raid by the Spaniards on British property on the New River. Caulfield recommended the stationing of a sloop of war in the Bay as a more effective defence than the building of forts.
29. Dobson, 58.
30. O. N. Bolland, *Colonialism and Resistance in Belize*, Belize (1988), 15–16.
31. Enc. to White/Townsend, 10 February 1783, CO 123/2.
32. ibid.
33. Bolland, 16–17.
34. ibid.

3

External Rivalry and Internal Dissent: The Eighteenth Century

As seen in the last chapter, in the early years of the eighteenth century Spanish assertion of control of the Yucatan peninsula displaced the focus of British activity southwards to the area around the Belize River or, as the settlement was more widely known for many years to come, the Bay of Honduras. Here the Spaniards were for the time less conveniently placed to disturb the logwood cutters, as is borne out by the fact that there were no significant attacks on the settlement during the War of the Spanish Succession from 1701 to 1713.

This war, involving the whole of western Europe, pitched Britain and Austria against France and Spain. It ended with the Treaty of Utrecht, which saw the transfer of Spanish territories on the Italian peninsula and in the Netherlands to Austria, and Gibraltar and Minorca to Britain. For the Caribbean, the treaty only reaffirmed, as far as territorial rights were concerned, the provisions of the agreement negotiated by Godolphin in 1670.[1] This, it will be remembered, had settled questions of sovereignty in the region wherever there was an established government, but had failed to acknowledge the rights assumed by British logwood cutters elsewhere on the basis of simple occupation before 1670. There was a further cause of friction in 1713. The Spaniards refused to agree in the treaty to more than one annual British shipment to and from the Caribbean of goods other than slaves, for which they reluctantly and with some resentment granted a British monopoly for thirty years.[2]

Early Spanish attacks

The War of the Spanish Succession, and the treaty arrangements ending it, left the Spanish government feeling aggrieved, while British merchants for their part were unwilling to accept either the severe trade restrictions imposed upon them or the Spanish practice of searching British shipping. Relations between Britain and Spain, especially in the Caribbean where the British were still regarded as interlopers, were therefore delicate. An inconsistent attitude on the part of the government in Madrid encouraged the Spanish colonial authorities in the region to take action against British ships and settlers when they saw opportunity or felt they had other reason to do so. A local British reaction was inevitable, as was referral of disputes to capitals. Thus local friction led to a Spanish demand to the British government in 1716 for the suppression of the logwood trade. This prompted a British declaration in 1717 for the first time publicly upholding the settlers' rights to carry on with it.[3] That in turn led the next year to an unsuccessful Spanish military expedition, mounted from Guatemala, against the Bay of Honduras settlement,[4] the first of a series of such attacks which continued sporadically for the next eighty years, both in times of war and in times of peace.

A Spanish writer referred to a further attack in 1726.[5] This was the year a further war broke out between Britain and Spain. The Spanish government agreed, under the terms of the Treaty of Seville that ended that war in 1729, to participate in a joint commission to look into the causes of continuing disputes.[6] Before that met there was a further Spanish attack on the Bay settlement, when many of the British settlers had to retreat to Black River on the Mosquito Shore.[7] When the joint commission met in 1732 there was no meeting of minds. For Yucatan, the Bay of Honduras, and the Mosquito Shore, the British side wished to focus on the settlers' rights, the Spaniards on abuses of Spanish sovereignty. Matters stalled when the British side insisted that the burden of proof for this charge rested with the Spaniards.[8] That was followed by a resumption of attacks on British shipping in the Caribbean, which in turn led in 1739 to the celebrated War of Jenkins' Ear between Britain and Spain. This was soon subsumed by the wider War of the Austrian Succession, with Austria and Britain fighting France, Spain, and, from time to time, Prussia over a wide range of European as well as colonial issues. Between Britain and Spain, the Treaty of Aix la Chapelle which ended the war in 1748 settled none of the causes except the British monopoly of slave trading in the Caribbean, which was not renewed.

When the logwood cutters on the Belize River were forced to evacuate their settlement in 1730, they took refuge on the Mosquito Shore. Here there were established by the early eighteenth century British communities in three places: Black River on the coast of northern Honduras, Cape Gracios a Dios where the coastline turns from east to south, and Bluefields on the eastern coast of Nicaragua. Because of a strong informal alliance between the British and the local Indians, the Spaniards had never been able to gain full control of this remote region, and were not in a position to make a serious attempt to do so until much later in the century. Following an unsuccessful Spanish attempt at occupation in 1709,[9] it was left in peace for the next seventy years. Together with Ruatan (captured by the British in 1742 and held until the end of the War of the Austrian Succession), it again provided a haven for the logwood cutters of the Bay when they were faced with a Spanish attack in 1747. At that time a small force of British troops was based there.[10] The Shore served the same purpose in 1754, when, despite supposed peace between Britain and Spain, the Bay settlers were threatened with attack by a sizeable Spanish naval squadron.[11] The British government had meanwhile become more active in their peacetime support for the Mosquito Shore settlers with the appointment in 1749 of a Superintendent, based at Black River.[12] During the next European war, the Seven Years War of 1756–63, they again signalled their will to defend the settlement. Although for Britain's ally Prussia this was a war of survival against Austria, France and Russia, for Britain itself the focus became a struggle with France for control of possessions outside Europe. Towards the end of that war, in early 1762, Spain once again took the side of France. Although her war aims included regaining Gibraltar and Minorca, one of three more specific current disputes with Britain was once again the logwood settlements. War had long been foreseen: the Governor of Jamaica had been instructed to take defensive measures on the Mosquito Shore as early as 1754.[13] As a result a company of British infantry and some artillery were once more based on the Central American mainland, again at Black River.

The first treaty and continuing friction

The Bay of Honduras settlers did not enjoy such support. They had built their own fort when they returned to the Belize River the year after the 1754 evacuation, the Spaniards having withdrawn on instructions from Madrid because their attack had not been authorised by the king. It may have been the fort which deterred further Spanish attacks over the next few years. When Spain entered the Seven Years War in 1762, their colonial authorities were forced onto the defensive by a successful British assault on Havana the same year. By this time the British had driven the French out of India and Canada, and out of almost all of their possessions in the Caribbean. They too were therefore ready to negotiate peace terms with both enemies. The result was the Treaty of Paris of 1763. Under Article 17 of that treaty the Spanish government, which had to surrender Florida in order to regain Cuba, for the first time acknowledged the right of the British settlers on both the Mosquito Shore and the Belize River to cut, load and ship logwood. The British government for its part agreed to demolish fortifications at both places and to withdraw all troops and equipment.[14] This caused considerable dismay at the several settlements. The Mosquito Shore Superintendent queried his instructions and delayed implementation, including demolition of the Belize River fort, until the following year.[15]

For the logwood cutters the Treaty of Paris was nonetheless undoubtedly a step forward. But it left considerable scope for further trouble because no geographical limits to their activity were laid down. The settlers as a result felt free steadily to extend their cutting despite the Spanish authorities' resistance to what they saw as encroachment. Nevertheless, for sixteen years after the treaty was signed there seems to have been no substantial Spanish attack on the Belize River area, although there was some harassment, possibly provoked by the local Indians, on the Mosquito Shore towards the end of that time. It is during this period that we again get glimpses of the rough and ready community at the former.

Unlike at Black River, there was still no British government presence at the Bay of Honduras settlement, let alone formal administration, during this period. Records are therefore sparse. As to the size of the settlement, by the time of the 1754 evacuation the total number was reported to have been about 500. The settlement seems likely then to have enjoyed a period of modest growth: a 1782 claim for loss of property shows that by 1779, at the time of the next major Spanish attack, there were 96 heads of families established on St George's Cay, the main residential centre.[16] We know too that 101 whites, 40 people of 'mixed colour', and up to 250 slaves were taken into captivity then,[17] while about 50 white men and another couple of hundred slaves avoided capture and made their way to Ruatan,[18] which had once again been seized by the British.

Descriptions of the society that had evolved, as well as the constant quarreling with their Spanish neighbours, show that the bucaneering spirit of the early camps was largely unchanged. Rear Admiral Burnaby, the British naval commander at Jamaica, visited the Belize River in 1765 to make sure that the terms of the Treaty of Paris were being observed by both sides. He saw a need to establish on a sounder footing an informal framework of rules for the maintenance of basic order. This led to the adoption of 'Burnaby's Code', a very simple set of powers for elected magistrates to deal with offences, settle disputes and grievances, and levy tax.[19] When reporting what had been agreed, Burnaby said that he had found the settlers 'in a state of anarchy and confusion', and, qualifying the success of the visit, that he had heard since then that they only complied with the arrangements he had introduced when it suited them.[20] Reports over the next few years by visiting warship captains must have been even more damning. In 1768 Burnaby's successor, Rear Admiral Parry suggested the impostion of military law to control 'a most notorious lawless sett of miscreants who are artful and cunning and who have practised every ill and fly from different parts thither to avoid justice where they pursue their licentious conduct with impunity'.[21] Nor did things improve with the passage of time. Twenty years later a member of the magistracy set up by Admiral Burnaby wrote of the settlement as 'an open receptacle for outlaws, felons, and foreigners and all such men who fly from justice or are fond of a licentious life';[22] and in 1793, during the interval when the settlement had no Superintendent, a visiting warship captain described the inhabitants as of a 'turbulent and unsettled disposition'.[23]

All of this will have inhibited the development of any satisfactory working relationship with the neighbouring Spanish authorities in both southern Mexico and northeastern Guatemala, more important as the Spaniards slowly strengthened their administration of those extremities of their Central American empire. Immediately after the end of the Seven Years War there was a series of clashes about woodcutting limits, with the Spaniards seeking to reduce the area of British activity. This was successfully resisted. Thereafter, with regular visits to the coast by British warships, the Spanish authorities broadly observed their peace treaty obligation not to interfere in the internal life of the Bay of Honduras settlement, and the British side upheld their agreement not to fortify it ashore. But those obligations were assumed under terms negotiated at the end of a war that the Spaniards had lost. It was therefore to be expected that as soon as they found themselves at war with Britain again, they should act quickly to suppress a settlement that had always been, and because of constant disputes about limits remained, a thorn in their side.

Spanish occupation, restoration and two further agreements

This next war was the American War of Independence, which started in 1776 as a rebellion by North American colonists against trade restrictions and taxation imposed upon them by a remote government in London. By 1778 the war was going badly for the British, and their difficulties were made worse by a French initiative that year to form an alliance with the colonists. This was followed by Spanish entry into the war in June 1779, with the aim once again of recovering Gibraltar and Minorca, together with, for the Caribbean, Jamaica and the Bay of Honduras. On the last they were not slow to move. Three months after they declared war, a small fleet of 19 Spanish ships arrived off St George's Cay, led by the commandant of the fort at Bacalar.[24] Settlers and slaves were seized and made to march overland to Merida. They were later imprisoned at Havana, from where they were not released until 1782. Ruatan, to which the remainder

of the settlers fled, was once again garrisoned by the British following successful Spanish raids on the Mosquito Shore's administrative centre, Black
River, in 1780 and 1782.[25] The Belize River remained under direct Spanish
control until the year after the war ended in 1783, when a joint commission supervised the transfer to the returning settlers of the land to the
north of it that they had traditionally worked.[26]

The American War of Independence was a war which the British lost
on the North American mainland, but not, thanks to Admiral Rodney's
victory over a large French fleet off Martinique in 1782, in the Caribbean.
Thus at the peace settlement, the Treaty of Versailles of September 1783,
British territorial concessions in the Caribbean were limited to the loss of
Tobago. But for the Bay of Honduras the terms that the British had to
accept, after agreeing a vaguer formulation in the peace preliminaries,
included for the first time details that were quite tough. While the
logwood cutters' right to work there was confirmed, geographical limits
were imposed that were tight: under Article 6 of the treaty, cutting was
limited to the area between the Belize and Hondo Rivers, and occupation
of the cays was ruled out. As bad, the only resource that was allowed for
exploitation was logwood, thus threatening to put paid to the increasingly
profitable mahogany trade and to secondary activity such as turtling.

This led to strong and repeated representations to the Secretary of
State by the agent in London for both the Baymen and the Mosquito
Shore settlers, Robert White. Not only did White protest against the
'narrow and insupportable limits insisted upon by the Spanish court' in
the case of the Bay settlement,[27] he also urged that both communities
should be allowed to exploit 'logwood, mahogany, and other produce of
the soil'.[28] In justifying this on behalf of the Bay of Honduras settlers, he
estimated that whereas the then current limit to the international logwood
market was 7000 tons per annum, the demand for mahogany there was ten
times that amount. In the same letter, White made much of the importance
for Britain of the Central American timber trade, in the context of both
the shipping industry and government revenue. But in his next representation, only two months later, he backed, as between the two settlements,
the one for which, records suggest, he had been acting for longer. He proposed to ministers in London that they exchange the Bay of Honduras settlement for rights of 'full possession' of the Mosquito Shore, of which no
mention had been made in the Treaty of Versailles.[29] White's proposal, to
which he reverted as late as November 1784 when further negotiations
were in train, may have been on the basis of arguments against demilitar-
isation there, put forward in 1763 by the settlers on that coast. Essentially
these were that the Spaniards had never taken possession of the Mosquito
Shore, and that in 1740, in order to pre-empt this, the native people had

sought the protection of the British government. These arguments were not available to the Belize River settlers, although the year before, when urging redress for the the losses suffered by the Baymen in 1779, White had emphasised that they had been the 'first occupants' of the area.

As it turned out a quid pro quo proved to be negotiable. But it was the Baymen's rights that were strengthened in exchange for British withdrawal from the Mosquito Shore rather than the other way round. Under the terms of the Convention of London of July 1786, the Spaniards agreed to expand the economic boundaries of the Bay of Honduras settlement southwards to the Sibun River; and to extend the resources to be harvested to cover all timber, including mahogany, and, (although 'plantations' were disallowed until a further concession in 1789), the 'natural fruits of the earth'. They also agreed that fishing rights should be extended, that St George's Cay should be inhabited, and that other cays traditionally used for careening ships should continue to be available to British seamen.

In return for these concessions, the British government agreed in the first article of the Convention that the prescriptive rights of settlement that they believed had been acquired on the Mosquito Shore should be given up. This had a direct consequence for the Bay of Honduras settlers beyond the treaty concessions they had gained, and one that was much less welcome. Most of the Mosquito Shore settlers and their slaves, having lost the notional protection of the British government, moved to the Belize River. The number of arrivals, at over 2000, at least quadrupled the post-1783 population of the Bay settlement, and caused considerable stress and strain there. Anticipation of this added to existing pressure for the appointment of some form of British government representative to regulate the affairs of the community.

The first Superintendent and his troubles

The creation in 1749 of the post of Superintendent on the Mosquito Shore had been broadly successful, although the third of the four incumbents had incurred the wrath of the settlers. At about the same time the creation of a similar post at the Belize River had been considered. Reports were written on the subject at least twice before the end of the Seven Years War, but without result despite subsequent petitions from the settlers themselves. The first fully developed case for a superintendency in the Bay of Honduras was presented by White to the Secretary of State in June 1783, ironically two months after his suggestion that the Bay should be evacuated in exchange for strengthened rights on the Mosquito Shore. White argued that such an official would have the necessary standing to impose internal order in the settlement, the state of which he described in a later representation as one of 'internal imbecility, weakness, and confusion'.[30] As, if not more, important, he would command the respect of the Spanish authorities who, under the terms of the peace treaty, were entitled to inspect this British foothold in their dominions twice a year. White felt able, moreover, to recommend the right person for the post: Captain Edward Marcus Despard, who had been the commander of the small garrison the British had established on Ruatan during the late war and who, according to White, had been the choice of the Mosquito Indians to command the expedition to recover the Black River settlement after the Spanish attack of 1782. Despard was described by White as 'mild and gentle' in his civil capacity, but 'vigorous and steady' when necessary.[31] The Bay settlers, who welcomed, as far as they went, the terms later enshrined in the 1786 convention, endorsed White's recommendation and added a proposal that a British warship should visit the coast from time to time to deter the Spanish coastguard from harassing British shipping.

Later in 1783 White went further, arguing for a 'regular magistracy and government' independent of Jamaica even if still looking to Jamaica for 'auxiliary assistance'.[32] Because they were concerned above all that there should be no compromise of their sovereignty, explicitly confirmed in the Treaty of Versailles, the Spanish government regarded that as quite unacceptable; and no progress was made in that direction in the continuing negotiations, beyond agreement on the post of Superintendent. That he was going to be regarded by the Spaniards as no more than an agent was to be predicted from the qualifications in Article 7 of the Convention of London: the 'formation of any system of government, military or civil' was prohibited 'further than such regulations as their Britannic and Catholic majesties may judge proper for maintaining peace and good order'.

Like the Treaty of Paris of 1763, the 1783 and 1786 agreements together nonetheless represented a substantial consolidation of the settlers' position. But obvious points of friction other than the question of government ensured that it did not bring a lasting stability to local relations. The arrival of so many Mosquito Shore settlers and slaves was bound to lead immediately to claims that the geographical limits laid down for woodcutting were too narrow. The Spanish inspections provided for in the Convention touched nerves already raw on account of continuing boundary disputes. The bar on plantations was resented as simply unreasonable. The issue of Spanish harbouring of runaway slaves, which had also led to considerable trouble on the Mosquito Shore, remained unaddressed. The situation in which the first Superintendent found himself was not therefore a comfortable one.

Despard, first notified of his appointment in November 1784, arrived at the Belize River settlement in June 1786, a month before the Convention was concluded. He did not like what he saw. In one of his earliest despatches he observed that the agreement had already been violated, and that 'a spirit of opposition' to it prevailed. He forecast that this would continue until the 'democratic form of government be superseded and such regulations established in lieu' as were 'agreable' to Article 7 of the Convention.[33] Meanwhile 'legislative, executive, and judicial powers' were 'in the hands of the people', and thus, by implication, beyond his control.

But a concern that quickly became more pressing was the imminent absorption of the Mosquito Shore settlers. By May 1787 they had arrived. That month Despard reported that the established woodcutters were claiming every tree within the 1783 limits as private property, despite the fact that they were considerably fewer in number than they had been before the 1779 evacuation. He therefore proposed to 'appropriate the augmentation' (i.e. the newly conceded territory) for the use of the new arrivals.[34] The number of woodcutters already established is put in this despatch at 55. Despard estimated that the settlers already at the Belize River were outnumbered by immigrants from the Mosquito Shore by 5 to 1. Assuming that there were about the same number of dependents as there were established woodcutters, this estimate would be consistent with the number (537) of white and free coloured settlers reported by the Mosquito Shore Superintendent as having left for the Bay. The number of slaves accompanying them was put at 1677.[35] With an increase in population of this order, the issue of government in the Bay settlement thus became as difficult internally as it had already become contentious externally.

An attempt had been made in London to clarify the legal position on the extent of British jurisdiction as early as 1766, three years after the Treaty of Paris had defined, albeit in the most general terms, the settlers' rights. That interpretation held that the granting by the Spanish government to British subjects of usufructuary rights in the Bay of Honduras gave the British government enough territorial right there to exercise a civil jurisdiction over those subjects.[36] Practice was, however, to prove more difficult than theory. The internal constraint was that the Superintendent had no apparatus to enable him to fulfill his duty to maintain order; whereas whatever apparatus he might propose to establish was to be subject to the agreement of not only the Spanish authorities but also the settlers.

The existing arrangements were a loose and no doubt partial system of self-regulation controlled in effect by the leading white settlers, the 'democratic form of government' noted and deplored by Despard on his arrival.

This was the framework of informal government Admiral Burnaby had codified during his visit in 1765 to strengthen such order as prevailed in the settlement. By means of a resolution adopted at the first recorded Public Meeting after the settlers' return in early 1784, it was re-instituted in no uncertain terms: 'The laws and regulations of 1765 be continued in full force'.[37] Burnaby's code was based on a magistracy of seven leading citizens who had been elected periodically since at least 1738, and a jury of thirteen householders who were also to be elected. This court was to convene four times a year on St George's Cay, and was empowered to seize property if its authority was challenged. Such laws as had been established covered fundamentals like stealing, payment of debt and hiring of servants. The other main plank of Burnaby's Code, as it became known, was the Public Meeting, also seemingly an earlier practice. The function of that was to discuss both existing regulations and proposals for new ones, and to take decisions on these rules by means of a majority vote. The franchise both for election to the bench and for voting at public meetings was of course limited, by means of property qualifications, to white settlers who were also heads of households. But by the standards of eighteenth century Europe the political structure of the settlement was indeed democratic, and to some would have seemed dangerously so.

That such a free-wheeling tradition ran contrary to Despard's ideas is shown by the first recorded request he made to the Secretary of State, Lord Sydney, in December 1786: that he be given 'powers to restrain the settlers'.[38] He meanwhile also asked the Governor of Jamaica whether the existing magistracy was not contrary to the terms of the Treaty of Versailles. For a military man with experience of civil administration only in wartime, these feelings were hardly surprising. But added impetus would have been given to them by the priority assigned in his instructions to the six monthly inspections by the neighbouring Spanish commandant provided for under the peace terms. He was told that the 'engagements' these were designed to monitor were to be 'punctually and faithfully fulfilled'.[39] Consequently one of the first actions he took on arrival was to uphold a Spanish complaint. Affirmed in a letter of February 1787, his efforts to cultivate good relations with the Spaniards met with success: one Spanish official referred in correspondence to 'the cordial friendship which unites us', while Despard for his part referred at the end of his time to the Spaniards' 'scrupulous exactness'.[40] But this predisposition, his evident distaste for the way the settlement had been run and his unilateral measures to resettle the refugees from the Mosquito Shore were bound to set him on a collision course with the most influential inhabitants.

From the middle of 1787 Despard was at loggerheads with the established settlers. They took the view that he had acted arbitrarily in allocating land to the new arrivals without consultation. He believed that they sought to destroy his authority and moreover had contravened the Treaty of Versailles by purchasing land for a court-house and appointing a Clerk of the Court, a Provost Marshal and a Collector of Revenue. From then until his recall relations deteriorated steadily. The old settlers, viewing the appointment as 'for the purpose of negotiating with the Spaniards only', bombarded the Secretary of State with complaints about the Superintendent's 'despotism' in interfering with the settlement's established self-regulation. Lord Sydney, while generally supportive of Despard, urged 'a more conciliatory demeanour'.[41] But Despard, although not without support from some of the new arrivals, failed to come to terms with the leading residents. Instead, infuriated by the magistrates' insistence that only they could make laws, he took advantage for internal purposes of his instructions to maintain good relations with the Spaniards: when he received a complaint from them in May 1789 that the existence of the magistracy indeed contravened the peace agreements, he dissolved it and abolished the Public Meeting. In their place he convened a new council chaired by himself, thus giving himself the greater degree of direct authority he felt he needed. But this made his relations with many, though not all, of the settlers even worse. They saw the new council as 'totally incompatible with the spirit of the British constitution and subversive of civil liberty'.[42] There followed both local demands for his recall and considerable concern in London. Shortly after Lord Grenville replaced Lord Sydney as Secretary of State in the second half of 1789, Despard, who had himself shown despair, was told that his post was suspended pending an enquiry. He was given the opportunity of returning to London for discussions. But after he arrived there in the summer of 1790 these failed to materialise. He remained unemployed for several years before becoming involved in an Irish separatist conspiracy that cost him his life.

A temporary successor and an interregnum

As a temporary replacement for Despard, Colonel Peter Hunter was posted from Jamaica to what was still called the Bay of Honduras. He was not impressed with what he found on his arrival in April 1790 describing the settlement as an asylum for 'the banditti of the West Indian islands' with 'at least one half of its present inhabitants ... of that description'.[43] His priority nonetheless was to mollify the settlers. On instructions from London, he reinstituted the magistracy while further consideration was given to the vexed question of administration. Meanwhile Hunter was told to avoid anything resembling a colonial government. What he therefore proposed to the Secretary of State was a structure based on the existing (i.e. 1765) system, but with twelve elected magistrates rather than seven and greater powers of appointment of other officials for himself.[44] This was broadly accepted in London but never put to the Spaniards because of a serious but short-lived dispute about fishing rights in the north Pacific. That caused the Admiralty to station a sloop in the Bay with a supply of arms and ammunition for the settlement in case of need.[45] When those differences were resolved Hunter was able to depart, after only a year's stay. He left the elected magistracy intact and autonomous, and reinforced only by a makeshift scheme of subordinate administration by half a dozen appointed officials. In this rudimentary way the community governed itself for the next five years.

Colonel Barrow and the Battle of St George's Cay

No further serious consideration was given either to administration or to British government representation in the settlement during that period. The Governor of Jamaica suggested that occasional visits by British war-ships would be an adequate substitute.[46] This advice was accepted in 1793.[47] The next Superintendent was only appointed when Britain was yet again faced with Spanish entry into a war already being waged against her by France, a war that had broken out four years after the French Revolution of 1789. By 1796, with Britain's allies falling away as France consolidated territorial gains in Europe, the Spaniards saw once again a chance to settle scores that went back nearly a hundred years. Lieutenant Colonel Thomas Barrow arrived in the Bay of Honduras at the end of the year, two months after Spain had declared war. His main task was to prepare defences for the settlement. This led to martial law being imposed, the restrictions and the economic disruption of which caused resentment. A further grievance was British reluctance to dispatch troops and warships from Jamaica, where both military and naval officers were preoccupied with other threats. In April 1797 the 20-gun sloop *Merlin* arrived.[48] But a Public Meeting in June to decide between defence and evacuation of the Bay settlement saw only a narrow majority in favour of the former.[49]

Morale was improved with the arrival of three companies of Irish troops in September 1797, though there was dismay when it was revealed that nearly half of them were sick. Work on fortifications continued, driven by Barrow, and a contingent of colonial troops and some artillery were added to the garrison in April 1798. But in June Captain Moss of the *Merlin* had to threaten to leave the settlement to its own devices in order to overcome 'tardiness, (and) want of unanimity and promptness'.[50] After a Spanish invasion fleet was sighted off Cozumel on 18 July, a unity of purpose was at last found; and in early August it was even agreed that St George's Cay should be evacuated and the buildings on it destroyed so that military resources could be concentrated at Belize Point and Haulover Creek.[51]

The Spanish expedition involved 32 ships and 2000 men. By the time they arrived off Cay Chapel many of the troops were sick with Yellow Fever.[52] The attack nonetheless went ahead on 3 September 1798. In a despatch to the Governor of Jamaica, reproduced in the London *Gazette* of 22 January 1799, Colonel Barrow reported that over three days five makeshift gunboats with mixed naval and civilian crews and assorted smaller craft had been able, thanks to their shallow draft, to outmanoeuvre and repel a force of up to seven Spanish ships as they tried to force a passage southwards towards St George's Cay through the narrow and tortuous channels inside the reef. Other roots of the defenders' success seem to have been good intelligence from 'scoutboats', knowledge of the waters, and denial, by removal, of navigational marks to the other side.

On the fourth day the Spaniards again approached St George's Cay, this time from outside Long Cay, but without pressing an attack. The last attempt, by fourteen ships four days later, was reported to have aimed at a landing on the mainland on the northern side of what is now Belize City. The *Merlin* and two armed merchant vessels, supported by the gunboats, barred the way ten miles offshore. After an exchange of fire involving only nine of the Spanish ships and lasting about two and a half hours, the Spaniards fell back to their anchorage off Cay Chapel. Over half their original fleet had never left it because they drew too much water. The whole force retreated to Bacalar and Campeche on 15 September.

Such was the nature of what was to be the last Spanish attack on the Bay of Honduras, or Belize River, settlement. In late 1801 hostilities were suspended, as negotiations opened for the Treaty of Amiens of 1802. During the three years before war was resumed, the Governor of Yucatan pressed Barrow's successor, Brigadier General Bassett, and then Barrow on his return, to 'deliver up' the settlement in accordance with the treaty provision that Britain would evacuate Spanish territory occupied by force of arms during the war.[53] But war broke out again in 1804, the year after it had resumed with the French and before matters could be clarified between capitals. During the next few years the Spaniards made no move. With Napoleon's invasion of Spain in 1808, Britain and Spain became allies and remained so for the rest of the Napoleonic War. By the time it ended in 1815, the Spanish Empire in the Americas was threatened with collapse, and the Bay settlement was, for a time, left to its own devices.[54]

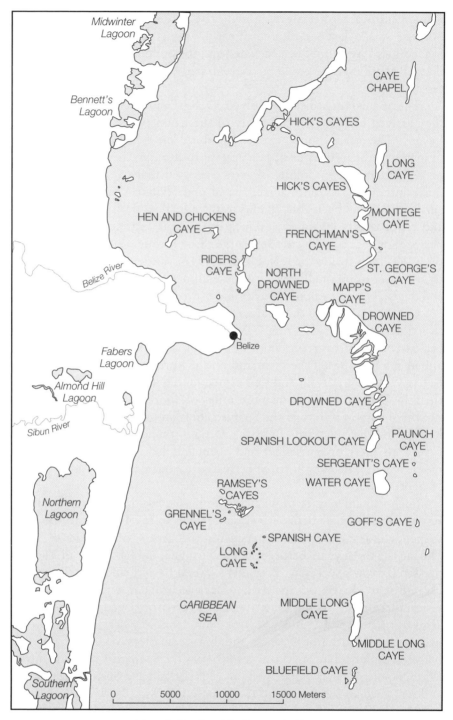

Map F Battle of St George's Cay

Notes

1. R. A. Humphries, *The Diplomatic History of British Honduras 1638–1901*, London (1961), 2.
2. J. H. Plumb, *England in the Eighteenth Century*, London (1950), 71. The monopoly (or 'assiento'), granted to the South Sea Company, was suspended in 1733 due to Spanish dissatisfaction with the way the trade was conducted, and terminated on the outbreak of the War of Jenkins' Ear in 1739 – see C. A. Palmer, *Human Cargo 1570–1650*.
3. This was based on a Board of Trade memorandum to King George I arguing that the sites of the camps had been occupied by British woodcutters before the 1667 Treaty of Madrid, at a time when there was no evidence of Spanish occupation. A precis of the text is reproduced in ABH Vol. 1, 64–6.
4. James McLeish, *British Activities in Yucatan and on the Mosquito Shore in the 18th Century*, unpublished MA thesis for the University of London (1926), 77–9.
5. Dobson, 69.
6. Humphries, 3.
7. ABH Vol. 1, 43, McLeish, 81, and Gilbert Joseph, *The Logwood Trade and its Settlements (Part 2)*, Belizean Studies Vol. 5 No. 3, May (1977), 8–9. According to A. R. Gibbs, *British Honduras: a Historical and Descriptive Account*, London (1883), 34, nearly forty settlers and slaves were captured in this attack.
8. McLeish, 84.
9. McLeish, 203.
10. McLeish, 204–6.
11. McLeish, 98.
12. Letter of appointment to Captain Robert Hodgson, 5 October 1749, CO 123/1.
13. Secretary of State/Governor of Jamaica, 8 July 1754, CO 123/1.
14. See detailed terms in CO 123/1.
15. See Hodgson letter of explanation of 23 December 1766 in CO 123/1.
16. See inventory of property loss at p.83 of CO 123/2.
17. Enc. ('Account of the taking of St George's Key Sept.15 1779') to Dalling/Germain, 29 October 1779, CO 137/76.
18. Bartlett/Dalling, undated, enclosed with Dalling/Germain, 28 December 1779, CO 137/76.
19. That this was not the first set of such regulations is indicated by a reference in the preamble to the 1765 code to the 'Original Laws and Regulations established for the benefit of this Community' – see ABH Vol. 1, 100. The formalisation of the elected magistracy may also have come at an earlier stage. The Governor of Jamaica at the time of Burnaby's visit (Lyttleton) refers in correspondence to the issue by a predecessor (Knowles) of commissions appointing Justices of the Peace in the Bay. Lyttleton took the view that such appointments would be inconsistent with the recent (1763) treaty with Spain – see Lyttleton/Conway 15 January 1766, CO 137/62.
20. ABH Vol. 1, 109.
21. Parry/Stephens, 12 December 1768, ADM 1/238. This correspondence was about the case for stationing a frigate in the Bay 'to prevent as much as possible murders, frauds and confusion which are notoriously practised amongst the Baymen and which cannot be checked but by military force'. That had been asked for by a settler within a few months of Burnaby's visit in 1765. He complained that 'the regulations appointed by Rear Admiral Sir W. Burnaby are very good and proper but for want of some vessel or man of war to enforce their execution' – see enc. to Lyttleton/Conway 15 January 1766 op. cit.
22. Letter to Colonel Hunter, 16 October 1789, CO 123/8.
23. Dobson, 74.

24. An enclosure with Dalling/Germain, 29 October 1779, CO 137/76 makes clear that the settlers were unaware of Spain's entry into the war and therefore quite unprepared. Dalling himself deplored the failure of subordinates to ensure the arrival of a warning he had sent.
25. McLeish, 212–5.
26. See record of Public Meeting of 12 June 1784 in CO 123/14.
27. White/Fox, 24 June 1783, CO 123/2.
28. White/Townsend, 10 February 1783, CO 123/2.
29. White/North, 8 April 1783, CO 123/2.
30. White/Sydney, 31 January 1786, CO 123/4.
31. White/North, 13 June 1783, CO 123/2.
32. White/North, 3 November 1783, CO 123/2.
33. Despard/Sydney, 20 December 1786, CO 123/5.
34. Despard/Sydney, 14 May 1787, CO 123/5.
35. Lawrie/Nepean, 26 January 1788, CO 123/6. A number of other Mosquito Shore settlers and slaves moved to the Cayman Islands – see Wallace Brown, *The Mosquito Shore and the Bay of Honduras*, Belizean Studies Vol. 18 Nos. 2–3, (1990).
36. See legal opinion in paper by R. Hodgson dated 17 October 1766, CO 123/1.
37. See record of Public Meeting of 12 June 1784, CO 123/14.
38. Despard/Sydney, 20 December 1786, CO 123/5.
39. Carmarthen/Despard, 1 September 1786, CO 123/4.
40. Despard/Hull, 25 November 1789, CO 123/9.
41. Sydney/Despard, February 1788, CO 123/6.
42. See precis of complaints against Despard dated May 1790 in CO 123/14.
43. Hunter/Grenville, 18 May 1790, CO 123/9.
44. Enc. to above.
45. See secret despatch to Colonel Hunter, 15 May 1790, CO 123/9.
46. Dobson, 74.
47. *Honduras Almanack*, Belize (1828), 100–1. This move may have had more to do with the outbreak of war with France that year than with concern for law and order in the Bay settlement.
48. H. F. Humphries, *The Battle of St Georges Caye: a New Analysis*, Belzean Studies Vol. 7 No. 4, July (1979), 4.
49. *Honduras Almanack*, 107.
50. ABH Vol. 1, 248–9.
51. H. F. Humphries, 6 and 8.
52. ibid., 5.
53. Barrow/Hobart, 23 June 1803, CO 123/15.
54. Although there were no further Spanish inspections, there were four protests between 1808 and 1816 against infringement of treaty restrictions. None was followed up.

4

The Settlement at the Beginning of the Nineteenth Century

It is around 1800 that the simple name Belize begins to appear in official correspondence. That seems to denote the emerging town, however, rather than the whole territory under British occupation. The latter was still generally referred to as Honduras, the Bay of Honduras, or even Yucatan. Thus there are references to the town, previously called Wallix River, Belize Rivermouth, or Belize Point, as Belize in Honduras or Belize in Yucatan. A variant of the spelling of the town's name was Balize. According to the longest account we have of the settlement in the first decade of the nineteenth century, it consisted of about two hundred shingle- or palm-roof dwellings. Outside the town there were no roads, and indeed only four or five miles of track for recreational horse-riding.[1] Travel into the interior was by pitpan, a 40ft. dugout canoe propelled by paddles and poles.

The composition of the society

We do not have precise figures for the population of the Bay settlement for 1800. At the time of the 1790 census that number, at 2655, was very close to the level reported by the Superintendent three years earlier, when the refugees arrived from the Mosquito Shore. By 1816, a generation later, the figure had increased by nearly a half, to 3824. A breakdown of these two figures sheds light not only on the structure of the society, but also on changes that took place in the decades either side of the turn of the century.

In 1790 there were 260 whites divided approximately in the proportions 4 : 1 : 1 between men, women and children. For the 370 'free coloureds and blacks' the division between the three was more or less equal; for the 2024 slaves the combined figure for women and children nearly equalled that for men. Thus there was an extreme shortage of white women and a significant shortage of women classed as slaves; and only in the 'free black and coloured' section of the community was there any possibility of family life as a norm. By 1816 the shortage of women in the white community had moderated, with only twice as many men as women; whereas it had grown somewhat amongst the slaves, with only 639 women to 1645 men. For the 'free coloureds and blacks' the change was that there were now significantly more women than men, no doubt partly because female domestic servants were more likely to be freed than male labourers.[2]

The breakdown also shows that in the years either side of 1800 the racial balance was changing quite fundamentally: the white population declined by over a third; the slave population expanded by the same proportion; and the 'free coloureds and blacks' soared in numbers by two and a half times, so that there were six times as many people in this category, representing a quarter of the population, as there were whites. The explanation here is probably complex. We know that poor whites from the Mosquito Shore found it very difficult to get started in the mahogany trade because of lack of capital, labour and land, and that some of them sought resettlement in the Bahamas. As significantly, the rate of reproduction in the white community will have been abnormally low because of the shortage of white women. That shortage is likely also to provide the main reason for the explosion of the 'free coloured and black' population, which continued to rise steadily through the 1820s: many white men will have consorted with black women, freed for the purpose, to produce 'coloured' children. The reason for the 50 per cent increase in the number of male slaves (against a 20 per cent increase in slave women) seems likely to have been a resort to importation as the cutting and transporting of mahogany became even more labour intensive as it spread to less accessible areas. We know that the rate of importation of slaves was a matter of concern during Colonel Barrow's second term, so much so that there was one proposal that only newly arrived settlers should be allowed to bring in slaves, and then only where the slaves concerned had been with them for five or more years.[3]

Such was the size and racial profile of the community as the nineteenth century opened. An indication of the economic profile is provided by a 1790 occupational breakdown of the white population.[4] This listed 71 woodcutters plus 49 more whites 'in their service'. Interestingly a further 71 whites were listed as turtlers, who must, as less than a ton of shell was exported each year, have been scratching a living providing meat for the community along with the 14 whites categorised as hunters; while another 50 were described simply as 'of no fixed abode', presumably longshoremen, beachcombers and other vagrants fitting some of the derogatory descriptions of the society at the time. A category that does not appear in this analysis is that of vegetable grower, possibly because that occupation had traditionally been done by slaves for their masters. But it was an emerging category as the custom of cultivating vegetables largely for the use of the grower and his family gave way to primitive commercial cultivation. So too was that of trader, of whom, together with 'tradesmen' (i.e. artisans), there were 42 amongst the white community. Already in 1803 there is a reference to a tender for the building of a market house, while by 1805 there was a system of licensing of vendors.[5] Cultivation and market-trading were steadily becoming the domain of the burgeoning 'free coloureds and blacks' section of the community. Their growing numbers would have made them an increasing economic force in the settlement, representing, as already noted, 25 per cent of the population by 1816, and nearly a half by 1832. Besides natural expansion through both birth and release from slavery, their numbers were swollen by the decision of 500 members of the 5th West India Regiment, which had provided the garrison during much of the war, to settle in the Bay when the regiment was disbanded in 1817, and by the subsequent addition of 200 former members of the 2nd West India Regiment which replaced it.[6] Most of these new arrivals took up small-scale farming, while others, like other 'free coloureds and blacks' already there, found work as wage earners in the commercial life of the one town that then existed.

The decisive feature of the economic and indeed social structure of the settlement is the simple fact that about a dozen white families held three-quarters of the land identified as suitable for exploitation.[7] The same dozen families 'owned' nearly 50 per cent of the slaves.[8] These were the leaders of the people who had laid claim to all the exploitable land in 1787, as the Mosquito Shore evacuees moved to the Bay, and who had opposed allocation only to the new arrivals of the extra territory just ceded by Spain. They were also the people who dominated the magistracy, the platform for opposition to the Superintendent on this and other issues which rumbled on after that post was re-instituted in 1796. Their grip on what was essentially political power in the settlement is well illustrated by the fact that five of the seven magistrates serving in 1790 were still in place ten years later; while two of those same five were still magistrates in 1816. One magistrate, who stood down in 1789 after ten years, returned to the bench in 1791 and then continued to serve until 1807; while another served for twenty-seven years between 1795 and 1827.[9] But the very fact that many other heads of white families owned only two or three slaves each suggests that while there may have been broad support for the existing order within the European community, the disparity of wealth and power across it would nonetheless have created tensions. It would have been those tensions that ensured that opposition to the Superintendent, though sometimes very substantial, was never total.

The Superintendent

Against this oligarchy the Superintendent in 1800 (first Lieutenant Colonel Barrow then Brigadier Basset) could only seek to bring influence to bear. Because the British government claimed no sovereign rights or powers, his legal status was nebulous. Like others charged with a regulatory function overseas, he had his Commission, in this case from the Governor of Jamaica, and his instructions from the Secretary of State. But both were couched more vaguely than those issued to colonial governors. The commission continued to emphasise in general terms the importance of maintaining good relations with the neighbouring Spanish authorities, the priority for the unfortunate Despard. A good example is the commission issued to Lieutenant Colonel Arthur in 1814, which urged him to use his 'utmost endeavours to prevent any cause of misunderstanding or disagreement between His Majesty's subjects and those of His Catholic Majesty inhabiting that neighbourhood'.[10]

The instructions, presumably because of the sharp reaction to Despard's attempt to change things internally, referred similarly to the government's policy of upholding existing customs and institutions. This policy is stated forcefully in the letter of appointment from the Secretary of State to Barrow on his return to the settlement at the beginning of 1803. He was told that 'the system of internal police that was re-established by Colonel Hunter in the year 1790 having been sanctioned by the experience which the British subjects residing at Honduras have had of its favourable operation and effects, it is His Majesty's pleasure that the same should be continued in force and no alteration should be made'.[11] In the case of Colonel Smyth in 1810 this instruction was even more specific, spelling out under the heading of existing customs the inclusion of 'convening of public meetings', 'election of magistrates and other public officers', and 'raising and application of the money required for the public service'.[12] This direct interest in London in what the Superintendent was up to is reflected in the orders Barrow received on reporting. He was to correspond directly with the Secretary of State for the Home Department, Lord Hobart, copying his despatches to his nominal superior in Jamaica. A further channel of correspondence for him, in his capacity of military commandant, was to the 'Commander of Forces', a general, in Jamaica. The affairs of the garrison kept the Superintendent busy enough for Lieutenant Colonel Arthur to ask for the appointment of a military secretary to ease the burden of military correspondence with which he and his civil secretary were having to deal.[13]

It was not until Arthur's long tenure from 1814 to 1822 that the Superintendent adopted a more interventionist stance in civil affairs, or began, as he put it, to 'assume authority over the proceedings of the settle-ment'.[14] As a result he gained some control over the filling of public appointments (such as Clerk of the Court, Keeper of Records, Public Treasurer, Provost Marshal, High Constable and Harbourmaster), which was finally endorsed in unequivocal terms by the Secretary of State (and the Prince Regent) in late 1819.[15] For progress of this kind, much depended on the Superintendent's personal relations with the magistrates and other leading citizens. Not all Superintendents had the right touch. Like Despard, Bassett became, even in his short tenure from 1800 to 1801, detested because of his 'propensity to ... exercise an arbitrary disposition repugnant to our regulations, customs, and usages';[16] and, again like Despard, he was alleged by the merchants to be 'an improper person to remain in his present situation'.[17] On the arrival of his successor, once again Barrow, the leading settlers, referring to his previous superintend-ency, expressed confidence that they could 'look up for that happiness and internal quietude which for some time past we have unfortunately been deprived of'.[18] In the nature of things personality continued to play a large part in the success with which a Superintendent's efforts were met, even as the post became better established. Thus Arthur, who arrived as a major, was both respected at the time and well remembered afterwards, whereas his successor, the much more senior Major General Edward Codd, left the settlement after six years in 'a state of mental imbecility'.[19]

The Public Meeting

It was also not until Arthur's time that greater use was made of the Superintendent's right to issue proclamations, thus enabling him to encroach on the Public Meeting's more general prerogative of making laws and setting taxes. In 1800, it seems that the Superintendent could only cajole. As the political and legal status of the Bay of Honduras settlement was unique in the evolving British Empire, so was the institution of the Public Meeting. An informal tradition from the first half of the eighteenth century, it had been semi-formalised by Rear Admiral Burnaby when he drew up his code for basic self-government in 1765. Until 1808 participa-tion was open only to heads of white households owning property valued at £80 or more. Thereafter free coloured residents of five years' standing were eligible subject to a property qualification of £200. The residential qualification was five times, and the property threshold twice, the revised amount for whites.[20] By 1820 the property rates were £500 for whites and £1000 for free coloureds.[21] Typically 25 to 40 people who met such criteria turned out as voters at this quarterly event. Despite the exasperation of successive Superintendents, who sometimes had to back up their cajoling with threats, the Public Meeting remained as the settlement's legislative body, with exclusive powers over the raising of taxes, until 1854, when it was replaced by a Legislative Assembly of elected members. By that time the Public Meeting, with over sixty people entitled to attend, had long become an unwieldy instrument for the making of laws; while changes in the British government's view of the status of the settlement at last made possible this substantive move towards proper constitutional development.

Although the Public Meeting was supposed to take place every three months after the quarterly meeting of the general session of the court, inspection of records for the second half of the year 1800 shows that in practice they were held somewhat more frequently and on an ad hoc basis. Thus five Meetings were held during that period, in August, October and (three times) in December. Matters taken varied from the fundamental, through the topical, to the ephemeral. The August Meeting voted on an address to the Governor of Jamaica seeking a widening of the limited 'commercial intercourse with America' allowed with the severe shortage of British shipping due to the war with France and Spain. In October the Meeting's concern was the failure of the Superintendent, two years after the defeat of the Spaniards off St George's Cay, to allow the settlement to revert entirely to traditional self-government. In a spirit of compromise arising from the exigiencies of war, they nonetheless agreed to accept the Superintendent's assurances of 'his disposition to respect the laws of this country'. By December the threat of attack must have increased because the next Meeting was devoted to discussion of defence measures. Interestingly one resolution granted the Superintendent £100 from the Public Treasury for 'secret expenditure'. The fourth Meeting, on Christmas Eve, dealt with public order over the Christmas holiday; while the last Meeting of the year, on 30 December, goes unrecorded.[22]

The magistracy

It was the Public Meeting that elected, each year, the seven members of the magistracy. Initially seven, the size of this bench had fluctuated since the adoption of Burnaby's Code in 1765 between five and nine before reverting to the original number in 1799. By custom they were white and British-born, although that was not formalised until 1809 when the further quite stiff condition was added of ownership of property worth £500.[23] As a result many of the same names, as we have already seen, appear on the lists of magistrates year after year. Although Lieutenant Colonel Arthur held them often to be 'persons of the worst character',[24] the magistrates had primary responsibility for the operation of the very basic judicial system. They held general courts (dealing quarterly with crimes, misdemeanours and significant debt cases); summary courts (dealing monthly with petty debt cases); transient courts (dealing as required with disputes involving visitors); and slave courts (dealing as required with offences against slave law). Verdicts in general and transient courts were decided by a jury of 12; those in summary and slave courts by a jury of 5.[25] All jurors were white property holders.[26] Despite uneasiness among the government's Law Officers in London, who in 1812 formally cast doubt on the legality of the arrangement, the bench continued to award punishments 'according to the customs of the Bay'. There were provisions for appeals to Jamaica and even to London in particularly contentious cases. A further device to overcome the obvious shortcomings of the local judicial system was resort by the Superintendent in serious cases to trial by court martial. This too raised doubts in London. These doubts must have increased with time. By 1815 the Law Officers in London were proposing that capital cases should be heard in Britain. Arthur's counterproposal of tribunals run on court martial lines but by militia rather than garrison officers was not accepted.[27] In 1817 an act was passed enabling murder cases in settlements outside the King's dominions to be 'tried, judged, and punished' in the territory concerned 'under or by virtue of the King's commission'.[28]

This Act of Parliament, and further legislation in London the following year, led to the establishment in 1819 of a Supreme Court in the Bay to deal with certain designated serious offences. The difficulty of applying British legislation in a territory where Spain was still the recognised sovereign power was tacitly set aside. Thereafter the only significant change to the judicial system during the first half of the century was the decision in 1832 that the magistrates should be nominated by the Superintendent rather than elected by the Public Meeting. Those two formal steps, following the *de facto* widening of the Superintendent's powers by Arthur, marked the beginning of the end of the eighteenth century system of government entirely by elected representatives of a section of the community.

By virtue of its powers of decision over spending of revenue from the taxes voted by the Public Meeting, the magistracy, which was itself unpaid, was also in 1800 in effect the executive arm of government. As it was put in the local *Almanac* in 1828, the magistrates 'manage the public funds and control the Treasurer; and no money can be paid without the sanction of four'. This was sometimes a further frustration for the Superintendent, and was the reason Lieutenant Colonel Arthur repeatedly proposed that the magistrates should be made responsible to the

Superintendent. It could also impinge very personally: in 1828 Major General Codd was not sure that the magistrates would agree to the British government's proposal that local payment of his full salary should be placed on a regular footing.[29] Influence on the management of public finances was perhaps the major preoccupation of the Superintendents of the early nineteenth century. Before 1828, the incumbent himself received a British government salary of £500, usually matched by a local grant, and otherwise had direct control only over the £500 he was allowed to charge to HM Treasury for 'contingent' expenses incurred in the public service. There were times in that period when there was a high level of local public debt despite the neglect of public works, and other times when there was a surplus despite an active works programme. Thus Arthur, who had succeeded in initiating a number of public works, left the settlement, in 1822, with healthy public finances; but by the time Lieutenant Colonel Cockburn arrived eight years later, tax had to be increased and a loan raised to pay off a public debt which had grown to £23,000.[30] One reason funds were often short seems to have been a reliance for revenue on import duties (generally 5 per cent, but 6 per cent for wines and spirits), harbour dues, liquor licence proceeds, and fines. Resistance at Public Meetings to any form of direct taxation continued throughout the period.

Another important function of the magistracy in the early years of the nineteenth century was to act as a 'committee of correspondence' with the London merchants with whom they did business. The London merchants formed their own committee. Much of the lobbying of government had been in the hands of the solicitor Robert White, who had been extremely active as the settlers' designated agent during and after the American war. But it had become increasingly clear that the interests he represented were not necessarily at one with those of either all the mahogany exporters or all the merchants in London. From the 1780s there are traces of separate representations to Ministers and Under Secretaries both by individual merchants and by the committee. White then seems, from the conclusion of the 1786 Convention, to have focused steadily more on the case for compensation for both the Mosquito Shore evacuees and those of the Bay settlers who had lost property at the time of the Spanish invasion of 1779. But in the early years of the nineteenth century these various channels of communication between the magistrates and their contacts in London, and through them with the government there, were something the Superintendent had constantly to bear in mind, as Despard had found to his cost. It was not until 1815 that the settlers proposed that all correspondence intended for government departments should be routed through the Superintendent.[31]

Again it is instructive to look at the record, in this case at meetings of the magistracy for the last quarter of 1800. There were seven altogether, two in October, two in November and three in December, attended by between five and seven members of the bench each time. The first two involved the magistrates in their judicial function: review of the case of an imprisoned member of the garrison and consideration of the need for prosecution of two keepers of 'tippling houses' where there had been drunken and disorderly behaviour. The November meetings were both concerned with public expenditure: funding of repairs to the forts at the mouth of the Belize River and payment for a boat to reconnoitre Spanish military preparations at Trujillo in Honduras. Of the December meetings only one dealt with internal administration, when someone had to be nominated to make arrangements for the effects of a deceased settler. The other two meetings considered reports of hostile moves by the Spaniards.[32] Thus other than sitting to take formal evidence as a court, and setting aside meetings about defence, civil matters only required the magistrates to meet once in three months. That it was not always like that is shown by the record for 1793, when they met no less than eight times in six weeks early in the year to discuss the winding up of a particularly complex estate.

Slaves, Free Coloureds and Blacks, and Caribs

As was held to be natural at the time, the settlement's slaves had neither part nor voice in any aspect of administration or in the election of those charged with it. But despite their supposed freedom and their numbers, the political status of the 'free coloureds and blacks' was also heavily circumscribed. When the bar on participation in Public Meetings was removed in 1808 they were burdened, as we have seen, with a property qualification twice as heavy as that for white settlers and a residence qualification five times as long. Seven years later Lieutenant Colonel Arthur sought unsuccessfully to reimpose that bar on even those 'free coloureds and blacks' who had qualified, claiming that 'our security certainly requires that [their privileges] should be curtailed rather than extended'.[33] But by 1819 the climate had changed, and he was comparing them favourably to the majority of whites, describing 'the better description of people of colour' as 'infinitely superior to the lower class of white inhabitants'.[34] They remained nonetheless unable during that period to serve as magistrates or jurors. Although they formed the main strength of the militia's artillery companies,[35] they were also ineligible for commissioned military service. Moreover when conditional eligibility for service as magistrates did come for 'free coloureds' in 1829, followed by full equalisation of rights and privileges in 1831, 'free blacks' were not included until after final emancipation of the settlement's slaves.[36]

On the periphery of the community was a fourth group, the Black Caribs (then spelt Charibs, now called Garifuna). They had originated from a mingling in the eastern Caribbean between aboriginal Red Caribs and escaped African slaves. They had been transported to the island of Ruatan in the Gulf of Honduras in 1797 following rebellions in Dominica and St Vincent. By 1802, 150 of them had migrated to the coast south of the Sibun,[37] where they worked first as labourers, then as fishermen and farmers. Physically more African than Carib, they remained culturally distinct from the much larger number of Africans brought to the territory as slaves. Because of the background to their tranportation they were at first regarded as 'a most dangerous people',[38] and only allowed to visit Belize town if they had written permission to do so. This prejudice changed with the passage of time. By 1835, when their number had increased to 500, they were described as 'quiet, industrious, and attached to the British' and looked upon as a resource to meet an anticipated labour shortage.[39]

Social, cultural and religious life

We have only glimpses of the social and recreational life of the settlement in the early 1800s. Christmas hilarity was opened with a 'discharge of small arms in every direction' and marked with singing and dancing, dory and pitpan racing, and much drinking. Other pursuits were fishing from the cays and shooting in the bush.[40] The cultural and religious life of all three sections of this very small and remote society was of course extremely limited. There was no school of any kind in the settlement at the turn of the century, when those who had the time and ability to do so taught their children at home. In 1807, by coincidence the year it was also decided to establish a gaol, a Meeting agreed that the public purse should fund a free school for ten poor boys, under the auspices of the Anglican church.[41] This grew steadily until by the early 1830s around a hundred boys were enrolled. Girls from better-off families were by then being taught in small classes, though mostly still privately.[42] But it was nonconformist missionaries who brought about the slow spread of primary education, especially outside Belize town, from the same period onwards.

They had not been the first priests to arrive. The very first had been a visiting Anglican clergyman who came to the Bay in 1776 to convalesce. He was persuaded to stay in return for a small stipend raised by subscription, and a place of worship was built for him on St George's Cay. In 1779 that was destroyed, but the Reverend Shaw escaped to the Mosquito Shore and then returned to the Bay for three years from 1786. After a five-year inter-regnum, the Reverend Stanford, an evangelical, took up residence in 1794. Although he is supposed on one occasion to have been too drunk to bury a visiting seaman, he was by the time of the Spanish attack in 1798, when he distinguished himself, a magistrate; and between 1800 and 1803, although he only married 7, he managed to baptise 109 and bury 35. Church services were held in the Court House. It was not until 1810 that a Public Meeting decided that a church should be built, the first Protestant church in Central America.[43] By the time it was consecrated by the Bishop of Jamaica in 1826, to whose diocese the Bay had been added in 1824, Stanford's successor, also an evangelical, had been in the settlement for fourteen years, during the first eleven of which he had baptised 1800 people. But, although reinforced in 1820 by an assistant, he was facing competition soon afterwards from the first of the non-conformist missionaries referred to above. These were Baptists, who arrived in 1822, and Wesleyans, who arrived in 1826.[44] Although they were left free to set up chapels and to preach in them, their right to perform marriage services was challenged because it was still (until 1836) not allowed in England, and because of concern among owners at the missionaries' readiness to marry slave couples. Legally this bar was not removed in Belize until 1852.[45] A later, but in the second half of the century more powerful, competitor for the Church of England was Roman Catholicism, the first ordained representative of which, a Franciscan, arrived in 1832 to minister to Carib refugees from Honduras at Mullins River.[46]

Logging

As we have seen, the settlement's traditional industry, the cutting and exporting of logwood, had been largely replaced in the three decades before 1800 by the exploitation of mahogany. A number of factors combined to make this a more labour intensive business, which in turn led to the concentration of its direction, and of ownership of the 'works' in the rain forest, in fewer hands. First, mahogany trees are bigger and thus required larger gangs to undertake the cutting and subsequent transportation. Second, new growth is much slower, and therefore to keep up with demand the cutters had to range ever further away from the banks of rivers. This in turn complicated the logistics of the operation, including the building of camps for the workers. It also called for the introduction around the turn of the century of oxen to haul felled trees to the nearest riverbank, representing further capital investment for the entrepreneur; while hauling over these greater distances involved the cutting of tracks through the jungle, the cost of which was a further overhead for him to bear.

Extraction of both mahogany and logwood, the felling of the second which seems to have reached its lowest point around the beginning of the century, was a seasonal affair. Identification and marking, and the building of camps, took place in the autumn, towards the end of the rainy season. Most of the cutting, and all of the hauling, was done in the dry months of the new year and spring. The timber was then floated down one or other of the rivers in enormous rafts when the rains returned in May or June. Mahogany was not, as we have seen, a resource that renewed itself quickly. It therefore became steadily more difficult to find within the treaty limits. This is what drove the woodcutters southwards in the unoccupied land south of the River Sibun, as we shall see. It took them ultimately, and certainly by 1825, to what later became the settlement's southern boundary, the River Sarstoon. The same shortage led to a change in attitude towards mahogany imported for shipment from Belize from north of the River Hondo. For many years 'foreign mahogany' was a prohibited import. By 1818 it was an accepted commodity, but subject to a heavy UK duty. By 1832 it was being proposed that this discrimination should be waived where the shipper was a British merchant.[47]

Trade

At the turn of the century this export trade involved clearance of about 8000 tons of shipping annually. The French Revolutionary War, and then, from 1803, the Napoleonic War led to some disruption. It is noticeable that in 1802, the one full year of peace between the two, mahogany exports increased by 50 per cent over the 1800 figure. As significantly, whereas half of all production was consigned to the United States in 1800, this proportion fell to 5 per cent, with 90 per cent bound to Europe, in 1802.[48] This represented a return to normality. In wartime, direct trade from British overseas possessions to European continental markets was blocked by both sides. But shipment to the United States for onward dispatch in neutral vessels overcame that constraint until the total blockade of the later years of the struggle. In peacetime, on the other hand, the British government was anxious to maximise revenue from duties firstly by encouraging export to or through Britain itself and secondly by maintaining the traditional monopoly of the trade for British ships.

This issue of freedom to trade both to the United States and in American 'bottoms' was one of a number of recurring themes in early nineteenth-century representations to the British government by the Belize timber producers and their correspondents in London, and indeed to an extent also by the Superintendents. Thus as the first phase of the war drew to an end in the autumn of 1801, a former magistrate, and resident of the Bay for 38 years, petitioned the Secretary of State for an end, because of its 'injurious consequence', to the peacetime bar on shipment of both imports and exports in American ships, a demand repeated the following year by the merchants collectively.[49] A secret despatch to Barrow at the end of 1803 makes clear that the waiver of that bar marked the resumption of war rather than a change of basic policy.[50] In 1815, after peace in Europe was finally made, Lieutenant Colonel Arthur was calling for reversion to a 'limited American intercourse', both to make imports more affordable for poorer inhabitants and to avoid damage from Spanish competition to the trade of the mahogany exporters.[51] Trade was not, however, finally freed until 1830.

The traders also took the opportunity of the peace of 1802 to press Lord Hobart twice, reminding him of earlier representations to Lord Hawkesbury, to seek Spanish agreement to a southwards extension of the settlement's boundaries.[52] This, as we have seen, would have been a simple legitimisation of an accomplished fact. A third concern, endorsed by the Superintendents, was the limited range of what might be produced in the settlement. Thus we have in 1802 and 1803 first the London merchants then the Superintendent urging the Secretary of State to press the Spaniards for the settlers to be allowed to grow cotton, with Barrow also suggesting sugar, coffee and ginger.[53] In 1805 the settlement's London agent reported that no prospect was foreseen of diversifying the economy in this way.[54] Arthur returned to the suggestion in 1817,[55] while more than one Superintendent drew attention to the inadequacy for the settlers' subsistence of the 'garden grounds' approved by the Spanish authorities in 1789.

War

The settlement's relations with its neighbours were of course complicated until 1815 by the shifting alliances of the war in Europe. Barrow on his return in January 1803, during the break in the war referred to above, assured the Governor of Yucatan that he sought 'a cordial and liberal understanding between the subjects of both crowns',[56] and three months later reported a reciprocal agreement with the Captain General of Guatemala on the return of runaway slaves.[57] But everyone knew that war was likely to resume. Consequently, while Barrow was satisfied that the settlement was in 'a very increasing and flourishing state', he was very concerned about the 'ruinous' state of its defences.[58] By the middle of 1803 he was ordering the construction of gunboats and considering the distribution of arms and stationing of look-out boats. Defence was centred on the newly constructed Fort George at the mouth of the Belize River, and supported by 'judiciously placed batteries'.[59] As to troops, he still had available the 5th West India Regiment, which had not been withdrawn because of the uncertainty of the peace, to whom he could add in support nearly 800 members of the local militia. But he received no extra supplies until the end of the year, shortly before Spain followed France into a resumption of the war. Then, interestingly he also received 'presents' for the Mosquito Indians, who, to the irritation of the Governor of Yucatan, had been in touch with him about arms with which to fight consolidation of the Spanish hold on their homeland.

In the event there was no Spanish attack on the Bay settement. This must have been due partly to the increasing grip in which the British Navy held the Caribbean and partly to experience in 1798 of the navigational difficulty of attacking the Belize River mouth when, unlike in 1779, it was defended by both a military and a naval force. For the first time therefore the settlers would have felt, even in time of war, some sense of security against external attack. This would have increased with the changes in Spain's position brought about first by developments in the war in Europe, then by the turn of events in her empire that followed the peace.

Notes

1. G. Henderson, *An Account of the British Settlement of Honduras*, London (1809), 12–13.
2. 'General Return of the Inhabitants in the Bay of Honduras', 22 October 1790, CO 123/9; and 'Census of the Population 1816 (Recapitulation)', BA (0016 CNS/1, 95)
3. Enc. to Barrow/Hobart, 31 March 1803, CO 123/15.
4. Summary of occupations by Hunter, late 1790, CO 123/14.
5. O. N. Bolland, *The Formation of a Colonial Society: Belize from Conquest to Crown Colony*, Baltimore (1977), 60.
6. ibid., 89.
7. Despard/Sydney, 31 October 1787, CO 123/6. This is confirmed in 'The Present State of the British Settlers in Honduras', undated 1790, CO 123/9. That document records that there were then 13 'cutters and exporters of wood possessed of considerable property', 34 'possessed of less property', and 24 'of small property', besides 49 settlers 'in the service of' the woodcutters.
8. O. N. Bolland, 'Slavery in Belize', *Journal of Belizean Affairs*, No. 6, January (1978), 23.
9. *Honduras Almanack*, Belize (1828).
10. Commission from the Duke of Manchester, Governor of Jamaica, filed as enc. to Arthur/Bathurst, 17 April 1815, CO 123/24. Arthur was the most distinguished of the early Superintendents in later life, becoming a Lieutenant General and Privy Councillor. But for ill health, he would have been appointed Governor General of India – see Narda Dobson, *A History of Belize*, London (1973), 104.
11. Letter of appointment to Barrow, 5 October 1802, CO 123/15.
12. Liverpool/Smyth, 15 June 1810, CO 124/3.
13. Arthur/Bathurst, 30 August 1817, CO 123/26.

14. Arthur/Bathurst, 17 April 1815, CO 123/24. Besides a degree of control of public appointments (see below), Arthur secured agreement that he should be informed when Public Meetings were to be convened – see Bolland in *The Formation of a Colonial Society*, 171.
15. ABH Vol. 2, 224.
16. Magistrates/London merchants, 18 September 1801, CO 123/15.
17. G. Dyer/J. King, 23 February 1802, CO 123/15.
18. Memorial leading settlers/Barrow, 25 January 1803, CO 123/15.
19. Cockburn/Messervy, 2 February 1830, CO 123/41.
20. ABH Vol. 2, 123.
21. ibid., 232. The wide gap in the residential qualification also remained. A white settler qualified after a year's residence, whereas a free coloured resident had to be locally born – see Bolland in *The Formation of a Colonial Society*, 172.
22. BA (Record of Public and Magistrates' meetings for 1800).
23. ABH Vol. 2, 127.
24. Arthur/Bathurst, 17 April 1815, CO 123/24.
25. Enc. to Barrow/Hobart, 31 March 1803, CO 123/15.
26. Lt. Col. Arthur reported that 'the only distinction between the whites and the (free) people of colour is that the latter cannot hold the office of magistrate or sit as jurors' – see Arthur/Bathurst 15 February 1815, CO 123/24.
27. Arthur/Bathhurst, 11 August 1817, CO 123/27.
28. CO 123/26
29. Codd/Murray, 1 January 1829, ABH Vol. 2, 304.
30. Cockburn/Messervy, 3 April 1830 and Cockburn/Twiss, 8 November 1830, CO 123/41; Cockburn/Marshall, 9 July 1835, CO 123/46.
31. Arthur /Bathurst, 26 July 1815, CO 123/24.
32. BA (Record of Public and Magistrates' meetings for 1800).
33. Arthur/Bathurst, 15 February 1815, CO 123/24.
34. Arthur/Bathurst, 4 November 1819, CO 123/28.
35. Honduras Almanack (Belize 1828).
36. Macdonald/Glenelg, 28 February 1838, CO 123/52.
37. Nancie L. Gonzalez, 'Garifuna Traditions in Historical Perspectives', *Belizean Studies*, Vol. 14 No. 2, (1986), 5.
38. ABH Vol. 2, 146.
39. Miller/Aberdeen, 4 February 1835, CO 123/47.
40. Henderson, 74–80.
41. W. R. Johnston, *A History of Christianity in Belize 1776–1838*, London (1985), 204. The school was enlarged in 1819, when it admitted girls for the first time.
42. Cockburn/Goderich, 10 January 1833, CO 123/44.
43. Johnston, 42. Construction started in 1812.
44. C. H. Grant, *The Making of Modern Belize*, Cambridge (1976), 47. In each case a chapel was opened in Belize a year after the arrival of the first representative – see Johnston, 101 and 127.
45. Johnston, 152.
46. Richard Buhler, *A History of the Catholic Church in Belize*, Belize Institute for Social Research and Action (1976), 7. His successor built a church there in 1836. The first Roman Catholic chapel in Belize opened in 1840. The rapid expansion of Roman Catholicism in the territory, especially among immigrants in the north and the Maya, followed the arrival of the first Jesuit mission in 1851.
47. Cockburn/Goderich, 20 November 1832, CO 123/43.
48. Enc. to Barrow/Hobart, 31 March 1803, CO 123/15.
49. Memorial London merchants/Hobart, 25 March 1802, CO 123/15.
50. Hobart/Barrow, 3 November 1803, CO 123/15.
51. Arthur/Bathurst, 26 July 1815, CO 123/24.

52. G. Dyer/J. King, 20 February 1802, and London merchants/Hobart, 15 October 1802 – both CO 123/15.
53. Enc. to Barrow/Hobart, 31 March 1803, CO 123/15.
54. ABH Vol. 2, 88.
55. Arthur/Bathurst, 2 April 1817, CO 123/27.
56. Barrow/Governor Yucatan, 27 January 1803, CO 123/15.
57. Barrow/Hobart, 19 April 1803, CO 123/15.
58. ibid.
59. Henderson, 72–3.

5

Slavery and Emancipation

The shipment of African slaves to the New World began with the early colonisation of the Americas. The general purpose was to provide a cheap but robust labour force for the plantations that were established in the region mainly, but not only, to produce sugar. In the eighteenth century the trade was dominated by the British, whose principal slave markets were in Jamaica and Barbados. At the beginning of the nineteenth century most (in 1803, three-quarters) of the people living in the town of Belize and the wider British settlement of the Bay of Honduras were slaves, imported as labourers for the mahogany 'works'. This remained the position until about 1825, when the proportion of slaves in the population dipped, declining also in absolute terms, to a level just below 50 per cent. It remained there until a limited freedom was granted in 1834. Until that time slaves were classified as the private property of their owners, and bought and sold like any other chattel. Although a commission of enquiry reporting in 1829 stated that it was 'the custom of the country' to sell slaves as families, the absolute right of property enjoyed by an owner could in law, and sometimes did in practice, over-ride such considerations as the keeping together of these or any other social units. The only difference between the nature of slavery in the Bay and elsewhere lay in the conditions in which most slaves worked and the consequently greater degree of interdependence between masters and men: the working environment was the untamed rain forest rather than the orderly plantation, and this did not lend itself to the very close control of labour that was a feature of the islands and the American southern states.

Development, demography and employment

The earliest report of the presence of African slaves in the Bay is by a Spanish missionary in 1722 or 1724, who indicated that they had then only recently been introduced.[1] Within the next twenty years they became a clear majority in the settlement. An appeal in 1745 by the settlers for help to deal with the threat of Spanish attack stated that their numbers did not exceed 'fifty white men and about a hundred and twenty negroes'.[2] By 1779, when the Spaniards seized the territory, the number had grown considerably. We know that 250 slaves were included with the white settlers that were taken into captivity then, and that a comparable number accompanied other whites who succeeded in escaping to Ruatan. Many others would have simply melted away, although the figure of a total slave population then of 3000 quoted in one source[3] seems almost certain to be an exaggeration.

As we have already seen, the reason for the sharp increase in slave numbers was the replacement, in the last thirty years of the eighteenth century, of logwood cutting by the much more labour-intensive business of mahogany felling. Whereas logwood cutting could be undertaken by a white settler 'with a single negro, some without one',[4] a mahogany works employed a substantial gang of labourers some of whom, such as the 'hunters' who identified the trees to be felled, the 'axemen' who cut them, and the 'cattlemen' who managed the oxen that hauled them, were skilled specialists. The extra numbers were brought in from the slave markets of Jamaica, a process which continued, because of the low local birth rate, well into the nineteenth century. At around the time the slave trade was formally abolished in 1807, the market price of a 'seasoned' adult male slave was between £200 and £300.[5] This implied a high level of capital investment for any one of the dozen major owners, for whom the average slave holding in 1816 was 92. There are indications that as late as 1823 up to 60 per cent of those on the slave register may have been African born.[6] Consistent with this is evidence that importation continued in the Bay after the trade was banned, presumably because of doubts about both the powers of the Superintendent and the applicability of the Abolition Act to a settlement still under Spanish sovereignty. This was not helped by an opinion from the Attorney General in Jamaica that, because the Bay settlement could not be considered to be in the West Indies, only naval and customs officers, of whom there were none in the Bay, had the powers to seize shipments of slaves.[7] This led to Lieutenant Colonel Arthur's recourse to a proclamation in 1815, giving himself the necessary powers on the basis that the act applied to British subjects everywhere.[8] A year later he claimed to have 'put an entire stop to that disgraceful commerce'.[9] By the beginning of the following decade closure of this external supply, together with a continuing low rate of reproduction due to the shortage of women, was beginning to make itself felt in the settlement's demographic structure. By then the proportion of slaves over forty had increased to about a fifth, and a continuation of the trend took that proportion to a third by the time of abolition in 1834.[10]

The main purpose of slavery in the Bay settlement, as on the Mosquito Shore until 1787, was to provide a cheap but hardy labour force to extract timber from the harsh surroundings of the rain forest. Statistics compiled in 1834, the year slavery formally came to an end, indicate that nearly 90 per cent of male slaves between the ages of 20 and 59 were engaged in woodcutting.[11] But, as a useful by-product of the system, female, child, and elderly adult male slave labour was also available for a range of other, physically less demanding, tasks in the areas where the setters lived. Here the two main categories of work were domestic service of all kinds, engaging largely, but not exclusively, women and girls; and cultivation by older male slaves of fruit and vegetable provisions in the 'gardens' or 'plantations' that date, at least legally, from 1789, when the Spaniards extended their approval of gathering the 'natural fruits of the soil' to subsistence cultivation. By 1809, although there is no sign of any export trade, the scale of this latter activity had become substantial enough for one observer to refer to the banks of the Sibun as 'thickly studded with plantations'.[12] As we have seen, it had also developed a rudimentary commercial dimension, with licensed vendors selling surplus production in Belize town to those who were not self-supporting. There was also a third category of employment for male slaves. Contemporary records show that among their number was a handful of more or less skilled tradesmen not directly connected with woodcutting: blacksmiths, coopers and boatmen, presumably working for white or free black or coloured people who had businesses in those or related fields.

Treatment

Many favourable comparisons have been drawn between the treatment of slaves on the British-occupied Central American coast and that meted out elsewhere, and also between social relations there and in other places. This surfaces in quite early records from both the Mosquito Shore and the Bay. For the former the last Superintendent stated shortly before the settlement was given up that 'neither whip nor overseer are necessary or practised to enforce labour' and that 'during late and former wars these negroes have been entrusted with arms'.[13] For the Bay it is clear from Lieutenant Colonel Hunter's correspondence that during the downturn in Anglo-Spanish relations in 1790, with the consequent possibility of attack on the settlement, there were plans to issue arms to at least some slaves. Later records make clear that during that Spanish attack of 1798 most slaves were actually armed and 'embodied' as militia troops.[14] Moreover the author of the longest account we have of local life in the early nineteenth century, an army officer who served with the garrison, stated that 'the whole of the slaves of Honduras are permitted to use arms, and possibly a more expert body of marksmen could nowhere be found'.[15] More generally, and as significantly, he observed that 'in no part of the world where slavery prevails can the condition of beings so circumstanced be found in milder or more indulgent form'.[16] At about the same time a visiting brigadier observed in an official report to the Governor of Jamaica that he had been struck by 'the robust and healthy appearance of the slaves' in the Bay, and by how well fed they were by their owners.[17] All these witnesses may have had in mind what they had seen of slave treatment in Jamaica, where whips and overseers were very much a part of the system. Furthermore, although the last two were writing at a time when slavery was being questioned, the current issue was the international trade in slaves, rather than the institution of slavery in Britain's Caribbean possessions and the status and treatment which that involved for its victims.

Perhaps partly because the climate of opinion was changing, but possibly also because they simply spent more time in the Bay, we have a very different view only a few years later of the reality of slavery both from a Superintendent who shortly after his arrival had written of the 'humane manner in which the slaves of this country have uniformly been treated[18] and from a clerical observer who was perhaps always more likely to be sceptical. In 1820, his sixth year in the settlement, Lieutenant Colonel Arthur, in the first of a series of letters to the Secretary of State, said that while there was an initial overall impression of humanity in the treatment of slaves, in fact there was a tendency towards increasing inhumanity amongst the 'lower class of slave owners'.[19] In a letter of the same month to Lord Bathurst he referred again to 'the increasing severity and cruelty which is now practised with impunity'.[20] Four years later, in 1824, the Reverend Armstrong summed up his view of the treatment of slaves at the end of his long stay by describing it as 'comparatively comfortable; but there are instances, many instances, of horrible barbarity practised here'.[21] The reality may be that enlightened self interest, beyond the powers of some of the totally uneducated poorer white settlers, led to a certain restraint in the treatment of their slaves by at least some of the bigger owners. They are likely after all to have been aware of their dependence on the initiative of their men when in the rain forest, and to have seen that slaves represented, by 1807, a non-renewable resource.

If the picture is mixed, it is nonetheless striking that in 1820 Arthur saw fit to recommend a Council for the Protection of Slaves.[22] What is in any case beyond doubt is that slaves both rebelled against their condition and sought escape from it to territory under Spanish control. The 1745 appeal for military assistance against threat of Spanish attack already quoted makes clear that any idea of slave loyalty to their masters in time of war could not be taken for granted ('we cannot tell how many may prove true in the time of engagement'), whereas constant complaints confirm that even in time of peace, flight was a continual problem for slave owners right up until the grant of full freedom in 1838. Indeed the problem of runaway slaves was one of the main complications in relations between Britain and Spain on the coast throughout the eighteenth-century history of both the Bay and the Shore settlements, and in the case of the former well into the nineteenth century.

Rebellion and flight

Three of the four significant slave revolts took place between 1765 and 1773, that is during the expansion of both mahogany extraction and the slave labour force needed to achieve it, and before the Spanish occupation of the settlement during the American War of Independence. Because there was no police organisation or standing military presence, all caused great alarm. The first two were small-scale affairs, involving less than twenty-five men. In 1773, however, when the slave population had probably grown to well over a thousand, fifty slaves took control of five logging camps and killed six whites in a rebellion that was only quelled after nearly six months with the assistance of seamen and marines from two British warships.[23] In the 1780s, during much of which there were no arrangements for the return of fugitives, desertion, judging from the settlers' representations, became more common. From 1796 the presence of a garrison, which remained with the return of peace in 1815 and was only reduced from four companies to two the year before full emancipation, may explain why there was only one further rebellion in the latter years of slavery in the Bay. Caused in the Superintendent's view by 'very unnecessary harshness', that revolt, in 1820, was only put down after a month by a combination of inducement, martial law and the use of troops.[24] But for years before that the white settlers had lived in fear of the possibility of the kind of upheaval that had brutally destroyed colonial society in French San Domingo (later Haiti) in 1804. That fear was aggravated by concern about the rapport between the slaves and the black rank-and-file of the 2nd West India Regiment which, by 1825, had been stationed in the settlement for nearly ten years.[25] It would have been reinforced by the knowledge that in the years shortly before the 1820 revolt, maroon communities had sprung up around the headwaters of some of the rivers that run through the territory. The numbers of maroons were enough for the Superintendent to describe them in 1817 as 'a considerable body of runaway slaves'.[26]

As for flight, the difficulty it caused the settlers was taken up by their representatives in London a number of times in the 1780s. In 1790 Lieutenant Colonel Hunter put it more succinctly: 'Many of the settlers of this country have been entirely ruined by these circumstances, and all experience frequent and heavy losses'.[27] What made escape practicable, of course, was the combination of the knowledge of the bush gained from working in it and the comparatively small extent of the territory. The favoured destination through most of the eighteenth century seems to have been the area just across the most accessible part of the border, that with the southern Yucatan, where, before working relations were established with the Superintendent from 1786–90 and again from 1802, the Commandant at Bacalar offered asylum. As cutting was pushed westwards in the 1770s the Peten region of Guatemala became an alternative. Possibly because of Barrow's agreement with the authorities in Guatemala in 1803,[28] and because, too, cutting in the previous few years had also been extended well south of the Sibun, there are more references in the early nineteenth century to Omoa and Trujillo in present-day Honduras. The problem became aggravated in the 1820s, with the independence of the neighbouring territories and the abolition of slavery by the governments of the new republics that took shape there. In 1823 it was reported that no less than thirty-nine slaves had escaped to the Peten in a little over two months.[29] For the first two months of 1825, the number increased to a hundred.[30] In 1826 nearly 10 per cent of those on the slave register were listed as runaways.[31] By 1830 one view in the Colonial Office was that 'if we persist in maintaining (slavery), we must look for a rapid depopulation of the settlement by the slaves passing the border line and returning no more'.[32] For individual settlers the result could be disastrous, because for many years there had been no more slaves available.

Slavery and the law

The slaves' general dissatisfaction with their lot would have been aggravated by the appalling treatment that individual slave owners could undoubtedly get away with if they were so minded, and by the reluctance of the magistrates to afford slaves any redress. In his letters of the early 1820s to the Secretary of State, Lord Bathurst, written against the background of the last of the slave revolts, Lieutenant Colonel Arthur gives some stark examples. In 1820 he cites a case of severe injury to a female slave caused by a whipping which the magistrates decided was legitimate because it had not exceeded the permitted maximum of thirty-nine lashes.[33] The following year he described an illegal punishment inflicted upon four slaves, which the magistrates decided not to take up because of the expense of a jury trial; and the staking and flogging of a female for no more than complaining, where the magistrates declined to find a suitable charge against the perpetrator.[34] Six months later, in 1822, he reported the failure of the executors of a deceased slave owner to free some of his slaves eighteen years before as decreed in the will, a decision upheld by the magistrates on the grounds that the deceased's debts exceeded his disposable property.[35] Where extreme punishment was awarded without the least demur was in cases of slaves found guilty of violence towards their masters. An example of that is the hanging of a slave in 1794 for injuring his owner with a machete, when three years before a slave owner found guilty of 'ill-treating and mutilating certain negro slaves his property' was merely fined ten pounds.[36]

Arthur also drew attention in 1822 to the situation of Mosquito Indians who had arrived with the British refugees when the Shore was evacuated in 1787 and had found themselves enslaved ever since. Their earlier petitions had been denied by the magistrates. But this was a fundamental contravention of current (though not earlier) Jamaican law, on the force of which Arthur had issued a proclamation after the recent slave revolt 'because doubts have arisen in the minds of several of our subjects' about its applicability to the Bay settlement and 'in order to quiet alarm amongst slaves at being deprived of all protection'.[37] Because of the unwillingness to act of the three commissioners he then appointed to look into the case, Arthur felt justified in this instance in taking steps himself, placing the unfortunate Indians under the care of the Provost Marshal. His decision was eventually accepted by the slave owners, but not without an initial strong reaction and subsequent monetary compensation. It was in this connection that he wrote that 'parties that hold the Indians in slavery seem to consider that their interest and their convenience are the primary objects to be consulted';[38] while his summary on the whole issue of slavery, in a letter to his successor also in 1822, was that 'upon this subject the woodcutters are jealous to an extreme of any interference'.[39]

The problem was not so much that the institution of slavery was carried on in a legal vacuum. From at least 1803, if not earlier, both slaves and owners were subject to the Consolidated Slave Law of Jamaica of 1800, 'so far as the local situation thereof will admit'.[40] Although hardly generous in its frame of reference, this did regulate the punishments that could be inflicted and did prescribe certain minima in other treatment. It also provided for the purchase of freedom and for an entitlement to own property. But interpretation of that law was in the hands of magistrates who were themselves slave owners; and as we have just seen they were not unimaginative in finding reasons for throwing out maltreatment cases brought against owners who believed in terror as a management tool. Moreover because of doubts in London about the legal authority of the Superintendent, he was urged as late as 1822 to exercise it 'sparingly and with great circumspection' even where it 'may be rendered necessary by the oppression, cruelty, or flagrant injustice of any of the inhabitants'.[41] Recourse to the court, where it could be achieved, was thus quite likely to be futile, leaving an aggrieved slave certainly with no incentive to stay and arguably with every incentive to flee.

But matters were worse than this for slaves, compounding any inclination to take things into their own hands, because they suffered from two fundamental and more formal legal disabilities. First, a slave had no direct access to the court himself, depending rather on the willingness of a free person to seek redress on his behalf. Second, having got to court, he faced the difficulty that until 1829 a fellow slave's evidence was inadmissible if it was directed towards a white person.[42] He therefore depended for testimony for his case, once again, on the agreement of a free person to come forward. The system of justice, such as it was when limited to the 'customs of the Bay', was thus, again indisputably, heavily weighted against the slave. It would have been for all these reasons that Lieutenant Colonel Arthur, otherwise not a natural social reformer, referred in a letter in February 1822 to the Secretary of State to the 'total and absolute impossibility of protecting the slave population under the present system';[43] and in a further letter the following month sought authority to introduce a 'more effectual means' of protection.[44] For corroboration of Arthur's concern, we have to look no further than to the Reverend Armstrong, who drew attention in his book to the special difficulty, 'even in cases of the most flagrant abuse and injustice', of convicting any slave owner for cruelty.[45]

Possibilities for freedom

There were possibilities for freedom other than by purchase. Some slaves were granted their freedom by gift, for others it was bequeathed on an owner's death. Statistics for the five years from the beginning of 1826 to the end of 1830 suggest that the greatest proportion of these 'manumissions' were by gift.[46] No doubt because of the shortage of white women, freedom, in the first thirty years of the nineteenth century, came to more female than male slaves; and the 1826–30 statistics suggest that, perhaps because of the economic value of mature male labour, not much more than half of the males who were freed were adults. Thus, given that the number of females, adult and child, in the slave population was only about half the number of males, the chances of freedom for women and girls were, pre-dictably, much better than they were for boys and, particularly, men. As a proportion of the slave population, which declined slowly from just under 3000 in 1803 to just over 2000 in 1829, the overall rate of manumission was in any case very low: around 20 males and females per annum between 1807 and 1820 (i.e. less than 1 per cent of the slave population), rising to about 40 per annum in the second half of the 1820s.[47] In total around six hundred slaves were freed between the abolition of the slave trade and the abolition of slavery, approximately a fifth of the slave population at the beginning of the period. Any slave who gained his freedom was therefore very lucky. The one quasi-legal advantage 'the customs of the Bay' did give him over his fellow slaves elsewhere was that if he did have that good fortune he was reasonably secure: it seems that the burden of proof in any challenge to his freedom was on the challenger rather than on him.

Abolition

As in all British overseas possessions where the economy was based on slavery, the freedom formally granted to all the settlement's 1913 slaves on 1 August 1834 was initially very limited. The Abolition Act, which authori-ties everywhere under British jurisdiction were obliged to apply on that date, had been passed in June 1833. It provided for part-compensation for slave owners for loss of 'property'; in the case of the Bay at more than twice the Jamaican rate per slave, and indeed at a rate (£53) that was higher than that awarded in any other colony.[48] But owners everywhere, supported by the governors of the colonies where slavery had been practised, had also argued that in order to avoid disruption of the economy a transitional scheme of employment was needed while the necessary adjustments were made to adapt local conditions to a free labour market. The point was con-ceded by the home government, and the concession took the form of 'apprenticeship'. In the Bay this meant, for former slaves, forty-five hours of unpaid labour for their masters each week, with only overtime work beyond that time being counted as eligible for cash payment.[49] Although the work pattern in the logging camps was based on specific tasks that could sometimes be finished by noon, elsewhere there was a twelve-hour day, with two one-hour breaks, five days a week.[50] Thus the likelihood must be that for many slaves during this period only five hours of their regular work each week was paid.

Against this background it is not suprising that Cockburn, who had correctly predicted there would not be trouble,[51] should have to report that the newly designated apprentice labourers 'neither feel benefited nor

gratified at what has been done for them'.[52] The records make clear moreover that former slaves continued to buy their full freedom and also to
escape from the settlement. Nonetheless a year later the Superintendent
felt able to state the view that the employers were satisfied and the apprentices' labour 'cheerfully performed'.[53] Indeed there is, perhaps strangely,
no record of complaint against the apprenticeship arrangement during the
four years it lasted. This may be partly due to the home government's
insistence on a degree of independent regulation. Special magistrates were
dispatched to all territories where this momentous change had been implemented to oversee its operation. The allocation to the Bay of Honduras
was one, a half-pay Army lieutenant. When he died, he was replaced by a
civilian whose background is unknown. In the interval a local settler who
had engaged no apprentices was appointed. To back up the special magistrate if necessary, a very small force of constables was raised. Although the
special magistrate had to initiate punishments against 117 apprentices in
the first year, the next year his successor was referring in a report to 'peace
good order and quietude',[54] and the constabulary was reduced.

Full emancipation, with the end of 'apprenticeship', also passed
smoothly when it came with due festivity in August 1838. Although it was
not long before the gaol was full as a result of drunken and riotous
behaviour,[55] the Superintendent felt able to report that the day after the
celebrations 'the emancipated persons were all industriously pursuing their
avocations'.[56] But the greater difficulty for the authorities was legal: there
had been simply no law with which to regulate labour contracts, such contracts as existed having been based on a system of custom biased in favour
of the employer. There was moreover no proper procedure for settling
labour disputes, a proposal for such a law having been rejected by a Public
Meeting in 1830.[57] Regulations under both headings had been rushed
through, after much argument, the month before the apprenticeship
system came to an end. But there was no experience of operating them on
which to draw, and they in any case remained to be tested more generally.
Consequently modifications had to be introduced within a month. The
result was an enactment obliging employers to issue written contracts to
employees and enabling labour disputes to be settled summarily by a panel
of three magistrates.[58] The relationship nonetheless remained fundamentally unbalanced, largely because of the employers' monopoly of
supplies at the camps and the penalties they could impose for non-
payment or late payment for them by their workers. Combined with a
system of enforceable six- and twelve-month contracts, the result for the
labourers was what has been described as 'debt servitude'.[59]

Meanwhile another issue began to brew which had a longer-term
effect. In one of his early proclamations, Lieutenant Colonel Arthur had

decreed, in 1817, that all unclaimed land belonged to the Crown. For the next few years Crown land was available for allocation without charge to those who were free. But by 1838 the Colonial Office in London had ruled that grants could only be made at a price of £1 per acre. This was reflected in instructions to Colonel McDonald in April and June 1839.[60] It frustrated the hopes of many former slaves of taking up small-scale farming on gaining their freedom, the one activity other than logging of which there was reasonably wide experience within their community. This specific bone of contention became caught up with, and aggravated, the more general question of the allocation, transfer and general status of land as ownership became concentrated in even fewer hands than it had been at the beginning of the century.

Notes

1. H. H. Bancroft, *History of Central America* (3 Volumes), San Francisco (1883–7), Vol. 2, 626.
2. Inhabitants/Major Caulfield, 8 June 1745, CO 137/48.
3. Unsigned letter to Dalling, 3 September 1779, CO 137/75.
4. Despard/Sydney, 17 August 1787, CO 123/5.
5. G. Henderson, *An Account of the British Settlement of Honduras*, London (1809), 60.
6. Codd/Wilmot, 23 February 1823, CO 123/34. By then slave numbers were 2400 out of a total population of 4100 – see Census of the Population 1823 (Recapitulation), BA (0015 CNS/1, 249–51). By 1826, while the number of slaves remained the same, the total population had increased to 5197.
7. Arthur/Bathurst, 14 March 1815, CO 123/24.
8. Narda Dobson, *A History of Belize*, London (1973), 146–7. One way round the restrictions imposed by the act abolishing the slave trade was to import Africans as 'domestic servants'.
9. Arthur/Bathurst, 7 November 1816, CO 123/25.
10. O. N. Bolland, 'Slavery in Belize', *Journal of Belizean Affairs*, No. 6, January 1978, 8.
11. 1834 Slave Register, BA (Slave Registers).
12. Henderson, 42.
13. Lawrie/Lieutenant Governor of Jamaica, 9 March 1786, CO 123/4.
14. AB H Vol. 1, 247.
15. Henderson, 73.
16. ibid. 59–60.
17. Montresor/Coote, 22 October 1806, CO 123/17 .
18. Arthur/Bathurst, 26 July 1815, CO 123/24.
19. Arthur/Bathurst, 7 October 1820, Correspondence Relative to the Condition and Treatment of Slaves at Honduras 1820–3 (hereafter CCTS), BA.
20. Arthur/Bathurst, 7 October 1820, CO 123/29.
21. J. Armstrong, *A Candid Examination of the Defence of the Settlers of Honduras*, London (1824), 61, cited in O. N. Bolland, *The Formation of a Colonial Society: Belize from Conquest to Crown Colony*, Baltimore and London (1977), 83.
22. Arthur/Bathurst, 7 October 1820, op. cit.
23. ABH Vol. 1, 121–4.
24. Arthur/Bathurst, 16 May 1820, CO 123/29.
25. See record of the Superintendent's meeting with the magistrates on 15 February 1825 enclosed with Codd/Bathurst 18 February 1825, CO 123/36. Codd

proposed, and the magistrates agreed, that he should ask for a white regiment to form the garrison instead. Nothing came of the request.

26. Arthur/Fraser, 12 June 1817, CO 123/26.
27. Enc. to Hunter/Grenville, 18 May 1790, CO 123/9.
28. Barrow/Hobart, 19 April 1803, CO 123/15.
29. Bolland in *Slavery in Belize*, 28–9.
30. Enc. to Codd/Bathurst 18 February 1825 op. cit. Later in the year there were hopes that the Guatemalan authorities would co-operate in the return of runaway slaves, but measures in that sense proposed by the Congress were rejected by the Senate – see Codd/Bathurst, 2 June and 10 July 1825, CO 123/36.
31. Bolland in *The Formation of a Colonial Society*, 80.
32. Stephen/Twiss, 13 October 1830, CO 123/41.
33. Arthur/Bathurst, 7 October 1820, op. cit.
34. Arthur/Bathurst, 28 September 1821, CCTS, BA.
35. Arthur/Bathurst, 2 March 1822, CCTS, BA.
36. Richard E. Hadel, 'Slave Trials in Belize', *National Studies*, Vol. 3 No. 2, March 1975, 2–3.
37. Armstrong, 67, cited in O. N. Bolland, *Colonialism and Resistance in Belize*, Belize (1988), 56.
38. Arthur/Bathurst, 28 February 1822, CCTS, BA.
39. ABH Vol. 2, 258.
40. Enc. to Barrow/Hobart, 31 March 1803, CO 123/15.
41. Bathurst/Arthur, 16 March 1822, BA (R3, 39–42).
42. See 1829 report of Commissioners of Inquiry into the Administration of Criminal and Civil Justice ... on the Settlement of Honduras, CO 318/77.
43. Arthur/Bathurst, 22 February 1822, CCTS, BA.
44. Arthur/Bathurst, 2 March 1822, CCTS, BA.
45. Armstrong, 59, cited in Bolland, *Formation of a Colonial Society*, 65.
46. Bolland in *Colonialism and Resistance in Belize*, 56.
47. Bolland in *Slavery in Belize*, 21.
48. ibid., 24, and Dobson, 175.
49. Enc. to Cockburn/Stanley, 10 July 1834, CO 123/45.
50. McLenan/Cockburn, 1 October 1836, CO 123/48.
51. Cockburn/Lefevre, 17 July 1833, CO 123/44.
52. Cockburn/Lefevre, 13 August 1834, CO 123/45.
53. Cockburn/Glenelg, 1 July 1835, CO 123/46.
54. Enc. to Cockburn/Aberdeen, 1 July 1835, CO 123/46.
55. Bolland in *The Formation of a Colonial Society*, 117.
56. McDonald/Glenelg, 10 August 1838, CO 123/53.
57. Cockburn/Messervy, 3 April 1830, CO 123/41.
58. McDonald/Glenelg, 28 August 1838, CO 123/53.
59. Nigel Bolland and Assad Shoman, *Land in Belize 1765–1871*, University of the West Indies (1975), 63–4.
60. ABH Vol. 2, 407 and 408.

1 A late classic (c.600–900) vase from Buenavista, Cayo District
(Belize Historical Society)

2 A Maya site, Altun Ha
(Belize Archives Department)

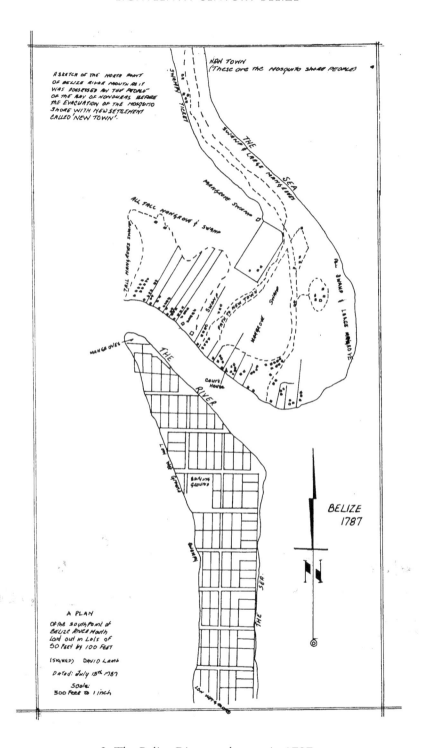

3 The Belize River settlement in 1787

4 The first bridge over the Belize River, built in the early nineteenth century
(Craig Family Collection)

5 St John's Cathedral, work on which started in 1812
(Nicholas Gillard)

6 The former Government House, built in 1815
(Belize Archives Department)

7 The Belize River mouth, from Fort George, 1842
(Craig Family Collection)

8 Woodcutters about to fell a mahogany tree
(Craig Family Collection)

9 Mahogany tree cut in lengths for transport to the river bank
(Craig Family Collection)

10 A cattle team loaded up with mahogany trunks
(Craig Family Collection)

11 Transporting logs by cattle team
(Craig Family Collection)

12 Mahogany logs in the lower reaches of the Belize River
(Craig Family Collection)

13 Squaring up logs for export
(Craig Family Collection)

6

Land

Occupation of strips of riverbank for the cutting of logwood over the first sixty years of the eighteenth century was unregulated. Custom, based on a rough and ready principle of first-come-first-served, was sufficient. Above all there was plenty of room for everybody, and a plentiful supply of good logwood was not hard to find. But with the emergence of a demand for mahogany, the greater effort called for in finding it, and the need for a more elaborate infrastructure to extract it, the case for some agreed system for the allocation of land became stronger. The occasion was the introduction of the simple set of principles for basic self-government drawn up by Admiral Burnaby in 1765 and accepted by the inhabitants as necessary for the improvement of public order. The rules on land tenure adopted around that time became known as the Location Laws. Like the main body of Burnaby's Code, they served the community more or less unchanged for over fifty years.

The Location system

The Location Laws were developed in three stages. At a Public Meeting in April 1765, when Burnaby's scheme was first presented, it was decided that a claim to a piece of land could be established by building a hut on it providing nobody else's hut was already there.[1] More significantly it was also agreed that no inhabitant could occupy more than one 'work' on the same river at the same time; and that a double 'work' exploited with a partner was only acceptable providing the partner was a settled inhabitant.[2] A further Public Meeting thirteen months later refined these very basic principles by setting both limits to the size of a site (2000 yards of river frontage) and a criterion for formal abandonment (the opening of another 'work').[3] At one of the first Public Meetings held after the return of the settlers at the end of the American War of Independence, in June 1784, all these rules were confirmed.[4] It was declared at the same time that 'possessions' held before the 1779 evacuation were to be restored. That second declaration contains for the first time specific references to mahogany. It also refers to acquisition by purchase as well as to possession by right of first claim, thus confirming that a 'work' was a tradable asset.

The third stage in the development of the Location Laws came in July 1787 as the refugees from the Mosquito Shore arrived, at least quadrupling the settlement's population, and, probably for the first time, putting pressure on the availability of exploitable resources. Again the further rules were adopted at a Public Meeting. They were clearly designed to accommodate the almost complete replacement of logwood by mahogany as the object of exploitation, and to maintain a degree of privilege for the established settlers over the new arrivals.

The first resolution relating to logging was that for a newcomer to the settlement to be eligible for title to a mahogany 'work', he must own at least four 'able' slaves with which to operate the site. This, if in fact discriminatory towards the evacuees, simply acknowledged the reality that mahogany could only be worked with a labour force of a certain size. The second resolution made the distinction more openly: whereas an established settler could own or 'locate' a 'work' of more than three miles in extent, a new arrival could only acquire such by purchase. The third resolution dealt on traditional lines with the case of abandonment of a 'work': if a claimant's slaves were withdrawn from his site (presumably during the cutting season), he would be deemed to have relinquished his interest in it . The final resolution at last established a public record of allocations: initial title, whether by 'location' or by purchase, together with subsequent transfers, of both logwood and mahogany 'works' were to be entered in a publicly available book within three months of acquisition.[5] A further Public Meeting the following month modified the established rule that no one operator, regardless of how many slaves he had, could hold more than a single 'work' on any one river by allowing two such works.[6]

We have already seen that what the established settlers saw at the time as interference in this system of land tenure, both in the newly ceded territory south of the Belize river and at the edges of the original settlement, was at the root of the first Superintendent's undoing. The dispute about the land south of the Belize River, which Despard wanted to allocate to the refugees from the Mosquito Shore, was the more serious. Some of the old settlers claimed that they had already cleared parts of the river's southern bank with the approval of the Spaniards. They incited the magistrates to act unilaterally, gaoling, for illegal possession, a refugee who had established himself on one such site. It was thus disposal of land that led to the complete breakdown in Despard's relations with the leading settlers and indirectly to his removal. It was also the reason why for the next twenty-five years, until Lieutenant Colonel George Arthur began gradually to assert a somewhat greater authority in internal affairs, successive Superintendents left land allocation, like administration of justice, well alone.

Allocation by the Crown

As we have seen, it was Arthur who began to make more use of the device of the proclamation to introduce measures which he thought were justified in terms of the settlement's interests but which might be voted down by the magistrates or the Public Meeting. One of his most important proclamations, which had been approved by the government in London, was on the subject of land. Arthur's proclamation of October 1817, based on instructions in a dispatch from Lord Bathurst dated 12 March 1817, was very much on lines he had proposed to the Secretary of State a year earlier, when he had reported the results of a land survey that showed much 'irregularity', deplored 'the monopoly on the part of the monied cutters', and drawn attention to the lack of reference to the subject in his initial instructions.[7] The main burden of the proclamation was that all unclaimed land was henceforth held to be Crown land, that is land disposable only by the British state.[8] The corollary was an at least notional increase in the hitherto very limited formal power of the Superintendent in internal civil affairs. It was to him, as the local representative of the Crown, that decisions on disposal would fall, although by 1819 he was complaining that his proclamation was being widely ignored.[9] This move had the disadvantage for the British government of embroiling it in the contentious issue of land allocation. On the other hand it lessened an administrative untidiness that had become a potential cause of public disorder. More immediately it enabled Arthur to avoid challenge to his allocation of land around the Sibun and Manatee rivers to the five hundred former members of the garrison who had chosen to settle in the Bay when their regiment disbanded.[10]

Designation of unclaimed land of course called first for the delineation of all claimed land. To this end Arthur also decreed that existing claims must be registered within six months. In March 1818 he appointed eleven commissioners to examine the claims he had received, and to consider whether those that were accepted should be formalised by the device of Crown grants.[11] The reluctance of the appointed commissioners to act, Arthur's threat to nominate military officers in their place, and the fact that their report took two and a half years to complete, are all indications of how sensitive this departure from 'the customs of the Bay' must have been. But what made the commissioners' work more sensitive still was their finding that the limit set in the Location Laws on the number of 'works' that could be held by one man had been widely ignored. But their only suggestion for reducing holdings referred to 'plantations' (also acquired by 'location') rather than 'works': any that had not been worked for five years should be forfeited.[12]

Arthur's response to this report was robust. He recommended to the Secretary of State that the limit should be two sites per woodcutter, and then only so long as they were worked. As contentiously, and as significantly for the future, he also recommended that land assigned for timber extraction should be granted on a leasehold rather than a freehold basis, with freehold tenancies only available for dwellings and for land assigned for cultivation.[13] Perhaps because of concern at what had happened when other Superintendents had sought to overturn established practice in the Bay, the government in London did not take up these suggestions. The result was as untidy a situation as before. Because land could no longer be acquired by 'location', there was less scope for dispute between competing new claims. But there were inevitably more disputes about the validity of old claims when sites in areas designated as Crown land were allocated. Moreover the British government, while facing as much extra difficulty as advantage internally in the Bay with this intervention, had to accept a further drawback externally. Simply by reference to Crown land, they had cut across their long-established acceptance, enshrined in successive treaties, of Spanish sovereignty within the settlement's agreed geographical limits; while by the very act of announcing a land policy, they had drawn attention to the gross infringement by the settlers of the even clearer Spanish rights beyond those limits.

Land outside treaty limits

Arthur's proclamation had been made at a time when the mahogany cutters, taking advantage of declining Spanish authority in Central America, had been pushing ever further south of the settlement's 1786 boundary. Having been active by the turn of the century on Deep River, a hundred miles south of Stann Creek (now Dangriga), by 1806 they had reached the Rio Grande, just north of what is now Punta Gorda; and by 1814 some were cutting as far south as the Moho River.[14] As the Superintendent's *raison d'être* was to oversee the activities of British subjects on the coast, this radical extension of the woodcutters' operations hugely enlarged the area over which he had to take at least a degree of responsibility. But a corollary of that was that he was able to apply to the area beyond treaty limits his proclamation ending acquisition by 'location' before such acquisition, in any formal sense, became extensive.[15] That in turn is why later in the century, when British sovereignty was established, most Crown land was in the south of the territory.

Meanwhile circumstances in the area south of the Sibun changed to an extent with the end of Spanish rule in neighbouring countries in 1821. Until then little had been said by anyone about the status of land occupied by British woodcutters in the south. Thereafter the settlers became bolder in asserting what they saw as their rights, as indiscriminate exploitation continued without definition of title.[16] In July 1825 the Superintendent, Major General Edward Codd, reported that the limits of the territory were generally held by the settlers to be the Hondo in the north and the Sarstoon in the south.[17] In October 1834 his substantive successor, Cockburn, stated that possession within these limits and as far west as Garbutt's Falls, before 1821, was a demonstrable fact.[18] The Colonial Office early the next year accepted that in the absence of other occupants, 'the ... tract lying between the Sarstoon and the Belize must be considered British'.[19] This view would have been behind the next decision, to try to negotiate Spanish acceptance of that position in advance of the prospective settlement between Spain and Mexico and in response to Guatemalan land grants in the area.

It would have been because of that diplomatic aim that in the mid-1830s the geographical area within which Superintendents were allowed to allocate land for exploitation was still confined to the treaty limits. This had its disadvantages: we have Lieutenant Colonel Cockburn confirming as late as 1835 that land settled south of the Sibun was not subject to 'regulation or restriction'.[20] That was in the context of a recommendation that land there, of which settlers were in full and undisturbed possession in 1821, when Spanish Central America became independent, should be registered as properly held. A strong reason for this recommendation was that the Guatemalan government was supporting claims by its citizens to parcels of land in what then became a disputed area.[21] In 1836, having agreed with the magistrates two years earlier that they should press for the Hondo/Sarstoon/Garbutt's Falls limits,[22] Cockburn went further, proposing to the Secretary of State that he should have authority to make grants south of the Sibun in order to show that Guatemalan pretensions were not accepted.[23] These representations had their effect. The next year Cockburn's successor, Colonel Alexander McDonald, made at least four grants in the name of the Crown of land on the southern rivers;[24] and in 1839 he was told that because there was now unlikely to be objection from Spain, further allocations were permissible.[25] But there was no more formal resolution of land policy in what had become the wider settlement until the 1850s.

Sale of Crown land

Only two decisions of significance on land administration seem to have been taken in London before the passing of the more fundamental Honduras Land Titles Act of 1858. In a sense they were contradictory. The second of these two interim decisions was straightforward. In 1839 the Superintendent was given greater freedom to allocate land, curiously still within treaty limits, for cultivation.[26] This would have been a consequence of the final emancipation of the settlement's former slaves the previous year. The other ruling, the decision referred to in the last chapter to introduce a charge for Crown land grants, had come the year before, in 1838, and was more far-reaching. It was a measure introduced at the same time in all the British West Indian possessions. For this reason of uniformity of policy the Superintendent's protests from the Bay settlement were ignored. The ruling had some benefit for the territory, because it increased the revenue available for local public purposes. But as we have seen, it also substantially increased the difficulties for freed slaves who wanted to take advantage of the new availability of land for agriculture. The result was that the great majority of inhabitants of African origin remained urban-based forestry workers. That would have suited the mahogany exporters because it lessened the possibility of a labour shortage following full emancipation. But as McDonald pointed out, the introduction of a charge of £1 per acre for any land granted was likely also to discourage necessarily heavy investment in larger-scale agriculture by anyone else.[27] As by this time new exploitable timber resources were already beginning to become more difficult to find, this raised questions about the settlement's longer-term economic future.

McDonald was over-ruled, and his successor Colonel Charles Fancourt was enjoined in 1843 to bear down on 'the gratuitous alienation of the Public Lands'.[28] Meanwhile disputes broke out quite quickly about whether specific tracts of land had or had not been claimed before 1817 or granted before 1838. This finally led to a proclamation by Fancourt in 1846, 'having for its object the prevention of cutting mahogany and logwood on ungranted lands'.[29] But the change from simple grant to sale of land had already had another result, albeit secondary, which was more beneficial. The Secretary of State had suggested to McDonald that he set up a council to decide on allocation of the funds which land sales brought in.[30] This became an embryo of the kind of Executive Council that advised colonial governors elsewhere, and at last formed an institutional bridge between the authority of the Superintendent and that of the Public Meeting/magistracy nexus. Although the range of its work was initially very limited, the council accustomed the leading settlers to working in a formal sense more closely with the Superintendent than they had done in the past.

Legal consolidation

The 1839 decision to open up (by sale) more land for cultivation had very little result for twenty years. In 1847 Fancourt asserted that 'the cultivation of the soil has been almost entirely neglected'.[31] An 1855 memorandum to the Superintendent reported that 'very few plantations have been established (and) none for the purpose of cultivating produce for exportation'.[32] The same document, however, in stating that many disposals of Crown land 'bestow land south of the River Sibun', does confirm that McDonald's initiative of 1837, granting to woodcutters for the first time land south of the Sibun, had been followed up over the intervening years. It was also in 1855 that the Legislative Assembly passed the Laws in Force Act, which gave security of title to landowners whose acquisitions had been recorded by confirming the legal validity of the system under which it had been acquired.[33] To give further comfort to the metropolitan interests now present, more doubtful cases were validated by the Honduras Land Titles Act in 1858 and by the establishment of a Land Titles Register the following year.[34] Those two measures, together with the underpinning of the Anglo-Guatemalan Convention also of 1859, at last fully regularised land tenure in the settlement.

If that regularisation was an administrative advance, the net benefit for the community is more doubtful. In Nigel Bolland's words, 'the structure of land ownership, which had been highly concentrated since the late eighteenth century, became one of increasingly extreme monopolization' as the nineteenth century continued.[35] Bearing this out are the entries in the Land Titles Register. By the early 1860s three firms (the British Honduras Company, Young Toledo, and Carmichael Vidal) shared 158 out of 191 mahogany claims recorded; and by 1875, when the British Honduras Company became the Belize Estate and Produce Company, the entries were all but divided between the first two of those companies.[36] As we shall see in Chapter 10, this process militated against the diversification of the economy that was increasingly recognised as necessary for a stable future for the territory. It also gave these London-based entities an exceptional degree of influence over the whole spectrum of British Honduras affairs.

A further contentious point on the regularised land sales system arose over the same period. With the establishment of a Legislative Assembly in 1854, the settlers expected that their representatives would be allowed to allocate both Crown land and the funds its sale generated. After a number of exchanges, the Secretary of State decided against this in 1862.[37] A further decision went against the wishes of the settlers in 1872. Following a proposal by the Lieutenant Governor in 1868, a Crown Land Ordinance four years later gave reservation rights to the inhabitants of Indian and Carib villages and plantations on Crown land in the south of the colony. No firm title was offered,[38] however, as was the case outside the designated areas, where a leasehold system had been imposed in 1857.[39]

Long-term consequence

The longer-term consequence of the eighteenth and nineteenth century history of land allocation in the settlement was, in net terms, negative. This was for reasons connected with McDonald's arguments against sale (rather than grant) of unallocated land. From the 1770s until 1838, the nature of the primary industry favoured bigger over smaller entrepreneurs in the acquisition of land, whether by 'location' or by grant. When in 1838 the demand for land for agriculture increased substantially with the full emancipation of former slaves, the new requirement that Crown land should be sold rather than granted severely restricted not only opportunities for these much greater numbers who now aspired to own land, but also the diversification of the economy that was going to be a necessary condition of future prosperity.

As it was, only the established timber exporters, who had capital and who did not face the cost of clearing land, could afford to pay the government's asking price. They were thus able to expand their holdings and consolidate their grip on the economy. Moreover they were then quite free to hold on to what they had acquired, even if they failed to exploit it. But neither these individuals, nor the companies who later in the century bought them out, seem to have been interested in agriculture. Apart from the slow growth of small-scale, mostly subsistence, tenant farming, which landowners had no incentive to support in any active way, agricultural development was left in the nineteenth century to other investors whose brave attempts mostly failed, as we shall see. The effect continued into the second half of the twentieth century. A 1959 survey showed that of two million acres of land in the territory suitable for agriculture, only 5 per cent was being used for it.[40] Three-quarters of that land was in private hands in the 1960s.[41] Half of that proportion was owned by the Belize Estate and Produce Company (BEC), and about 80 per cent of the remainder by forty-six foreign owners of estates of more than 10,000 acres each.[42] It is arguable that as a result of this concentration of land ownership since the

1850s in the hands of large absentee landowners, both the economic and the social development of British Honduras were unnecessarily stunted.

Notes

1. *A Consolidated Digest of the Laws of British Honduras from the Earliest Times*, Belize, (1857), 65, held in the Belize Archives under reference L 340.
2. ibid.
3. ibid.
4. ibid., 65–6.
5. ibid., 67–70.
6. ibid., 70.
7. Arthur/Bathurst, 17 October 1816, CO 123/25.
8. Proclamation of 28 October 1817, CO 123/28.
9. Arthur/Bathurst, 4 November, 1819, CO 123/28.
10. Arthur/Bathurst, 30 August 1817, CO 123/26.
11. Nigel Bolland and Assad Shoman, *Land in Belize 1765–1871*, University of the West Indies (1975), 37–8.
12. ibid., 40.
13. Arthur/Bathurst, 13 September 1820, CO 123/29.
14. Enc. to Smyth/Bathurst, 24 May 1814, co 123/23.
15. Bolland and Shoman, *Land in Belize*, 42.
16. ibid., 47.
17. Codd/Horton, 8 July 1825 in Horton/Planta, 23 September 1825, FO 15/4.
18. Cockburn/Lefevre, 22 October 1834 in Hay/Backhouse, 6 February 1835, FO 15/17.
19. CO memorandum of 20 January 1835 in CO 123/46.
20. Cockburn/Aberdeen, 17 April 1835, cited in Bolland and Shoman, *Land in Belize*, 47.
21. Cockburn/Aberdeen, 17 April 1835, CO 123/46 and Cockburn/Spring Rice, 15 September 1834, CO 123/45.
22. Cockburn/Grey, 22 May 1836, CO 123/48.
23. Cockburn/Grey, 22 May 1836, CO 123/48.
24. R. A. Humphreys, *The Diplomatic History of British Honduras 1638–1901*, London (1961), 24.
25. Bolland and Shoman, *Land in Belize*, 48.
26. ABH Vol. 2, 408.
27. McDonald/Normanby, 9 February 1839, CO 123/54.
28. Bolland and Shoman, *Land in Belize*, 60.
29. Fancourt/Governor, Jamaica, 15 December 1846, ABH Vol. 3, 89.
30. Normanby/McDonald, 29 June 1839, CO 123/55.
31. Fancourt/Grey, 19 June 1847, cited in Bolland and Shoman, *Land in Belize*, 66.
32. Chief Justice/Superintendent, 30 July 1855, ABH Vol. 3, 184.
33. O. N. Bolland, *The Formation of a Colonial Society: Belize from Conquest to Crown Colony*, Baltimore and London, (1977), 184.
34. Bolland and Shoman, *Land in Belize*, 75.
35. Bolland, *The Formation of a Colonial Society*, 187.
36. Bolland and Shoman, *Land in Belize*, 81–2. In the early 1860s, the British Honduras Company was still largely registered in the names of the founding partners, James Hyde and John Hodge. The Carmichael Vidal land was acquired by Young Toledo in 1864.
37. Enc. to Eyre/Newcastle, 4 April 1862 (confirming Secretary of State's decision passed to Legislative Assembly), CO 123/104.

38. O. N. Bolland, *Colonialism and Resistance in Belize*, Belize (1988), 110. Bolland goes on to show (p. 139) that the system of reserves was still not properly established by the end of the century.
39. Bolland and Shoman, *Land in Belize*, 90–1.
40. Narda Dobson, *A History of Belize*, London (1973), 273.
41. Bolland and Shoman, *Land in Belize*, 108.
42. ibid., 103 and 107–8.

7

Constitutional Development

Justice

As we saw in Chapter 4, the two Superintendents who began to strengthen the authority of the post in internal civil affairs, as distinct from external relations and defence, were Lieutenant Colonels George Arthur (1814–22) and Francis Cockburn (1830–36). It was in Arthur's time that the British Parliament for the first time enacted legislation that covered the Bay of Honduras, with a general Act in 1817 dealing with jurisdiction for the most serious offences in British settlements 'outside the King's dominions', followed by more specific legislation in 1818. These measures enabled a criminal court to be legally constituted in the Bay for the first time. Further measures the following year enabled the appointment of its members by commission.

The impulse behind this was growing recognition, after an 1801 opinion by the Attorney General in Jamaica, of the difficulty of allowing a court with no legal basis (the magistrates' court) or a court designed for a different purpose (the court martial) to award the extreme penalties that followed conviction for the most serious offences. As Arthur put it, it was 'indispensible' that 'some tribunal be erected before which the offenders might be brought, and authority somehow vested for carrying extreme punishment into execution'.[1] Eight commissioners were duly appointed by name, besides Arthur himself as First Commissioner, of whom the Superintendent thought three were unsuitable. A quorum consisted of any three members provided they included either the Superintendent or the garrison commander.[2] In due course this criminal court became known as the Supreme Court. The magistrates' court, which now sat as a civil court, was then restyled as the Grand Court to distinguish it from the summary and slave courts.

The introduction of the Supreme Court was an advance, but it left a number of judicial issues unresolved. First, it was only empowered to deal with the specific offences of murder, manslaughter, rape, robbery and burglary. This meant that other serious charges, such as arson and shooting with intent to kill, could only be heard in the lower court (the summary court) and treated as petty offences. They could thus not be punished with due weight. Second, qualified legal advice was still lacking, despite Arthur's offer for the settlement to fund the appointment of an Attorney General, on the lines of what had been done at Gibraltar.[3] Third, the quality of the jury, to whom the responsibility of a verdict fell, was usually low. With eight leading settlers disqualified by virtue of their membership of the court and the more capable among the rest of the white population often away in the bush, juries were usually made up of clerks, apprentices and others whose independence was questionable. In 1819 Arthur complained that while jury corruption continued to exist, the appointment of judicial commissioners was in vain.[4] None of these issues was tackled in the 1820s or 1830s, despite repeated representations by successive Superintendents.

There was also a growing recognition of the inadequacy of the civil court (the Grand Court), much of the business of which concerned debt and property. A solution proposed by Arthur was the introduction of a right of appeal to the Superintendent, on the basis that he could claim to be disinterested.[5] Cockburn went further, suggesting that the Supreme Court might act as an appeal court, but also insisting that the Grand Court too should be legally constituted.[6] He was concerned too about the authority of the law which the magistrates sought to interpret: they referred specifically to the customary law of the Bay, which had evolved by the simple vote of a section of the population; but there were also more general references by the magistrates to the 'Laws of England', which had never been formally applied to the settlement, and to the spirit of those laws. Nor had worries about the practical functioning of the criminal court (the Supreme Court) been laid to rest by the time Cockburn arrived. On taking up his appointment in 1830 he was dismayed to find that of the eight commissioners appointed in 1819, only two were left. By the following year there was only one, which meant he was deprived, as he put it, of his only legal tribunal.[7] Hence when recommending in 1834 that the Supreme Court should be empowered to try all cases where conviction was punishable by death or transportation, he also urged the Secretary of State to authorise him to fill vacancies in the court's membership. In the same letter he sought guidance on whether the court's jurisdiction might extend to territory under British occupation but outside treaty limits.[8] Question marks thus remained over a range of issues surrounding the administration of justice. Nor were they removed during the next decade with Cockburn's successor's unauthorised (but never disavowed) proclamation of 1840 that the laws of the settlement were to be the laws of England (with 'local customs, laws, and regulations' subordinate to them), and by the appointment in 1843 of a Chief Justice who caused years of controversy about his powers and status.[9] In particular there was still no legally constituted civil court.

The Public Meeting, the magistracy and executive government

These concerns were aggravated by what seemed to the Superintendents obvious deficiencies in the body which made the specific laws and regulations governing the settlement, the Public Meeting, or, as it gradually be came known, the Legislative Meeting. Arthur repeatedly complained about the 'irregularity' of these Meetings. In 1819 he reported that one such assembly had been conducted so badly that he had annulled the proceedings.[10] Whilst he would have preferred more radical change, he proposed that 'if the present defective system of legislation must be continued … laws voted on should not take effect until approved by the Superintendent'.[11] The following year he was indeed more radical in his recommendations, proposing that legislative authority be vested in a Council of twelve members, chaired by the Superintendent, and that only the Superintendent should have the power to call meetings and to execute whatever laws were adopted.[12] This was a reversion to what Despard had imposed in 1789.

Cockburn, whose briefly acting predecessor reported that 'nothing like law or justice has been known in the settlement since Colonel Arthur left it',[13] took up the proposal for what would have essentially been a legislative council. In one of the first letters he wrote to the Colonial Office, as it had now become, he argued for 'enactment of a law delegating to the Superintendent, with the advice of a few of the principal inhabitants and such restrictions as may be requisite, the power of making all necessary regulations for the better government of His Majesty's subjects'.[14] Seven months later he followed this up with the corollary, a proposal for the outright abolition of the Public Meeting, which he described in a further representation in 1831 as 'ill-governed, undefined, uncontrollable'.[15] It had grown to an assembly of as many as seventy people, and was, in Cockburn's view, constituted by a deeply flawed system of qualification for those taking part. He shared Arthur's opinion that if abolition was impossible, at the very least the Public Meeting should only convene when summoned by the Superintendent.

One reason Cockburn pushed hard for reform was that he had been led to believe on appointment that change was on the way. Like Arthur before him he then heard nothing of substance, until in 1832 a new Secretary of State explained that the previous three sessions of Parliament had been 'unpropitious' for taking forward any except the most urgent business. This of course referred particularly to the Great Reform Bill of that year, which, with a nice irony for Belize, widened the franchise in Britain just at the time ministers were considering moving, in a sense, in the opposite direction in the Bay. That they were still minded to do so is confirmed by Viscount Goderich in the same letter to Cockburn, when he added, keeping his options open, that he hoped fairly soon to act 'with the view of making some effectual provision for the enactment and execution of laws for the better government of the settlers'.[16]

That same letter did at last bring more tangible progress, from the Superintendent's point of view, in the executive operation of government. Indeed this was the principal 'constitutional' change that was made in Cockburn's time. For years Superintendents had been complaining about the intransigence of the magistrates in any discussions about public expenditure. In 1814 Arthur complained of 'the self-interest and ignorance that influence their decisions'.[17] On other important issues Arthur, as we have seen, had resorted to use of proclamations as he had done, for example, on land and the slave laws. But these had had to be used sparingly. In 1819 he had found himself in deep dispute with the magistrates, after they simply set aside a proclamation he had made on a bond requirement for coastal trading vessels as a measure to deter smuggling.[18] Consequently he was very reluctant the following year to impose a restriction on firearms,[19] observing that any interference by the Superintendent in internal civil affairs 'is received as an act of usurpation'.[20] Even the greater standing he was supposed to have been given in selection of public officers had been challenged by the magistrates, who had chosen an interpretation of the relevant letter from the Secretary of State at odds with the clear intent perceived by Arthur.[21] It was not until 1820 that he had received unambiguous support on that in the form of a further letter telling him 'in no case to recognise or admit any person in any public capacity whose actual momination or appointment shall not have originated with yourself'.[22]

On executive administration Cockburn had again taken up where Arthur had left off. Eight months after his arrival in 1830 he was deploring the magistrates' power of disposing of public funds without any control.[23] What made matters worse was that to him they represented the interests of a small faction within the community. The issue that then brought Cockburn into open confrontation with the magistrates was the funding of long-overdue repairs to the garrison barracks. Cockburn wanted to threaten to have the troops withdrawn. In his letter expressing his urgent wish to provide more effectively for the enactment of laws, the Sectretary of State also ruled that a different, but even more fundamental, lever should be applied on the barracks issue. This was authorisation of the withdrawal of the magistrates' right to collect taxes unless 'the first objects of public necessity' were provided for.[24] The threat was enough and the necessary appropriation was agreed. It was moreover in this same letter that Goderich announced his further decision, taking up a recommendation by Cockburn the year before, that henceforth magistrates should be nominated by the Superintendent rather than elected by the Public Meeting. Surprisingly this was also accepted without demur,[25] as was another ruling by the Secretary of State, that motions to be put to the Public Meeting must be approved by the Superintendent in advance. Although, unlike the establishment of the Supreme Court, these measures came about by decree rather than by Act of Parliament, they represented, as observed in Chapter 4, a second significant step in bringing the affairs of the settlement under the control of the Crown, and thus on to a more regular, if not yet constitutional, basis.

The change to a nominated magistracy came in 1832. It by no means ended disputes between the Superintendent and the magistrates, but it did enable the former to debar from service those he knew would make trouble. In Cockburn's remaining four years in the Bay, the focus of his efforts towards reform returned to the Public Meeting as the 'enactor' of laws. In 1834 he sent the settlement's Keeper of Records to London with detailed recommendations for its replacement by a Council of Advice, on the basis that, with sixty-five members, the Public Meeting was simply too large and unwieldy a body for constructive law-making. In case abolition was impracticable, Cockburn again recommended as a minimum change 'withdrawal of the power of assembling and dissolving without the authority of the Superintendent'.[26]

These recommendations were presented in early 1835. The following year Cockburn himself was in England and was able to approach the Secretary of State directly. His language was strong. Because the Public Meeting had 'arrogated to itself ... exclusive control even over the minutest items of its expenditure', he foresaw, in the absence of 'decisive measures' for better government, 'a state of anarchy and confusion'.[27] While reiterating his recommendation for an advisory council, he added to his earlier position a limit of twenty, to be achieved by election, on the number of participants in any Public Meeting that might have to be allowed to survive. Cockburn also took this opportunity to repeat his views on the extra powers needed for the Supreme Court and the legal authority required for the magistrates' court.

Cockburn's energetic and persistent lobbying seems to have got nowhere. Two years later, in April 1838, we find his successor Colonel Alexander McDonald, a veteran of Waterloo who had acted as Superintendent in 1829, returning to the charge. Like Arthur nearly twenty years before, McDonald proposed a council of twelve or thirteen which would, he argued, represent every interest in the settlement.[28] Having had no response to that recommendation, McDonald then suggested that the council of principal officials and leading inhabitants authorised by the Secretary of State in June 1839 to help with the administration of land sales might also serve to replace the Public Meeting as the legislative body and the magistracy as the financial authority.[29] That was turned down at the end of the year. But only seven months later, after a further plea in April 1840,[30] McDonald was at last allowed to form an Executive Council of 6–8 members to assist him in the day-to-day running of the settlement's wider affairs.[31] The settlement's administration was further reinforced by the creation of the post of Colonial Secretary in 1842.[32]

The Public Meeting, however, remained as the body which passed laws and, in particular, authorised 'supply', i.e. taxes and the rates at which they were set. This state of affairs was to continue for another fourteen years after the creation of the Executive Council, despite the best efforts of successive Superintendents. Inevitably there were tensions between the Public Meeting and the new executive body, which was even more under the Superintendent's control than the appointed magistracy. In the early 1840s this was not helped by McDonald's uncompromising nature. After the Executive Council's first session in early 1841, a Public Meeting was convened to protest against the new body's assumption not only of powers of financial administration, which it arguably needed in order to function, but also of legislative powers, which the Secretary of State had clearly not intended it to assume. The Meeting resolved that it could not 'cede to an Executive Council the power of legislation, the imposition of taxes, and the expenditure of public funds'.[33] This bickering led the Colonial Office to instruct the Governor of Jamaica to take a more active role in the settlement's affairs, and indeed for the Superintendent to 'apply' to the Governor 'for instructions on all matters of importance'.[34] But despite the Governor's emollient advice, McDonald, 'one of the most military-looking men' an American visitor had ever seen,[35] failed to establish a working relationship with the leading settlers. At the end of the same year, 1841, a further special Public Meeting drew up a memorandum to the Governor of Jamaica with the familiar complaint that the Superintendent was usurping his powers.[36] As a result, in early 1842, McDonald had to be told by the Governor of Jamaica that he 'should conciliate the Public Meeting, and carry on the affairs of your settlement in harmony with that body';[37] and, four months later, by the Secretary of State that 'Her Majesty's Government are not disposed to dispense with the services which the Public Meeting has been in the habit of rendering', as McDonald had proposed.[38]

McDonald's successor from 1843, Colonel Charles Fancourt, did not find the task much easier. He blamed the 'independent executive authority assumed by the magistrates'[39] and proposed as a solution that they, as a body and together with the Superintendent and the senior public service officers, should constitute the Executive Council and sit independently only as a judicial authority. This step was approved in London and implemented in July 1844.[40] The arrangement lasted for nearly two years, after which the magistrates, who had always been unpaid, gave up their judicial role and their title, remaining simply as executive councillors. With the approval of the Public Meeting in March 1846, the basic level of judicial authority, chairmanship of the Summary Court, passed to a newly created paid Police Magistrate who had no other function.[41] In the Grand Court, dealing with the bigger civil cases, the chair had already passed to the Chief Justice, and he hencforth was to be assisted by the commissioners who already assisted him in the Supreme Court.[42] But harmonious relations between the Superintendent and the leading settlers remained elusive as the Executive Council evolved into a body made up entirely of public service officials. In 1848, when the Public Meeting resolved that it 'does not possess the confidence of the inhabitants', the Council consisted only of the Chief Justice, Attorney General (a post created in 1847), Colonial Secretary and Public Treasurer.[43]

But it was the general behaviour of the Public Meeting as the legislative authority that continued to drive efforts by successive Superintendents to replace it with a more manageable and business-like entity. In November 1843, five months after Fancourt's arrival, membership, albeit for life, came to be by election. Both candidates and those who voted for them had to be established and self-supporting British-born settlers; and for candidates there was an additional requirement for ownership of property worth £500.[44] Although this change was regressive in that it enhanced the political power of the leading settlers, it did remove some of the rougher participants in earlier Meetings. Notwithstanding, Fancourt was complaining six months later of the 'numerous disreputable persons who are members of the meeting'.[45] By early 1848, relations had deteriorated to a point where the Public Meeting not only expressed its dissatisfaction with the Executive Council, but also approved the dispatch of a highly critical memorandum to the Secretary of State.[46] Fancourt flatly rejected the charges. As a result ill-feeling continued to simmer, although by the time Fancourt's departure was announced in late 1850 it had subsided enough for him to receive a warm tribute from the settlers.[47]

Introduction of a Legislative Assembly

By this time, however, both sides wished for change. In November 1850 the Secretary of State received a petition from the settlers, with Fancourt's endorsement, for colonial status.[48] With ministers' approval, ideas on governance were put forward throughout 1851. In January Fancourt gave his opinion that any proposal for specific arrangements should framed by a General Meeting, and that any Legislative Assembly should be on the 'British Model'.[49] In April a General Meeting was duly held and voted for colonial status and consequent constitutional change. A Legislative Council of four nominated and three elected members was proposed, together with a Legislative Assembly of 17 members elected for three years.[50] For Legislative Assembly membership it was resolved that the property qualification should be assets worth $3000 (i.e. £600); for the right to vote in the elections a property income capacity of $35 (i.e. £7). In reporting this, Fancourt queried the property qualification for membership, and suggested a distribution of five Assembly members each for the northern and southern districts and seven for Belize, all to be elected on a somewhat wider franchise. Opinions differed on the case for a small Legislative Council in addition to the Assembly. In July Philip Wodehouse, the newly arrived first non-military Superintendent, opposed the idea of a second chamber, suggesting instead one Assembly of 21 elected members. He thought that the Superintendent should preside with a casting vote, and that three or five of the Assembly members should be nominated to join the Executive Council.[51]

After further exchanges the British government's response came in a letter from 10, Downing Street, dated 16 November 1852, to the Governor of Jamaica. Ministers came down in favour of a single chamber of 21 members, of whom only 14 should be elected, chaired by a Speaker rather than the Superintendent. The original qualification for the franchise was upheld, but the property qualification for membership was reduced to $2500 (i.e. £500). This scheme was to be put to the Public Meeting for approval.[52] In January 1853 there were counter-proposals. The Public Meeting decided that they wanted 21 elected and 4 nominated members, while Wodehouse favoured 18 elected and 4 nominated members.[53] The British government remained reluctant to impose new arrangements on the settlement. This was also reflected in the concern expressed by Wodehouse just before his departure on leave early the next year, echoing the sentiments of a long line of predecessors, that the Superintendent's prerogative and authority was still undefined, with a home government unwilling to intervene.[54]

At last in August 1853 the Governor of Jamaica forwarded the Secretary of State's final decision on the establishment of a Legislative

Assembly[55] and his authority for its creation. Elections were duly held for 18 members; and the Assembly met for the first time in January 1854 reinforced by 3 nominated members. The property qualifications were finally settled at £400 for membership, £100 for the right to vote. Election was to be for a term of four years.[56] Three months later the Executive Council was reconstituted with three official and three unofficial members under the chairmanship of the Superintendent, who was obliged to consult it.[57]

The settlers had wanted the territory to be proclaimed a British colony. But the outcome of the exchanges of the early 1850s was a largely elected Legislative Assembly rather than the largely nominated Legislative Council that was a feature of nineteenth century Crown colonies. For the next eight years they had to be satisfied with an identity for the settlement as simply 'a part of the dominions of Her Majesty', under the terms of an 1851 ruling by the British government's Law Officers made in the context of the debate on whether the sovereignty issue should be pursued with Spain.[58] Although regularisation of the status of the civil court only came after the settlement did become a colony, the 1851 ruling at last also allowed formal extension of English law to the Bay in 1855 and to the consequent enlargement of the jurisdiction of the Supreme Court.[59]

Colonial status

Three years after the Legislative Assembly met for the first time, the Superintendent reported on the improvement in the conduct of affairs brought about by the new body as compared to 'the former irregular assemblages called Public Meetings'.[60] But by that time violence and the threat of further incidents on the northern border was feeding the wish for the perceived security of at least titular colonial status. This continued to gain momentum until in March 1861 a petition to the Queen was drawn up asking for the settlement to be formally declared a colony with its own governor now that 'the institutions of the country have been placed on a firm basis'.[61] With the Anglo-Guatemalan convention of 1859 signed by both sides, the Secretary of State felt able to support the proposed change of title, but doubted the 'expediency' of ending the settlement's subordination to Jamaica.[62] The name change was formally agreed at the end of the year. The Legislative Assembly expressed its appreciation, but urged severance of the Jamaica connection.[63] The British government was not, however, to be moved, and formal instruments for the inauguration of the Colony of British Honduras, administered by a Lieutenant Governor under the oversight of the governor of Jamaica, were received in May 1862.[64]

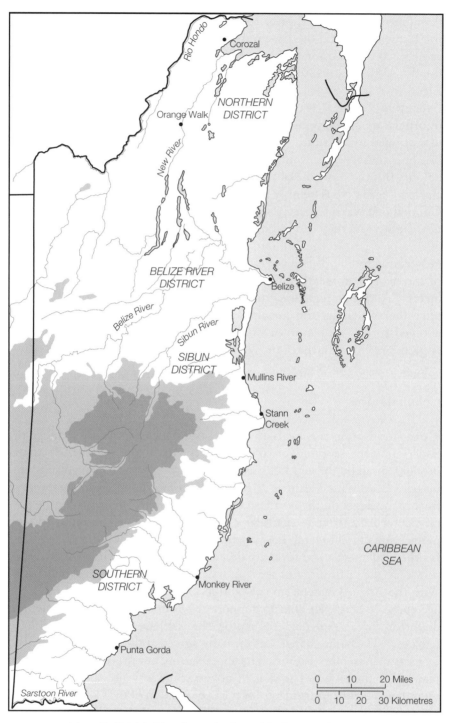

Map G British Honduras in the mid-nineteenth century

As the newly designated colony developed, there were increasing calls on the Legislative Assembly. By 1867 Lieutenant Governor John Austin was finding it difficult to transact necessary business there: avoidable and unavoidable absences together often made it difficult to achieve a quorum of fourteen members, and the Assembly seems to have been characterised by a general feeling of apathy.[65] This led Austin to support a proposal for a restructured Assembly of five elected and five nominated members,[66] a move which the Colonial Office recognised would take the settlement closer to the Crown colony model. Austin went further later the same year, suggesting the outright abolition of the Assembly. Nothing having come of either of these proposals, Austin's successor James Longden rehearsed the case in more detail in 1869, adding to it the geographically unrepresentative nature of the Assembly and the difficulty of finding candidates for by-elections. He advocated at the very least a reduction in the quorum to seven, a proposal which had been rejected by the Assembly the previous year.[67]

By late 1870, however, the settlers were again ready for change, impelled by a sharply deteriorating security situation and the knowledge that only full Crown colony status could relieve them of at least some of the cost of the extra troops which that situation demanded. Unable to agree whether, under existing arrangements, these costs should be met by a permanent tax on land or by higher import duties, and encouraged by the Colonial Office, who wanted greater administrative uniformity in Britain's Caribbean territories, their representatives voted for an Act to replace the Legislative Assembly with a Legislative Council consisting five official and four 'unofficial' members, all nominated. There were doubts about the validity of this move because of detailed amendments inserted in the Bill and because of the lack of a quorum.[68] A second vote was taken in December 1870 which met these objections, and the Royal Assent was finally received in April 1871.[69] The settlement became the Crown Colony of British Honduras. With the adoption of a nominated Council, two hundred years of autonomy in the settlement's internal affairs, and indeed government that was representative of at least a small section of the population, was thus brought to an end, an end which within a very few years was bitterly regretted.

Notes

1. Arthur/Bathurst, 11 August 1817, CO 123/27.
2. ABH Vol. 2, 229.
3. Arthur/Bathurst, 4 November 1819, CO 123/28.
4. ibid.
5. Arthur/Bathurst, 16 May 1820, CO 123/29.
6. Cockburn/Stanley, 10 June 1833, CO 123/44.

7. Cockburn/Goderich, 10 March 1831, CO 123/42.
8. Cockburn/Spring Rice, 7 November 1834, CO 123/45.
9. In 1845 the Chief Justice complained of the Superintendent's 'improper interference' (see Fancourt/Elgin, 15 February 1845, BA (R25, pages 37–50); and in 1845 he had to be 'cautioned' by the Superintendent, on the instructions of the Secretary of State, 'not to endeavour to apply with two much strictness the technical positions of the English Law in a state of society which necessarily requires a less artificial administration of justice' (see Grey (Secretary of State)/Grey (Governor of Jamaica), 26 January 1848, BA (R30, 21–2).
10. Arthur/Bathurst, 31 July 1819, CO 123/28.
11. ibid.
12. Arthur/Bathurst, 7 October 1820, CO 123/29.
13. McDonald/Messervy, 28 September 1829, CO 123/40.
14. Cockburn/Messervy, 27 January 1830, CO 123/41.
15. Cockburn/Goderich, 9 March 1831, CO 123/42.
16. Goderich/Cockburn, 18 August 1832, CO 123/43.
17. Arthur/Bathurst, 2 December 1814, CO 123/23.
18. Arthur/Bathurst, 4 November 1819, CO 123/28.
19. Arthur/Bathurst, 7 October 1820, CO 123/29.
20. ibid.
21. Arthur/Bathurst, 31 July 1819, CO 123/28.
22. ABH Vol. 2, 224.
23. Cockburn/Twiss, 9 August 1830, CO 123/41.
24. Goderich/Cockburn, 18 August 1832, CO 123/43.
25. Cockburn/Goderich, 4 January 1833, CO 123/44.
26. Miller memo. to Colonial Office, 2 January 1835, CO 123/46.
27. Cockburn/Grey, 22 May 1836, CO 123/48.
28. McDonald/Glenelg, 28 April 1838, CO 123/52.
29. McDonald/Normanby, 24 September 1839, CO 123/55.
30. McDonald/Russell, 11 April 1840, CO 123/57.
31. Russell/McDonald, 30 July 1840 and enc., CO 123/57.
32. *Handbook of British Honduras 1888–9*, Belize (1889), 37.
33. Enc. to McDonald/Russell, 12 March 1841, CO 123/59.
34. Acknowledged in McDonald/Russell, 21 April 1841, CO 123/60.
35. Lloyd Stephens, *Incidents of Travel in Central America, Chiapas, and Yucatan*, New York (1841), 14.
36. ABH Vol. 3, 53.
37. Metcalfe/McDonald, 6 May 1842, BA (R21, 45).
38. Stanley/Elgin, 1 August 1842, enclosed in Elgin/McDonald, 2 September 1842, BA (R21, 187–195).
39. Fancourt/Elgin, 16 January 1844, CO 123/679.
40. Fancourt/Stanley, 17 July 1844, BA (R19, 163–80).
41. Summarised in retrospective minute by Colonel Fancourt, 5 February 1848, BA (R25, 312–22).
42. Superintendent/Magistrates, 19 December 1845, ABH Vol. 3, 85–6.
43. ABH Vol. 3, 101.
44. ABH Vol. 3, 68–9.
45. Fancourt/Stanley, 15 April 1844, CO 123/68.
46. Fancourt/Grey, 11 March 1848, BA (R25, 309–11) and Fancourt/Grey 11 March 1848, BA (R25, 323–37).
47. Enc. to Fancourt/Grey, 18 September 1850, CO 123/79.
48. Fancourt/Grey, 11 July 1850, CO 123/79.
49. Superintendent/Petitioners, 20 January 1851, ABH Vol. 3, 141.
50. Fancourt/Grey, 19 April 1851, CO 123/82 and enclosures.

51. Wodehouse/Governor, Jamaica, 4 July 1851, ABH Vol. 3, 146–7.
52. Pakington/Governor, Jamaica, 16 November 1852, ABH Vol. 3, 1602.
53. Wodehouse/Grey, 15 January 1853, CO 123/87.
54. Wodehouse/Barkley, 15 November 1853, CO 123/88.
55. Governor, Jamaica/Wodehouse, 29 August 1853, ABH Vol. 3, 171.
56. D. A. G. Waddell, *British Honduras: a Historical and Contemporary Survey*, London (1961), 52, citing T. D. Vickers, *The Legislature of British Honduras*, Belize (1955), 3–5.
57. ABH Vol. 3, 177.
58. Narda Dobson, *A History of Belize*, London (1973), 212–3.
59. ibid., 125.
60. Stevenson/Governor, Jamaica, 20 February 1857, ABH Vol. 3, 195.
61. ABH Vol. 3, 234–6.
62. Secretary of State/Governor, Jamaica, 4 July 1861, ABH Vol. 3, 241.
63. Enc. to Darling/Newcastle, 20 February 1862, CO 123/109.
64. Seymour/Eyre, 13 May 1862, CO 123/105.
65. Austin/Grant, 13 July 1867, CO 123/128.
66. Austin/Grant, 1 July 1867, CO 123/128.
67. Longden/Grant, 26 July 1869, CO 123/137.
68. Cairns/Acting Governor of Jamaica, 12 September 1870, CO 123/141, answered in Dillett/Cairns, 29 December 1870, CO 123/141.
69. Cairns/Grant, 24 December 1870, CO 123/141, and ABH Vol. 3, 324.

8

Mexico and the Maya

Mexican independence from Spain was declared in February 1821. After a brief period of rule by a self-styled emperor, a republic was established. In 1824 the geographical extent of Mexico was declared to be the territories of the former Viceroyalty of New Spain (which included the former Captain-Generalcy of Yucatan) and the breakaway Guatemalan province of Chiapas.[1]

Early exchanges

Mexican independence was recognised by Britain in 1825 with the opening of negotiations for a Treaty of Friendship, Commerce and Navigation. After British rejection of a first draft which referred to the Bay settlement, defined as in the 1783 and 1786 treaties, as a part of Mexico, these talks were concluded successfully in December 1826. The article (Article 14) in the agreed text referring to British standing in the Bay settlement asserted the continuation of existing rights without any mention of the status of the territory to which they applied, and reserved future arrangements for discussion at 'some more fitting opportunity'.[2] In this way the British side avoided any reference that might imply acknowledgement of Mexican sovereignty.

The northern border of the Bay settlement had been the subject of more protests from the Spanish authorities than the southern or more loosely defined western edges because it was both inhabited and administered on the Spanish side. On the other hand British penetration in that direction, the subject of such complaints, had been limited to temporary woodcutting and trading a comparatively short distance into Spanish territory. It was quite different from the establishment of land claims and mahogany works further and further south of the Sibun and ever more upstream on the main rivers flowing eastwards through the settlement to the sea. Consequently there was no attempt to assert British rights north of the River Hondo in sporadic contacts with the

Mexican government over the next seventy years, before British sovereignty south of the river and the precise line of the border along it were formally acknowledged in 1897.

The main reason Britain declined to discuss these two issues with the Mexican government during the first ten years of that period was that Spain, Britain's partner in the treaties enshrining her rights, had not recognised Mexican independence. That was finally enacted in 1836. In the negotiations leading up to that independence agreement, the Mexicans had initially sought to insert a reference to the boundary provisions of the 1783 and 1786 treaties; but the Spaniards, partly at British prompting, had refused to oblige.[3] But the Spaniards had also declined to reply to a pre-emptive British request in 1835 for cession of sovereignty over the whole of the territory between the Rivers Hondo and Sarstoon, a proposition based on a combination of earlier treaty rights, British occupation of the area south of the Sibun during the years (1796–1808) when she was at war with Spain, and Mexican and Guatemalan independence.[4] Thus the treaty between Mexico and Spain finally contained no reference to Mexican boundaries, to the Bay settlement or to British rights there. The Spanish government never returned to the subject and Britain remained formally silent, *vis-a-vis* the Mexican government, for over twenty years.

For Britain the logical next step towards agreement on the definition of boundaries with neighbouring territories was in any case a settlement, likely to be long delayed by disagreement over the Peten region, between Mexico and Guatemala. There could then be no dispute as to which part of the Bay settlement's border was with Mexico and which with Guatemala. But following a Mexican protest caused by a misunderstanding about the source of the Hondo, the British did in 1838 agree to the commissioning of a joint survey of the *de facto* northern border.[5] The Mexicans appointed a representative at the end of the following year, but the work was never pursued. One reason may have been Mexican reluctance to do anything prejudicial to their position on inheritance of Spanish sovereign rights in the settlement. But with the opening of the new decade they were soon in any case overtaken by other events that were to preoccupy them. First the Yucatan became convulsed by civil strife over relations with the central government. Then the authorities were faced with the political and social upheaval of the Caste War, as the Maya took the opportunity to rise against the divided descendants of their former colonial masters. From then on the main concern of the Mexican government in relation to the Bay settlement was British support for the Indians who were at the centre of this storm.

The Caste War and the Santa Cruz threat

The Caste War of 1847–55 is estimated to have halved the population of the Yucatan.[6] The immediate effect on the Bay settlement was large-scale immigration. The population of the previously sparsely inhabited northern district increased quickly to about 6000.[7] For the settlement this had the benefit of providing labour for a slowly developing agriculture. But for the Mexican authorities the territory had the appearance not only of a refuge for rebels, but also of a source of supply for those who stayed behind. In 1849 they felt entitled to ask the British government formally to put a stop to the trafficking of arms across the border.[8] That was followed in 1854 by a protest, in the same context, about alleged British encroachments on Ambergris Cay, off Corozal Bay.[9]

In 1857, when there was again fighting between political factions in Merida and in Campeche, the Santa Cruz (or Cruzob) Indians retained control of much of south-eastern Yucatan, having defeated both the Mexican authorities and rival Indian tribes. This created considerable alarm in the Bay, because it seemed likely that they would seek to extend their reign of terror southwards. That alarm was heightened when the Santa Cruz demanded payment from the Young Toledo Company for a mahogany 'works' close to the River Hondo.[10] The Superintendent, who had been told to resort to military action only in case of 'absolute need',[11] was then authorised to station troops on the border and to resort to hot pursuit of any attackers where this could be justified. After the massacre by the Santa Cruz in February 1858 of the Mexican garrison at Bacalar for whose lives British mediators had been bargaining, almost the whole of the small military force in the settlement was deployed to Corozal. Although reinforcements, in the form of a second company of colonial infantry, were dispatched from Jamaica[12] and 5000 refugees given asylum,[13] the British government otherwise insisted on a policy of strict neutrality, refusing to cooperate in a punitive expedition. In particular, no doubt partly to avoid provoking the Indians but also partly to avoid compromising British sovereignty, they refused to allow Mexican forces to use British territory or territorial waters for this purpose.[14]

From 1859 to 1861 there was an uneasy stand-off on both sides of the border. Initially tension remained such that in April 1860 it was decided to build a permanent barracks in the north, at Punta Consejo, for the 160 extra troops sent from Jamaica two years before.[15] But a year later the Santa Cruz were assuring the British of their peaceful intentions and interest in trade[16] and the martial law that had been imposed on the Corozal area was rescinded.[17] With a further reduction in the threat over the next few months, the project for a permanent barracks close to the border was dropped in February 1862.[18]

The Icaiche threat

Subsequently the pattern of relationships changed more markedly, as a rapprochement developed between the British and the Santa Cruz Indians on the one hand and between the Mexicans and the most significant rival Indian tribe, the Icaiche (or Chichuanha), on the other. Certainly the latter tribe, who had come to terms with the Mexicans in 1853,[19] emerged as the main threat to the security of northern British Honduras, as it now was, over the next few years. Whereas the Santa Cruz had come to regard the British settlers as useful suppliers, the Icaiche found that they had, probably for that very reason, at least tacit Mexican support for increasingly bold raids on British territory. There was also, as we shall see, a connection with a reassertion of Mexican sovereignty claims, together with a probably more legitimate Icaiche grievance about British settlers' and Mexican refugees' failure to honour agreed payments for wood-cutting around Indian villages.[20]

Following an initial incident in June 1864, when twenty-three local inhabitants were kidnapped,[21] and further threats the next year, a more serious clash took place in May 1866. A 125-strong Icaiche gang led by 'General' Canul, who claimed to hold a Mexican commission, killed two local residents in the northern district and took another 79 as hostages from a logging camp close to the northwestern border.[22] The prisoners were released on payment of a ransom. The first contact that took place after the British army then instituted a system of patrols around border villages started with an Indian ambush southwest of Orange Walk. The outcome, much criticised by the Lieutenant Governor, was British losses of five dead and sixteen wounded, abandonment of both Orange Walk and the Civil Commissioner, and a hasty withdrawal.[23] Early in 1867 a larger number of troops from the garrison, again reinforced from Jamaica, undertook a series of further skirmishes against the Icaiche in the border area and against allies from the same tribe who had settled in the Yalbac Hills, in the northwest of the territory, around 1860.[24] These actions, which included burning of villages, were, thanks to help from Santa Cruz Indians, broadly successful from the British point of view. By April of that year, when the Lieutenant Governor confirmed the friendly relations developed with the Santa Cruz, the threat from the Icaiche was deemed to have diminished enough for martial law again to be lifted.[25] The following month the nature of British relations with the Santa Cruz was borne out by a report that the latter had pre-empted the possibility of an Icaiche raid on the colony.[26] By August 1867 security had improved to a point where the military presence in the northern district could be reduced to a single small detachment at Orange Walk.[27]

In July 1868, after a couple of minor incursions by the Icaiche, the Lieutenant Governor reported that, although rent disputes continued, all was quiet on the frontier.[28] This was confirmed in September 1869.[29] But by the end of the year troops were back in Corozal because of a kidnapping and threats by Indians to take possession of the town.[30] There then followed two significant and, for the British, damaging raids by Icaiche Indians, both again led by Canul. In April 1870, a month after British troops were again withdrawn, he achieved a temporary occupation of Corozal; and in 1872, when there was again a second company of colonial infantry in the Bay,[31] he penetrated the territory as far as Orange Walk, where he fought a six-hour action with the detachment of the West India Regiment that formed the local garrison. Both sides suffered losses, but for the Indians theirs were the more serious because they included their leader.[32] Canul died of wounds shortly after being carried back across the border. A combination of that loss and the construction of more substantial fortifications at the British military posts at Corozal and Orange Walk (Forts Cairns and Barlee) deterred further cross-border violence apart from occasional kidnappings and robberies. Although anxiety remained in the north throughout the 1880s, there were no significant reports of threatened larger-scale action after 1882, when a meeting was held between the Icaiche leader and the Lieutenant Governor.[33] The last company of the 2nd West India Regiment, detachments of which had been stationed in British Honduras since the Napoleonic War, was withdrawn in 1888.[34] In their stead security was provided by a much enlarged constabulary, built up to a strength of 170 by recruitment in Barbados and then stationed largely at former military posts in the north.[35]

Mexican assertion of sovereignty

At that time the British and Mexican governments had recently resumed diplomatic relations, broken off in 1867 following the execution of Emperor Maximilian and also because of the formal Mexican assertion of sovereignty over British Honduras already referred to. That position had been declared during the brief reign of Maximilian, imported from Austria after French, American and British intervention over foreign debt. The declaration, in 1864, had followed a British attempt in 1857, following discussions on the same subject with the Guatemalans, to interest the Mexican government in a border treaty,[36] an attempt which had foundered because the Mexican minister in London was not given the necessary powers and instructions.

With the Mexican declaration of 1864 both sides for the first time put their cards on the table. In response to the Mexican claim the British government immediately asserted exclusive sovereignty. They then protested at reported Mexican support for the Icaiche Indians' campaign of harassment of northern British Honduras, which they saw as linked to the sovereignty claim. That claim they again denied, together with its stated basis, the inheritance of earlier Spanish rights. Instead they suggested a final settlement of the border question without prejudice to British sovereignty.[37] The Mexican government, who claimed that they were unable to control the Icaiche, responded by protesting against British complicity in the arming of the Santa Cruz Indians and urging the British government to join with them in efforts to pacify both sides of the border. They also argued that they had succeeded to the treaty rights of the Captain-Generalcy of Yucatan; that that succession had been recognised in an agreement of 1838 governing relations between Mexico and Spain; and that the associated rights had in any case been consolidated under the Anglo/Mexican Treaty of Friendship, Commerce and Navigation of 1826.[38] Despite these diametrically opposed positions, however, both sides had an interest in a settlement: the British because of the security threat to their territory, the Mexicans because of the arms supply and the hot pursuit the British were only likely to stop once the border was respected. They therefore agreed to try to draw up a new friendship treaty satisfactory to both sides. Negotiations then foundered in 1866 on the difficulty of agreeing language on all those contentious issues. As a result of the hostile climate engendered by these exchanges, and then by the execution of Maximilian in 1867, diplomatic relations were broken off.

Such exchanges as there were by direct correspondence between governments in the next few years were sterile. Accusations were repeated, the British alleging Mexican encouragement of Icaiche incursions, the Mexicans alleging British support for the Santa Cruz. In 1874 the British reasserted their right of hot pursuit, which arose 'out of the extinction of all law and lawful authority in the particular tract in which it might take place'.[39] In 1878 the Mexican government once again, on the basis of earlier treaties, formally asserted their country's sovereignty over British Honduras. The British response was that they were not prepared to discuss the matter, as British sovereignty had been 'fully established by conquest subsequent to the treaties of 1783 and 1786 and long prior to the existence of Mexico as an independent state'.[40] A resumption of diplomatic relations was proposed in 1880, but came to nothing because of Mexican insistence that British claims to sovereignty over British Honduras be abandoned.[41] But by 1882, when the Icaiche threat to the settlement's northern border finally subsided, both sides again had an interest in rapprochement. Whereas the Mexicans needed foreign investment, the British were concerned that the boundary agreement signed that year between Mexico and Guatemala might add to their difficulties with the latter. Two years later relations were resumed on the basis of no reference by either side to rights or boundaries. The British then began to demarcate the border unilaterally. This seems not to have offended the Mexicans, for in 1886 they agreed to discussions on British terms, for the first time for sixty years. That was subject to the condition that steps would be taken to stop an allegedly continuing supply of arms to the local Indian population. The British for their part stipulated that no questions should be raised as to their sovereign rights. Because of both the security difficulties they had experienced and a wish to reduce their military forces in the Caribbean, they also demanded that the Yucatan Indians be brought firmly under control.

Resumption of negotiations

Negotiations opened in the spring of 1887, when the Mexicans were alarmed by reports that the Santa Cruz Indians were seeking to put their land under British protection.[42] These Indian overtures were in fact gently deflected by the British, who urged the Santa Cruz to negotiate a settlement with the Mexicans.[43] By this time the British demarcation of the border had been completed. The lines proposed were that of the River Hondo westwards until it met Blue Creek, and the line of the latter until it reached a point due north of the intersection of the borders agreed in 1859 between Guatemala and Britain (for British Honduras) and in 1882 between Guatemala and Mexico. The western border between Mexico and British Honduras was then to be the north–south line joining those two points. A draft agreement handed to the Mexicans contained these provisions, together with passages providing for prohibition of arms supply and prevention of incursions.[44] The Mexicans sought to introduce a minor variation of the northern border alignment plus preambular language implying Mexican sovereignty, neither of which the British were prepared to accept.

The Mexicans then decided to wait until they had completed pacification of the Indians before proceeding further. This they thought would make the proposed agreement more acceptable to public and political opinion in Mexico. But the British were concerned that if the

Santa Cruz Indians were denied arms with which to resist pacification, or were otherwise faced with British cooperation with the Mexicans, they would cause serious trouble in northern British Honduras. This dilemma prompted the suggestion in 1889 that British good offices might help bring about the southern Yucatan settlement that they (the British) had urged on the Santa Cruz, and thus both dispose of the arms issue and hasten a border agreement.[45] But talks between the Santa Cruz and the Mexicans failed to materialise because of ill-feeling about the rapid collapse of an earlier agreement reached in 1884;[46] and four more years passed before the Mexican side felt able, in 1893, to finalise the border agreement with Britain. Moreover when they did it was at the specific request of the Yucatan legislature, who were concerned about encroachment by British settlers,[47] rather than because of progress with pacification. Indeed what might also have persuaded the Mexican government to move was the argument that British co-operation in the security of southern Yucatan was both more valuable and more necessary than the small slice of northern British Honduras that was left to Mexico for a possible sovereignty claim after the Mexican-Guatemalan border agreement of 1882.

The 1893 treaty and its aftermath

The treaty between Mexico and Britain was signed in July 1893 in very much the form proposed in 1887. Ratification however was held up for yet another four years because of opposition in the Mexican Senate. In 1895 the British moved some way to meet the Mexican wish for security cooperation, by accepting the possibility of involvement in non-military pacification.[48] This seems to have meant undertaking a mediating role. But resistance to ratification continued in Mexico City, and it was to overcome this that the British government further agreed to the addition of an article providing for free navigation for Mexican merchant vessels (extended as a courtesy to warships) in the strait between Ambergris Cay and the mainland and elsewhere in British Honduras territorial waters.[49] That finally unblocked ratification in July 1897. It also enabled the Mexicans to build up their military forces around the northern edge of Chetumal Bay, and then in 1900 to launch their long-planned expedition against the Santa Cruz Indians. Attempts by British officials, who even offered the colony as a meeting place, to persuade the Santa Cruz to sue for peace continued until the last moment, but were finally recognised as futile.[50] Although the Governor felt some concern about the possible long-term strategic implications,[51] for British merchants the new business opportunity created by such a hefty Mexican presence just across the border more than compensated for the treaty obligation for them to stop supplying the Santa Cruz Indians. By 1902 pacification of southern Yucatan was more or less complete, and the beginnings of a modern cross-border economic relationship were being made.

With ratification of the 1893 treaty came at last, seventy-six years after the departure of the Spaniards, both Mexican recognition of British sovereignty and final settlement of the northern and northwestern borders of what is now Belize. There has since then been no serious suggestion by the Mexicans to the British or independent Belizean governments of reopening those questions, although they have in the past indicated to the Guatemalans that they might do so if the latter acquired rights in the territory.

Notes

1. R. A. Humphreys, *The Diplomatic History of British Honduras 1638-1901*, London (1961), 18–19.
2. British and Foreign State Papers, London (1841), XIV, 625.
3. The Spanish decision on this point is reported in a letter of 27 February 1836 from the British Minister in Madrid to Lord Palmerston in FO 72/457.
4. The British request had its origin in a letter of 22 September 1834 from the Foreign Office to the Colonial Office in FO 15/15. The Colonial Office then developed the justification of the case in a detailed memorandum dated 20 January 1835 (FO 72/452). The two approaches by the British Ambassador in Madrid to the Spanish Foreign Minister are described in Karl R. De Rouen, *Cockburn, Miller, and the Shift in British Policy in Belize* (Belizean Studies Vol. 19 Nos. 2 and 3, December 1991). Miller, Cockburn's emissary to London, was sent to Madrid by the British government to advise the Ambassador on details.
5. Palmerston/Ashburnham 15 December 1837, FO 50/104; and Ashburnham/ Palmerston 6 March and 4 April 1838, FO 50/113.
6. Narda Dobson, *A History of Belize*, London (1973) 218. An excellent account of the war is to be found in Nelson Reed, *The Caste War of Yucatan*, Stanford, California (1964).
7. Wayne Clegern, British Honduras: Colonial Dead End 1859–1900, Baton Rouge (1967), 10.
8. Doyle/Palmerston 16 March 1849, FO 50/227.
9. Superintendent/Governor, Jamaica, 4 October 1851, ABH Vol. 3, 150.
10. Seymour/Darling, 17 August 1857, BA (R52, 82–4). The Santa Cruz Maya espoused an amalgam of Christian and Maya religious beliefs with the "talking cross" an important symbol of their faith.
11. See reference in Seymour/Bell, 14 July 1857, BA (R52, 72–5).
12. Darling/Seymour, 27 March 1858, BA (R60, 165–172).
13. Superintendent/Governor, Jamaica, 17 May 1858, ABH Vol. 3, 206.
14. In a letter of 17 March 1858, the Superintendent urged the Governor (in Jamaica) to send a British warship to preserve the settlement's neutrality – see ABH Vol. 3, 203–4.
15. Darling/Rice, 5 April 1860, BA (R67, 43).
16. Magistrate, Northern District/Superintendent, 26 April 1861, ABH Vol. 3, 240.
17. ABH Vol. 3, 240, quoting Gazette of 18 May 1861.
18. Superintendent/Officer Commanding Troops, 28 February 1862, ABH Vol. 3, 245.

19. Nigel Bolland, *Colonialism and Resistance in Belize*, Belize (1988), 96. The Icaiche, a lowland Maya tribe who came from the Yucatan, are quite distinct from the Ketchi Maya living in southern Belize today. The latter arrived from the Guatemalan highlands in the late nineteenth century to work on the Kramer coffee and cocoa plantations established then in the Toledo district.
20. Austin/Storks 21 June 1866 in Rogers/Hammond 17 October 1866, FO 15/145.
21. Governor, Jamaica/Governor, Yucatan, 22 June 1864, BA (R86, 25–33). The Indian leader, Zuc, had claimed provocation by the theft of some mules by a resident of British Honduras. The hostages were ransomed the following month.
22. British Honduras Company/Lieutenant Governor, 2 May 1866, BA (R93, 1–2).
23. See opinion of Court of Inquiry with Grant/Buckingham, 6 July 1867, CO 123/128.
24. Bolland, 97.
25. Lieutenant Governor/Secretary of State, 5 April 1867, ABH Vol. 3, 284.
26. Enc. to Grant/Buckingham, 24 July 1867, CO 123/128.
27. Austin/Grant, 6 August 1867, CO 123/128.
28. Lieutenant Governor/Governor, Jamaica, 21 July 1868, ABH Vol. 3, 308–9.
29. Longden/Grant, 3 September 1869, CO 123/137.
30. Lieutenant Governor/Governor, Jamaica, 30 December 1869, ABH Vol. 3, 317.
31. Ordinance of 13 January 1872, ABH Vol. 3, 326.
32. Johnston/Cairns, 11 September 1872, ABH Vol. 3, 327–9.
33. Bolland, 99. The improvement in relations with the Icaiche will have been helped by the work of Roman Catholic missionaries amongst them from the 1860s – see Richard Buhler, *A History of the Catholic Church in Belize*, Belize Institute for Social Research and Action (1976).
34. Goldsworthy/Knutsford, 10 May 1888, CO 123/189.
35. ibid. and Fowler/Secretary of State, 11 July 1887, CO 123/184.
36. Lord Clarendon to the Mexican Minister in London, 27 June 1857, FO 50/327.
37. Russell/Scarlett 1 July 1865, FO 15/144B.
38. Castillo/Scarlett 9 December 1865, FO 15/144B.
39. Lord Derby/Mexican Minister of Foreign Affairs 28 July 1874, FO 50/433.
40. Lord Salisbury/Mexican Minister of Foreign Affairs 8 June 1878, FO 50/434.
41. Lyons/Granville 24 November 1881, FO 27/2498.
42. The offer was refused – see Salisbury/St. John 6 April 1887, FO 15/241 – although it was conceded that any Indians 'who may take refuge in the Colony should be allowed to remain on giving up their arms'.
43. Fowler/Secretary of State, 18 June 1887, CO 123/184.
44. Enc. to St. John/Mexican Minister of Foreign Affairs 12 May 1887, FO 15/242.
45. Goldsworthy/Knutsford, 4 July 1889, CO 123/192.
46. The agreement had been brokered by the acting Governor (technically Administrator) of British Honduras, Henry Fowler. But the Santa Cruz subsequently refused to ratify it because of a perceived insult by the Mexican delegation leader – see Grant D. Jones, *Belize, Santa Cruz, and Yucatan: the 1884 Articles of Peace*, Belizean Studies, Vol. 6 No. 2, (March 1978), 1–9.
47. St. John/Rosebery 28 January 1893, FO 15/279.
48. Clegern, 150. The policy seems to have originated with a letter from the Under Secretary at the Colonial Office to his counterpart at the Foreign Office (dated 14 October 1895, in FO 15/298) pointing out the risks of large numbers of armed Indians being displaced into British Honduras by Mexican military action.
49. The Mexican request for this was conveyed in a letter from the British Minister in Mexico City to Lord Kimberley as early as 31 March 1894.
50. Enc. to Wilson/Chamberlain, 1 February 1900, and Wilson/Chamberlain, 16 March 1900, CO 123/235.
51. Wilson/Chamberlain, 22 March 1900, CO 123/235.

9

Disputes between Britain and Guatemala

The Captain Generalcy of Guatemala decided on independence in September 1821, seven months after the Mexican declaration. Early the next year political leaders further decided to accept a Mexican invitation to join them in a union.[1] In June 1822 a Mexican army duly arrived at Guatemala City. But the next month, after the fall of the Mexican revolutionary leader Iturbide, there were second thoughts, and the old Captain Generalcy became instead the independent federal republic of the United Provinces of Central America (UPCA), comprising modern Guatemala, Honduras, Nicaragua, El Salvador and Costa Rica. A constitution was adopted three years later, but the precise extent of the new entity's territory was left undefined.[2] This was because the former Guatemalan province of Chiapas had chosen to remain a part of Mexico. That became the cause of a long dispute between the two countries. In the shorter term it gave Britain reason to withold recognition of the federal government of the UPCA and the constituent state government of Guatemala. That suited the British, because the Guatemalans had already made known their belief that they had inherited Spanish sovereignty over at least part of the Belize River settlement.

Early exchanges

The first of many exchanges between the British and Guatemalan governments on sovereignty claims came in February 1826. It concerned a reference by the Secretary of State of the UPCA, in an explanation of the text of a treaty with Colombia, to the Bay settlement as 'the only British establishment within the territory of the Republic'.[3] This may have hastened further contact. In April of that year Canning, the British Foreign Secretary, declared that the time was ripe for settlement of boundaries with the newly independent states bordering 'Her Majesty's possessions'.[4] The following month an emissary from the UPCA federal government arrived in London to negotiate a border agreement. But that overture came to nothing because of doubts about the visiting representative's instructions and because the British decided that the government of the United Provinces did not at that time have effective internal control.[5] For the latter reason it was not until 1831 that the opening of talks on a commercial treaty was agreed. Again no progress was made, this time because the Central American representative was recalled.[6] No greater success attended a British suggestion in July 1834 of a Treaty of Friendship, Commerce and Navigation with the state of Guatemala. The Guatemalans wanted a reference to the 1786 treaty in the text, as had been included in Britain's treaty with Mexico. The British would not agree. They were willing to see the talks suspended because they were hoping for retrospective recognition by the Spanish government, with whom they had signed that agreement, of British sovereignty over territory between the Rivers Hondo and Sarstoon.

By this time relations were soured by two grants of land, to a company and to an individual, by the Guatemalans in the area between the Rivers Sibun and the Sarstoon – the area partly occupied by the British but not covered by the eighteenth-century treaties. This climate was aggravated by the imposition of discriminatory import duties on products from the British settlement and on cargoes landed by ships which had called there.[7] The British response was to inform the Guatemalans for the first time, through the company granted land in the disputed area, that Britain claimed the territory between the Hondo and the Sarstoon as far west as Garbutt's Falls on the Belize River.[8] The question of precise boundary delineation was not taken up because by that time the Colonial Office had concluded that it must await a border agreement between Guatemala and Mexico.[9] But the British declaration was enough to choke off investment in the development schemes floated with the Guatemalan land grants, and both were given up.

The next British protest, in 1838, concerned a Guatemalan invitation to the inhabitants of the Bay settlement to send a representative to a constituent assembly called to revise the state constitution, so that they might 'concur with the other inhabitants of the territory of Guatemala in the political reorganisation of the state'.[10] This was overtaken by the collapse later the same year of the federal government of the United Provinces of Central America, and indeed of the federation itself. From this Guatemala emerged as an independent republic in April 1839. At that point the Colonial Office wanted to take the opportunity to set aside the treaties with Spain as 'obsolete and wholly inapplicable to the present circumstances of the contracting parties', to assert British sovereignty, and to regularise the Bay settlement's institutions.[11] That came to nothing because the Prime Minister, Lord Palmerston, was unwilling (for party political reasons) to present proposals to Parliament, and in any case believed that 'the best thing we can do is quietly to let the Spaniards forget it'; while his successor, Lord Aberdeen, was concerned about the effect of a unilateral move on relations with Spain.[12] Both sovereignty as an issue for the British government and substantive contacts with the Guatemalans were then allowed to lie until, in the first case, the British government's Law Officers gave their opinion in 1851 that the Bay settlement was 'a part of the dominions of the Crown' and, in the second case, the Guatemalan government, as an insurance against US 'interference' or even 'annexation', unsuccessfully proposed a secret treaty in 1853.[13]

The 1859 Convention

The Guatemalan claim, however, though dormant, was not dead. Moreover the British government had been coming under pressure from the United States to settle, in the spirit of the US interpretation of the 1850 Clayton–Bulwer Treaty on limits to the two powers' ambitions in Central America. They finally agreed to do so within two years under the terms of a further and more specific Anglo–US agreement, the Dallas–Clarendon Treaty of 1856. Under this accord Britain also agreed not only to give up the protection of the Mosquito Indians which had been formally re-assumed in 1847, but also to cede to Honduras the Bay Islands (i.e. Ruatan and Bonacca) which, before designation as a separate colony in 1852, had been a *de facto* dependency of the Belize River settlement administered by a magistrate appointed by the Superintendent.

These developments led the Guatemalan Minister in Paris to visit London in 1857 for substantive negotiations. These proceeded smoothly. Under the draft treaty that was agreed in 1858, after it became clear that a tripartite border agreement to include Mexico was unattainable, the Guatemalan representative accepted the boundaries between his country and 'the British Settlement and Possessions in the Bay of Honduras' as the Sarstoon as far as the Gracios a Dios Falls, a line from there to Garbutt's Falls on the Belize River, and a further line due north to the parallel of whatever Guatemala–Mexican frontier was agreed in the future. The reference in the past as well as the present tense to the existence of British 'possessions' clarified the nature of British sovereignty. The draft text also provided for the marking 'where necessary' of the agreed boundaries. But the proposed agreement was linked by the Guatemalan side to a separate and unilateral memorandum seeking an 'indemnity' relating to their earlier claims.[14] The terms in the agreed draft text, which also included an article on freedom of navigation, were subsequently accepted by the Guatemalan government subject to a provision in an additional article that would reflect the intention of their Minister's memorandum.

By this time final negotiation of the document to be signed had moved to Guatemala City. There the British Consul General was prevailed upon to agree on his own responsibility to add to the agreed draft the extra article referred to above, committing both sides to use their best efforts to establish the 'easiest communication' between Guatemala City and the Caribbean shore 'near the settlement of Belize'. To the Guatemalans this would supply the compensation they sought for what to them was cession of territory. To the Consul General it was no more than the inducement needed to secure the boundary agreement he had been told to use every endeavour to achieve, and moreover an arrangement that might help recover for British Honduras some of the regional trade lost to newly developed Pacific coast ports. To the British government it was a potentially very expensive commitment, which they accepted as a necessary inducement provided it was minimised so as to reduce any impression, offensive to the US, that British sovereignty had somehow been bought (and thus extended) rather than simply recognised. This last consideration became more important when it emerged that the most practicable route for the purpose would lie entirely on Guatemalan territory.

As each side saw the reason for the extra article (Article 7) differently, so each side had different ideas about implementation. For the Guatemalans it was a British concession which the British should in principle pay for. For the British it was a joint endeavour rather than a gift, and one for which they might appropriately provide technical knowledge but neither provide nor fund materials and labour. But as the Consul General had indicated to the Guatemalans, before signature, that the British would pay half the labour cost, the Secretary of State, in order to save the agreement, undertook, without entering into specifics, that 'Her Majesty's Government will honourably fulfill its obligations'.[15]

Unfortunately for both sides, not only did views on allocation of responsibility harden after signature on 30 April 1859, but investigation showed that the project was a much bigger undertaking than had been foreseen. Thus the Guatemalans took up the position that while they should provide materials and labour, payment for the latter should fall entirely to the British side; and the British military engineer who surveyed the route in 1860 estimated the cost (£121,315 for labour and materials alone) at nearly double the figure arrived at before. For both sides the resulting difficulty was political. For the Guatemalans, and especially for their Chamber of Representatives, the proposed road was the centrepiece of the Convention. For the British side, Parliament was most unlikely to agree an unexpectedly large payment for a scheme that, far from benefiting

British Honduras, might, in the form now recommended, actually further reduce its share of regional trade.

What further complicated implementation of the Convention was the issue of marking the western boundary of what was soon to be the colony. Marks were placed at Gracios a Dios Falls on the Sarstoon and at Garbutt's Falls on the Belize River. But the Guatemalan commissioner appointed for the survey refused to agree to marking more than a few miles south of Garbutt's Falls because the text of the Convention did not make that necessary; while the British commissioner was restrained by his own side from marking the border more than a few miles north because of a wish not to offend either the Mexicans or, more immediately, the Santa Cruz Indians (who then controlled most of southern Yucatan), and thus prejudice the interests of British loggers active in the area.[16]

The Additional Convention

For all these reasons the British government decided in November 1861 to propose further talks with the Guatemalans to discuss what they saw as necessary modifications to the 1859 Convention. Negotiation was to focus on practical fulfilment of the obligations placed on each side by the controversial Article 7.[17] The aim was a convention spelling out how the road project was to be managed and resourced. The British claimed to be willing to contribute a proper share provided that the Guatemalans were too. On the other hand, although they did not want to suggest it themselves, they were quite willing to set Article 7 aside.[18]

The Guatemalan opening position in May 1862 remained that Britain should bear the whole cost of the road scheme, although now subject to a limit of £100,000 for labour, the upper end of the initial estimate for the overall project. The British Minister in Guatemala City, again on his own responsibility, counter-proposed a maximum of two-thirds of the labour cost up to a limit of £50,000. The Guatemalan Foreign Minister agreed to the two-thirds share, but not to the £50,000 limit.[19] What became increasingly clear as the talks stalled was that the Guatemalans were not to be shaken from their convinction that the language of the 1859 Convention bound the British to bear the greater part of the cost of the project; and that they (the Guatemalans) were constrained by an acute shortage of funds.

In December 1862 the British Minister was instructed to propose a £25,000 down-payment by each side to cover at least part of the labour cost, with the British providing technical knowledge and the Guatemalans materials.[20] The Guatemalans not only rejected the British cash offer as less than half the likely labour cost, but also asserted that they could not confirm their relinquishment of rights between the Sibun and the Sarstoon without what they had envisaged as proper compensation.[21] Negotiations were then transferred, at the Guatemalans' suggestion, to London.

It was the Guatemalans who made the next move, with a draft supplementary convention presented by their Minister accredited to London in May 1863. This set at £60,737 (half the 1860 estimate) the amount the British should contribute towards the cost of labour and materials, with the Guatemalans bearing any balance.[22] As before, the British were to provide technical knowledge, the Guatemalans materials. As it stood, this was unacceptable to the British government, but it was a position both sides were willing to consider as a starting point for bargaining purposes. In subsequent negotiation, the Guatemalans lowered their sights, and within three months agreement was reached. The Additional Convention, signed in August 1863, provided for a straightforward payment by the British, in instalments as work progressed, of £50,000 against the construction of a road from Guatemala City to the Caribbean coast on a line to be proposed by the Guatemalan government. There was to be no other British involvement in the enterprise. The new agreement committed the Guatemalans to implementing the scheme within four years and to accepting the British payment as a full discharge of obligations entered into under the 1859 Convention.

Further exchanges

With fateful consequences for the future, ratifications of the Additional Convention were never exchanged. It had been agreed that this would be done within six months. But, for both fiscal and political reasons it was two years before the text was laid before the Guatemalan Council of State, and another ten months before their Minister in Paris was ready for the exchange. When he arrived, it was with proposals for 'clarification' of the Additional Convention. But by 1866 enthusiasm in London for the road project had cooled further, and it was doubted whether Parliament would now sanction such an outlay from which no likely British benefit could be seen. There was also the new complication of a revived Mexican sovereignty claim. The British government decided that the delay in ratification released them not only from commitments under the Additional Convention but also from those under the article of the 1859 convention to which it related. This was on the basis that their 'best efforts' to implement that article had failed to identify a means of undertaking the project envisaged in the Convention at a reasonable cost in relation to 'any commercial benefit which might be expected to arise from it'.[23] The Guatemalans, who perhaps did not help their case by referring again to compensation, pressed for agreement on a new Additional Convention identical to the original. They argued repeatedly over the next three years that Article 7 was an essential component of the 1859 Convention, and that, if clarifications were unacceptable, either it remained in force unelaborated or the whole of the Convention, including the provisions on recognition of British rights, fell away.[24] But the British government was not to be moved. It was the beginning of a deadlock that was to last for over a hundred years.

From 1869 the British were content to allow exchanges on this subject to lapse. Thereafter the Guatemalans made no serious move to reopen the unsettled questions for eleven years. Then, in July 1880, their newly appointed Minister in Paris (also, as before, accredited to London), presented the British Foreign Secretary, Lord Granville, with a long memorandum rehearsing all the points made in previous exchanges, and proposing arbitration by a third power.[25] Granville's response to this initiative was predictable: because, like his predecessor in the late 1860s, he saw no case for the British to answer, he could not agree that there was any basis for arbitration.[26]

Four years later the Guatemalans raised the subject again. This followed a somewhat doubtful argument by the US government, in response to British objections to ideas which in due course resulted in the Panama Canal, that the British, with the consolidation of the old Bay settlement as a larger colony, had violated the Anglo–US Clayton–Bulwer Treaty of 1850, which had sought to avoid competition between the two powers for influence in Central America. Although the British government rejected this, on the basis that British occupation of even the enlarged territory long pre-dated the 1850 treaty,[27] it was enough to encourage the Guatemalans to reopen the question of, as they saw it, full implementation of the 1859 Convention. The line the Guatemalan Minister took in a note of protest in April 1884 was that the Convention could only be considered to be in force if it was fully implemented; that without full implementation it was null and void; and that if null and void, the original Guatemalan claim to territorial rights stood.[28] The reassertion of the claim took the form of a 'solemn protest against the increasing occupation *de facto* on the part of Great Britain of an integral part of Guatemala's territory'.

The British reaction to this second approach, which threatened but did not declare repudiation of the 1859 Convention, was less intransigent than before. Their first move was to consult the Law Officers of the Crown on the implications for the Convention of the position Ministers had taken on Article 7, which they regarded as fulfilled if not implemented. The Law

Officers' somewhat convoluted view, first given in August then elaborated in November 1884, was that although the articles of the Convention were not of themselves interdependent, it was open to the Guatemalans to refuse to observe any one article if they had reason to believe that another remained unfulfilled by the other side. They also concluded that the British commitment under Article 7 extended at least to a moral obligation to use their best efforts to secure funds for the road project.[29] This opinion provoked some new thinking, and as ideas emerged the Lord Chancellor was also consulted. In response he went further than had the Law Officers. In his view the measures taken by the British in pursuit of Article 7 could not be considered the best efforts called for in that article; and nor was it unreasonable for the Guatemalans to link recognition of British sovereignty to that article being given 'substantial effect', because they had agreed to the former 'in consideration' of the latter.[30]

Railway proposals and deadlock

Meanwhile it had been established that the Guatemalans would not accept a simple payment of £50,000 if it were tied to construction of a railway from Guatemala City to the Guatemalan Caribbean shore to complement the line to the Pacific coast that had just been completed.[31] By April 1887, when the Colonial Office put to the Cabinet, as an alternative, a similar contribution towards a rail link from Belize (town) to Guatemala City, Treasury opposition had hardened to the point where it was considered no application to Parliament could be made for that or any other scheme. The Colonial Office repeated their proposal in January 1891, but it met with the same objections. As attempts by the administration in the colony to attract outside investment and Guatemalan land concessions for such a project had also come to nothing, the whole matter once again lapsed after a somewhat hollow British assurance that they would consider any mutually beneficial proposal to connect the two territories.[32]

After a further unsuccessful attempt in 1893 by the Colonial Office to revive discussion between departments, there was an informal approach two years later to try to interest the Guatemalans in a railway from Belize to the Peten linked to timber concessions and supported by a £50,000 British subsidy.[33] The Guatemalans responded positively to the notion of a railway linked to timber extraction, but preferred a wholly commercial arrangement, with the subsidy offer left, implicitly, for some other scheme. This proposal was taken up by the British, but negotiation of the necessary land concessions in Guatemala proved abortive. The plan finally collapsed in 1898 when the Treasury refused to contemplate the £50,000 loan to the

British Honduras administration that the Colonial Office and Foreign Office had agreed to seek in order to attract private capital and which might also, they hoped, somehow discharge the residual obligation under the 1859 Convention. The British Treasury saw inadequate economic justification for the public expenditure proposed for the rail link, and denied that any commitment remained under the Convention.[34]

A last attempt to promote a project financed entirely from commercial sources, without any government loan, ended in 1901 when the Guatemalans failed again to respond to approaches on land concessions. Construction of their own railway from Guatemala to the Caribbean coast at Puerto Barrios was well in hand by then, and was to be completed in 1908. By the end of the nineteenth century, Article 7 of the 1859 Convention appeared to be a dead letter; both the Guatemalans and the US had, for different reasons, lost interest.

Notes

1. R. A. Humphreys, *The Diplomatic History of British Honduras 1638–1901*, London (1961), 18.
2. ibid, 19.
3. Enc. to O'Reilly/Canning, 17 February 1826, FO 15/5. In the record of a meeting in February 1825 between the Superintendent and the magistrates, however, Major General Edward Codd refers to a letter from the Guatemalan authorities dated as early as 22 July 1823 in which he was informed that the settlement was 'in their territory' – see enc. to Codd/Bathurst 18 February 1825, CO 123/36.
4. Planta/Horton, 26 April 1826, FO 72/323, seeking the views of the Colonial Secretary.
5. Humphreys, 33.
6. Guatemalan Minister in London to Lord Palmerston 27 September 1831, FO 15/11.
7. Enc. to Miller/FO, 18 February 1835, FO 15/17.
8. Humphreys, 42–3.
9. Grey/Fox-Strangeways, 10 September 1835, FO 15/17.
10. Chatfield/Palmerston, 21 November 1838, FO 15/20.
11. Stephen/Fox-Strangeways, 28 August 1838, FO 72/521.
12. Palmerston/Glenelg, 15 September 1838, FO 15/21 and Foreign Office minuting attached to Hope/Canning, 11 November 1841, FO 72/596.
13. Dodson, Romilly and Cockburn/Grey, 14 March 1851, FO 15/114 and Wyke/Clarendon, 27 November 1853, FO 15/79. Britain had concluded a commercial treaty with Guatemala in 1849, which recognised Guatemala as an independent republic; but it contained no reference to British Honduras – see D. A. G. Waddell, *British Honduras: a Historical and Contemporary Survey*, London (1961), 35.
14. Humphries, 72–6.
15. Russell/Hall, 7 April 1860, FO 15/114.
16. Humphreys, 98–103.
17. Russell/Mathew, 26 November 1861, FO 15/143.
18. Hammond/Mathew, 16 June 1862, FO15/143.
19. Humphreys, 112.
20. Russell/Mathew, 15 December 1862, FO 15/143.

21. Guatemalan Foreign Minister/Mathew, 10 February 1863, FO 15/144A.
22. The proposals were elaborated in a long memorandum from the Guatemalan Minister in London dated 18 May 1863 – see FO 15/144A.
23. Stanley/Guatemalan Minister, 30 July 1866 and 29 August 1866, FO15/145.
24. Guatemalan Minister/Stanley, 13 September and 21 December 1866, FO 15/145; enc. to Corbett/Stanley, 14 November 1867, FO 15/146; and Guatemalan Minister/Clarendon, 24 September 1869, FO 15/146.
25. Guatemalan Minister/Granville, 15 July 1880, FO 15/207.
26. Granville/Guatemalan Minister, 18 August 1880, FO 15/207.
27. Humphreys, 154.
28. Guatemalan Minister/Granville, 5 April 1884, FO 15/222.
29. Law Officers/Granville, 12 August and 25 November 1884, FO 15/222.
30. Memorandum by Lord Herschell, 30 April 1886, FO 15/231. The opinion was requested by the Foreign Office for Lord Roseberry in a letter dated 31 March 1886 on the same file.
31. Gastrell/Roseberry, 2 and 3 July 1886, FO 15/232.
32. Salisbury/Gosling, 30 March 1891, FO 15/279.
33. Initiated in Selborne/Bertie, 25 October 1895, FO 15/298.
34. Treasury/Colonial Office, 6 May 1898, enclosed with Colonial Office/Foreign Office, 15 June 1898, FO 15/322.

10

Development of the Economy in the Nineteenth Century

Timber boom and bust

For the first half of the nineteenth century the industry that was the *raison d'etre* of the settlement continued to function as before. The 'works' were managed by the established white settlers who had 'located', been allocated, or purchased them; and the necessary labour was provided, first as slaves, then as 'apprentices', finally as 'free' hands, by the bulk of the male half of the black population. After some recovery in the early years of the century, logwood exports generally remained at between 2000 and 4000 tons per annum. Mahogany exports on the other hand rose more gradually from an average of 3.6 million 'superficial' feet between 1782 and 1802[1] to an average of around 5 million superficial feet between 1823 and 1833.[2] The industry then experienced a marked boom from 1835 to 1850 due to demand for mahogany for railway carriages and ships' hulls as well as for furniture. This led to shipments that peaked in 1846 at nearly three times the average level recorded in the late 1820s and early 1830s.[3]

In order to finance the expansion of their businesses to meet this increased demand, the settlers who had dominated the industry began to develop partnerships with metropolitan companies which, taking advantage of new measures to promote joint-stock enterprises, were looking to increase their investment overseas. Demand was duly met, but supply of the more accessible timber was run down. The boom subsided in the 1850s as the effects of British trade liberalisation of the late 1840s were felt, and as wood began to give way to iron and steel in shipbuilding. By 1857 exports, at 7.2 million superficial feet, had fallen to hardly more than half the 1846 level, and prices, moreover, had tumbled too.[4] There was thus less money to be made just at the time when the cost of extraction was rising. This depressed the local economy to an extent that caused the Public Treasurer to describe the beginning of 1859 as 'remarkable for the uneasiness and apprehension which pervaded the whole community'.[5] It also led to most of the old settler families having to sell their forestry interests to the British-based companies which had entered the industry.[6] That in turn led to the emergence as the new dominant force in the local economy of four or five large companies, the strongest of which were Young Toledo, with substantial holdings in the south, and, the biggest overall, the British Honduras Company. Incorporated in 1859 from a partnership between James Hyde and John Hodge, the British Honduras Company, (from 1875 under the name Belize Estate and Produce Company) was to have a decisive influence in the colony's affairs for over a century.

In the mid-1850s, the timber companies were in an even stronger position to exercise such power than they were later. As we saw in Chapter 6, although larger-scale cultivation had been authorised in 1839, sixteen years later there was still no agricultural export trade from British Honduras. Export earnings remained very largely based on shipment of timber, as they had been for two hundred years. They were otherwise supported only by an entrepot trade with neighbouring republics that had developed in the 1820s, when civil strife in those countries made Belize an attractive base for merchants with regional, as well as local, interests. This began to drop away as order returned, particularly to Guatemala, in the 1840s, and did so sharply with the opening of the coast-to-coast railway in Panama in 1855.[7] The lack of diversification in a settlement that was by then well consolidated has a number of explanations. The companies that had largely bought out the established settlers were in a position to take a long view of the timber industry; most individual residents could not afford to buy land; and there was in any case no experience of commercial agriculture and no labour surplus. All these considerations were to change in the next few years.

The establishment of a sugar industry

The impulse came first from the immigration into the settlement's previously very thinly populated northern district of refugees from the civil wars and rebellions that raged in the Yucatan throughout the late 1840s and most of the 1850s. Thus the local magistrate reported to the Superintendent in December 1850 that 80 per cent of the district's population, which had grown to 5000, were 'foreigners'.[8] By 1859 that population had more than doubled to 11,000, with 4000 of them living in Corozal alone.[9] The settlement's 1861 census then revealed that by then as many people lived in Corozal as in Belize town,[10] and that in the territory as a whole almost as many of the inhabitants had been born in Yucatan and Central America as locally.[11]

The advantage of this influx for British Honduras was that some of the refugees were in a position to buy or lease land suitable for agriculture, others were available and willing to work it, and almost all of them came from an agricultural background. In 1852 the Superintendent reported that the refugees 'have already commenced the cultivation of sugar, corn, tobacco, and other articles'.[12] By 1857 they had 800 acres under cultivation for sugar in small plots[13] and a very small initial shipment was sold in Europe.[14] In 1859 the Superintendent reported that the new arrivals had captured, albeit with this small-scale cultivation, the local market for sugar. He also foresaw that the production price advantage they enjoyed should lead to a regular export trade.[15] The following year he went further, reporting that 'agriculture is beginning to command a larger share of public attention' and that 'abundant scope for enterprise will soon be valued by capitalists, now that the capabilities of the soil have been practically tested by small planters'.[16] Sugar exports were duly established in 1862. This was at a very low level, but as production trebled over the next five years,[17] exports grew to 544 tons out of 868 tons manufactured in 1867.[18] By 1868 ten small commercial estates equipped with steam milling machinery had been established. These cultivated 1700 acres, about half the total area under cane.[19] Hope for further progress had risen the previous year with plans for the lease of land in the southern district to emigrants from the US former Confederate states who found it difficult to come to terms with the Union victory in the American Civil War. The target was 200 families within five years.[20]

Unfortunately, as was to happen more than once in the history of what is now Belize, these hopes for an economy diversified enough to ride out market fluctuations were not to be fulfilled. By 1870 northern sugar production still remained largely, in the Lieutenant Governor's words, 'experimental' due to lack of further investment, and most of the first wave of US emigrants that had by then been attracted to the southern district had returned home because of the inhospitable surroundings there. Timber still accounted for 80 per cent of export earnings.[21] But mahogany export volume had fallen to only a fifth of its 1846 peak of 13.7 million superficial feet[22] and, although logwood volume had increased in the 1860s, both mahogany and logwood prices had fallen significantly by 1868.[23] Moreover the entrepot trade had fallen further as neighbouring states began to develop their own infrastructure and, in the case of Guatemala, to open up the Pacific coastline. It was altogether, the Lieutenant Governor reported, 'a time of much depression'.[24]

There were two reasons why development of the nascent sugar industry had stalled, and each affected both northern and southern districts. First the price of Crown land, until 1867 $5 an acre, was high for investment that unavoidably, given both production and market conditions, remained speculative. An offer that year by the Young Toledo company at the new Crown land price of $2.50 an acre did something, as already indicated, to draw about fifty US former Confederate families to settle in the far south inland from the Carib village of Punta Gorda[25] but they did not stay. The second difficulty for potential investors was a shortage of labour. Again efforts were made to to resolve the problem, in this case by importing Chinese indentured workers. But as with US emigrants, comparitively few were attracted, and of 474 that were in 1865, only just over 200 were working on the land three years later.[26]

Sugar production remained an uncertain proposition for most of the 1870s, partly because of investment conditions, and partly also because of the continuing threat of Indian raids in the north, the district that lent itself best to larger-scale cultivation. There was moreover, for the same reasons, no serious attempt to develop production of other crops. But with the pacification of the north, a resulting new source of labour, and some fresh initiatives introduced by Lieutenant Governor Frederick Barlee, who arrived in 1877, the colony entered a phase of more substantive economic development which was to last for just over fifteen years.

A boom in sugar and bananas

Three measures were particularly effective in this sense. Most importantly for the overall investment environment, the price of Crown land, the central factor, was reduced at a stroke to $1 an acre, a measure followed up in 1879 by a Bill designed to streamline the sale procedure. For sugar, the excise tax, a substantial inhibitor for entrepreneurs, was abolished. For bananas, hitherto cultivated almost entirely for domestic consumption, access was opened on favourable terms to a large export market by an administrative rather than a fiscal adjustment: the route of the colony's postal connection with Europe and the US was changed so that the ships carrying the mail, necessarily offering a regular service, touched on the way at New Orleans rather than Jamaica.[27]

The response of the market to these incentives was marked. For sugar, impetus was given by a second wave of US immigrants who had arrived in the far south in the early 1870s, following an active promotion of the district by Young Toledo in the former Confederate states and also an outbreak of political unrest in former Spanish Honduras.[28] The new arrivals had first tried, unsuccessfully, to grow cotton. When they reverted more successfully to sugar, they overcame the continuing labour shortage by importing indentured labourers from India. These, who were fed, housed, and paid by but bound to their employers, proved to be excellent field workers.[29] By 1882 sugar exports, from commercial estates in both north and south, had built up to a level of 2500 tons for the year.[30] At the same time, banana cultivation, which had developed steadily apart from a dip in the early 1880s, by 1886 occupied 6300 acres behind both Punta Gorda and Stann Creek and had come to be regarded as the basis of a staple export.[31] Expansion, supported by a five-mile tramway in the Stann Creek valley, continued into the 1890s, with nearly half a million stems exported in 1891.[32] By that time the German-run Kramer company had also generated a small export surplus in coffee.[33]

One of the features of this period in the colony's development history is a further consolidation of enterprise. In 1880 the Young Toledo company sold out, and some of its land was bought by the former British Honduras Company, now renamed the Belize Estate and Produce Company (BEC).[34] From then the BEC's domination of the colony's economic life was complete. The major shareholders were the Hoare banking family. The biggest landowner and timber producer since the 1850s, the company had already also, by 1868, become the colony's biggest sugar producer.[35] Then holding a total of nearly a million acres of land and 100 mahogany 'works',[36] BEC's influence became predominant not only locally but also, on British Honduran affairs, in London. Moreover this kind of rationalisation went further during the decade that followed, with other mergers amongst smaller firms. By 1890, there were four companies holding more than 200 square miles of land each, with headquarters in Britain rather than in British Honduras and with their business largely focused on timber. The position of the Belize Estate Company had been further strengthened and, with 1646 square miles of land, it now held nearly five times as big an area as the next biggest proprietor, Sheldon Byass.[37] If this consolidation of ownership brought benefits of scale, it reduced the likelihood of more diverse development.

Collapse of sugar and decline in bananas

It so happened that the question of further diversification very soon became more relevant than it seemed in the late 1880s and early 1890s. The economic buoyancy of that period was not to last. In the last years of the nineteenth century exports in both the new sectors plunged. The sugar industry, hit by 'bounty-fed' competition from beet growers in Europe, saw production in 1893 fall to less than a third of the figure for three years before.[38] In 1898 the American settlers in the south complained of 'a great difficulty in finding a suitable market for their sugar'.[39] By the end of the century export volume had collapsed by 90 per cent.[40] Because export market prices in Britain and the US had fallen below the cost of production and shipment, the Governor urged the Colonial Office to grant the British Honduras growers the financial assistance already offered to the British West Indian island plantations. But the view in Whitehall was that labour costs in the territory were such that it was 'absurd for British Honduras to pretend to be a sugar colony'.[41]

The banana industry, which was also now up against cheaper and larger-scale production elsewhere, became affected by lower prices to a point where in 1898 export earnings had fallen by nearly 70 per cent over the previous seven years.[42] As a result, in both 1898 and 1899 the District Magistrate for Stann Creek reported that many of the smaller growers were giving up their plantations.[43] In the early years of the new century production recovered but prices remained at about half those received ten years before. The much smaller coffee and cocoa industries, developed over the previous fifteen years and seen by government officials in both Belize and the districts as promising alternatives to sugar, never generated a reasonable return, and in due course collapsed.[44]

To make matters worse, this decline of agriculture was accompanied in the mid-1890s by a sluggish timber market first for mahogany, then, at the end of the decade, for logwood. Although diversification remained stalled, the overall depression was then partly offset by a recovery in the mahogany trade. Thanks to increased demand in the US, exports rose from 5.3 million superficial feet in 1892 to 8 million superficial feet in 1900.[45] But the turn of the century nonetheless saw a reversion to the struggling economy of the early 1870s, with British Honduras almost entirely dependent once again on an uncertain timber export trade. As a consequence of the failure of these attempts at diversification, the colony was also again stuck with an adverse reputation for new investment. It was not until 1913 that the first foundations were laid for what eventually turned out to be, arguably, British Honduras' most successful twentieth-century industry, citrus.

Proposals for infrastructure development

Both the Governors who held office during the 1890s, Sir Alfred Moloney and Sir David Wilson, were convinced that economic diversification could only be brought about if the colony's transport infrastructure were radically improved. Concerned in 1895 that, with the slump in mahogany, sugar and banana prices, the colony was left only with the volatile market for logwood, Moloney strongly promoted railway construction to open up some of the agriculturally more promising but geographically less accessible parts of the territory. He saw this as necessary for any prospect of developing such alternatives as cocoa, coffee, tea, rubber and palm oil. He believed that competitive proposals for possible routes would reveal the best economic proposition. His solution to the problem of attracting investment in the railway was government borrowing to enable it to acquire a 50 per cent stake in the loan stock of the enterprise ('analogous to that of the debenture holder'), for re-sale as it prospered.[46] The Colonial Office thought a loan for such a purpose undesirable and the purpose itself impractical.[47] But they agreed to the completion, proposed by the Legislative Council in January 1896, of an 1892 route survey, work on which resumed in the March.[48]

Nothing came, however, of Moloney's scheme for a railway built for internal purposes because of rejection in 1898 by the Treasury of any British government loan either for that or for the Belize–Peten rail link discussed in Chapter 9. Wilson for his part reverted to the desirability of railway construction for economic development when the Peten scheme was resurrected in 1899. He was persuaded that the necessary capital might be raised if the British government simply guaranteed a suitable bond issue organised by commercial investors. That proposal got no further than the Colonial Office.[49] As we have seen, further discussions on a rail connection between the two territories finally ended in 1901 when the Guatemalans lost interest in offering the necessary land concessions to go with it.

In the event infrastructure improvement in British Honduras during this period was much more limited. Only one scheme was of direct help to the development of the economy. In 1886 a contractor began to dredge the approaches to Belize harbour. Work ceased the following year owing to disagreement about extension of the time allowed. The dispute rumbled on after arbitration failed to settle it in 1888.[50] Dredging, by another contractor, resumed in late 1890. That contract was cancelled the next year because of the government's wish to have greater control of use of the spoil.[51] The project was eventually continued by the Colonial Engineer's department with its own dredger. When completed it enabled ships to load more quickly. Two other schemes, proposals for which were initiated by Moloney towards the end of his term, in due course helped stimulate economic development albeit indirectly. In 1896 he notified the Colonial Office of his support for the establishment of a bank to provide wider access to credit, and for the installation of an inland electric telegraph to ease communication with and between district centres.[52] His successor, Wilson, took both projects forward. Incorporation of the bank and completion of the telegraph were both achieved at the end of 1902.

Otherwise public works on any scale were only undertaken in the capital itself, Belize. With steady growth over the nineteenth century, it had spread more and more into swampland. As the risk to public health became more evident, the government introduced in 1854 an Act compelling property holders to fill their land; then, in 1873, amended that legislation to enable their own authorities to fill it at property-holders expense. With the failure of both measures largely because of lack of fill, little headway was made despite the appointment of a Municipal Board in 1865[53] and annual outbreaks of yellow fever in the late 1880s. This changed thanks to the opportunity to use spoil from the dredging operations in Belize habour. Even then progress was slow because of labour shortage.[54] But with this long drawn-out programme, together with the dredging of the harbour and, in 1891, agreement on the provision of electric street lighting,[55] Belize began to look like a centre of trade and administration by the end of the century. But of British government tangible support for that or for wider development in the hinterland, there is little evidence.

Notes

1. John C. Everitt, *The Growth and Development of Belize City*, Belizean Studies Vol. 14 No. 1 (1986), 7.
2. *Honduras Almanack 1828*, Belize (1828), 258–9, and O. N. Bolland, *The Formation of a Colonial Society: Belize from Conquest to Crown Colony*, Baltimore (1977), 159 and 175.
3. Bolland, 175.
4. Nigel Bolland and Assad Shoman, *Land in Belize 1765–1871*, University of the West Indies (1975), 71.
5. Bolland in *The Formation of a Colonial Society*, 177.
6. Assad Shoman, *Thirteen Chapters of a History of Belize*, Belize (1994), 94.
7. ibid.
8. Salmon/Fancourt, 30 December 1850, ABH Vol. 3, 141.
9. Carmichael/Seymour, 16 March 1859, ABH Vol. 3, 212.
10. Superintendent's address to the Assembly, 22 January 1861, ABH Vol. 3, 233.
11. Narda Dobson, *A History of Belize*, London (1973), 250.
12. Record of Public Meeting, 20 January 1852, cited in Bolland and Shoman, *Land in Belize*, 68.
13. Bolland and Shoman in *Land in Belize*, 83.
14. Seymour/Darling, August 1857, BA R55.
15. Seymour/Governor, Jamaica, 22 June 1859, ABH Vol. 3, 221.
16. Treasurer/Superintendent, 4 April 1860, ABH Vol. 3, 229.
17. Longden/Governor, Jamaica, 19 June 1868, ABH Vol. 3, 305–6.
18. Longden/Grant 19 June 1868, cited in O. N. Bolland, *Colonialism and Resistance in Belize*, Belize (1988), 104.
19. Longden/Grant 17 May 1869, cited in O. N. Bolland, *Colonialism and Resistence in Belize*, 104. Four of the ten estates were owned by the British Honduras Company.
20. Austin/Grant, 9 July 1867, CO 123 / 128.
21. Bolland in *Colonialism and Resistance in Belize*, 105–6.
22. ibid.
23. Bolland in *The Formation of a Colonial Society*, 175–6.
24. Cairns/Grant, 24 December 1870, CO 123 / 137.
25. Bolland and Shoman in *Land in Belize*, 87.
26. Longden/Governor, Jamaica, 23 October 1868, ABH Vol. 3, 310.

27. Wayne M. Cleghern, *British Honduras: Colonial Dead End, 1859–1900*, Baton Rouge (1967), 60–1.
28. Michael A. Camille, *Historical Geography of the US Confederate Settlement at Toledo, Belize, 1868–1930*, Belcast Journal of Belizean Affairs Vol. 3, Nos. 1 and 2, June 1986), 40.
29. ibid.
30. *Alamack for British Honduras 1886.*
31. *Handbook for British Honduras 1888–9.*
32. Moloney/Knutsford, 6 April 1892, CO 123/198.
33. Dobson, *A History of Belize*, 268.
34. Peter Ashdown, *The Belize Elite and its Power Base*, Belizean Studies Vol. 9, Nos. 5–6 (1981), 38.
35. Bolland in *Colonialism and Resistance in Belize*, 104.
36. Ashdown, 38.
37. Goldsworthy/Knutsford, 20 June 1890, CO 123/194.
38. British Honduras Government Blue Books for 1890 and 1893, BA (Blue Books). See also Wilson/Chamberlain, 25 February 1898, CO 123/228.
39. Wilson/Chamberlain, 25 April 1899, enc. by District Magistrate, Toledo, CO 123/22.
40. Blue Books for 1898 and 1900, BA (Blue Books). From the middle of the decade the growers had abandoned the British and US markets and were only exporting to neighbouring Central American countries.
41. CO minute attached to Wilson/Chamberlain, 25 February 1898, CO 123/228.
42. Blue Books for 1891, 1892, and 1898, BA (Blue Books).
43. Wilson/Chamberlain, 21 April 1898, CO 123/228 and Wilson/Chamberlain, 25 April 1899, CO 123/232, encs. by Distict Magistrate, Stann Creek.
44. Bolland and Shoman in *Land in Belize*, 109.
45. Blue Books for 1892 and 1900, BA (Blue Books).
46. Moloney/Ripon, 24 January 1895, CO 123/210.
47. CO minute on above.
48. Moloney/Chamberlain, 13 March 1896, CO 123/217, reporting start of survey.
49. Wilson/Chamberlain, 5 July 1899, CO 123/232 and associated CO minuting.
50. Goldsworthy/Knutsford, 3 July 1888, CO 123/189.
51. Melville/Knutsford, 4 June 1891, CO 123/196.
52. Moloney/Chamberlain, 27 February 1896, CO 123/217.
53. Everitt, 17.
54. Melville/Knutsford, 12 March 1891, enc. by Colonial Surgeon, CO 123/196.
55. Melville/Knutsford, 19 February 1891, CO 123/196.

11

The Colony at the Beginning of the Twentieth Century

If by 1900 the economic development of British Honduras had come to resemble the motion of a see-saw, constitutional development had inched forward, albeit only slightly, in the years that followed acceptance of Crown Colony government in 1871. There had been two significant changes since the abolition of the elected legislature then, one a clear net gain, the other at the time more controversial. They were to be the last until the 1930s.

In 1884, following representations that had continued since the changes of 1854, the subordination of the British Honduras government to the Governor of Jamaica was ended. On 1 October of that year Sir Roger Goldsworthy was promoted from Lieutenant Governor to Governor in his own right, reporting directly to the Secretary of State in London. Ironically Goldsworthy proved to be the least popular occupant of the post on account of the partiality and bad judgement he showed in a dispute about a dredging contract to fill swamp land in and around Belize in 1886 and 1887 and in the subsequent court case. But his elevation brought to an end a structure that had been disliked since it was imposed forty-three years before to moderate the actions of a particularly headstrong superintendent. Thereafter the only constitutional link that remained between the two colonies was judicial: appeals against Supreme Court decisions went to the Supreme Court in Jamaica, an arrangement that continued until 1911.[1]

The other major change was to the balance of authority in the Legislative Council. The model adopted in 1871 had been a council of five official members (Chief Justice, Colonial Secretary, Officer Commanding Troops, Treasurer and Attorney General) and four 'unofficial' members nominated by the Lieutenant Governor. It was not long before the local elite, used to control of the territory's public finances through an elected assembly, felt they had reason for dissatisfaction. In the 1870s they found that far from the increased prosperity they had looked forward to with Crown Colony rule, British Honduras was faced with both a weakening economy and increased taxation. Then in the 1880s, with what they saw as a continuing Indian threat on the northern border, they had to accept the prospect of withdrawal of the garrison they had thought Crown Colony rule would consolidate. Next they were faced, as taxpayers, with the cost of compensation awarded by a court in London in 1890 for the cancellation by the Council of the 1886 dredging contract. The handling of that affair by the Governor, and in particular his decision to ignore the warning of his Attorney General about the bias of the arbitrator, led to the resignation of the four unofficial members and the refusal of other residents to take their places.[2] There followed both a paralysis of government and a strong campaign for an unofficial majority on the Legislative Council. Despite initial resistance from the Colonial Office, that proposal was eventually conceded on the recommendation of the new Governor, Sir Alfred Moloney, and was duly implemented in 1892.[3] For the next twenty years the Council was composed, under the chairmanship of the Governor, of three official members (Colonial Secretary, Treasurer and Attorney General) and five unofficial members. As we shall see, even though the balance was reversed the divergence remained.

The Governor in 1900 was Sir David Wilson. Aged 62, he had come to British Honduras in 1897 from Trinidad, where he had served, first as Private Secretary to the Governor then as a District Commissioner, for over thirty years.[4] He presided over the affairs of a colony with a population that had grown to 35,226, of whom just over a third, mostly creoles, lived in Belize, and around 10,000, mostly mestizos, in the north. Smaller minorities included about 4000 Maya living in the hinterland of both north and south, and 3000 'Black Caribs' (now Garifuna) living in the southern coastal villages. Peter Ashdown, in a 1981 *Belizean Studies* article on the colony's elite in the 1890s, describes a society in which the mestizos had only a subsidiary and the other minorities a negligible role, with the creole community dominating both the mainstay of the economy (logging) at all levels and also the colony's professional and commercial life.

Preoccupied with the need to open up the territory and to diversify the economy, the Governor was assisted by an Executive Council. This consisted of his senior officials together with, as a minority, two nominated local residents sitting as 'unofficials'. But the Executive Council had to base its work on the legal and fiscal framework set by the Legislative Council with its 'unofficial' majority. Although he had certain reserve powers, the Governor was expected by the Colonial Office in London to obtain the consent of 'Legco' for any legislation he wished to introduce, for any changes to taxation, and, crucially, for his annual plans for public expenditure, or 'estimates'. An example of the constraint Wilson was under was the Council's decision in 1900 to overturn, against his strong recommendation, earlier legislation to limit the credit that companies could offer employees to one month's wages.[5]

Day-to-day administration of government was the responsibility of the Colonial Secretary, who in 1900 was F. J. Newton, soon to be promoted into the same post in Barbados.[6] Reporting to him were the heads of government departments, such as the Treasurer (who was also the Collector of Customs), the Surveyor-General, the Colonial Surgeon, the Colonial Engineer and the Auditor, each of whom was responsible for a budget within the overall spending plans set out in the approved estimates for the year. By far the largest single source of revenue funding public expenditure was customs duty. Because trade was once again depressed there was little or no surplus, and almost the whole budget was taken up with recurrent costs. In 1901 and 1902 the only significant capital spending items were the electric telegraph system connecting Belize, Orange Walk and Corozal, completed at the end of 1902, and a new wing for Belize hospital.[7]

The Colonial Secretary was also responsible for supervising the six Commissioners who administered the Districts of Belize River, Cayo, Corozal, Orange Walk, Stann Creek and Toledo. These had evolved from the unpaid Belize River, Sibun, Northern and Southern Magistracies established in the mid-nineteenth century when settled populations took root in those outlying areas.[8] The District Commissioners too had small budgets for local maintenance and improvement, funded in their case from the proceeds of liquor licences, market rents, property tax and some fines.[9] Helped to a limited extent by grants from the central government, some improvements were made. In 1900 the District Commissioner in Corozal, who had been in post for no less than 23 years,[10] was able to report that 'for the first time in its history Corozal can say there are no streets that cannot be traversed in comfort even at the height of the rainy season'.[11] That patience was needed, however, is clear from his report the following year that only if progress with the metalling of the main road south from the town were continued for three years would a point be reached where 'it may no longer be impassable for the six weeks of the rainy season'.[12]

Below the level of the District Commissioner's office, the degree of social control in the outlying villages varied with different parts of the territory. In the Maya and Carib villages in the south, leadership was institutionalised through the Alclade and his council. This elected body was responsible not only for administering a basic level of justice, but also for organising communal activity and works. In the mestizo villages of the north, a looser authority was vested in an elected 'Patron' or 'Mayor', who settled disputes and acted as a representative. In the Creole villages of the Belize River valley, the community tended to look less formally to a leading inhabitant such as the local teacher.

At the turn of the century the garrison of West Indian troops that had been stationed in the territory for so long had been gone for twelve years.

Their place had been taken in the Northern District, where the main security threat lay, by an expanded British Honduras Constabulary. In 1900 the strength of this paramilitary force had fallen back, with a reduction of the Indian menace, to 3 officers and 80 NCOs and constables, 35 of whom were mounted.[13] Law and order in the rest of the country (except for Cayo, where a small detachment of the Constabulary was posted) lay with the British Honduras Police. This mustered a Superintendent and 75 NCOs and constables. There were 56 of them stationed in Belize, and the rest at small outlying police stations in Ambergris Cay, Mullins River, Stann Creek, Monkey River and Punta Gorda.[14] Interestingly only just over a third of police strength were of the colony, with the rest coming from elsewhere in the West Indies. With Mexican determination to pacify the southern Yucatan now clear, it was decided the following year to merge the two forces, with most of the Constabulary members who wished it absorbed into an enlarged British Honduras Police of 116 all ranks.[15] This measure, completed in January 1902,[16] led to significant savings.[17] The only other security force, available for emergencies, was the Belize Light Infantry Volunteer Corps, a 180-strong 'territorial' body which met once a month for basic military instruction by a sergeant-major seconded from the British Army.[18]

Government-supported education in the Colony was still limited to primary level. Even in this field there were reductions, with budgetary difficulties leading to 15 per cent cuts in grants over two successive years.[19] As a result the number of such schools fell from 49 in 1897 to 36 in 1901, with an enrolment in the latter year of 3423 children[20] and an average attendance of about two thirds of that figure. Included in the closures was the only school in Cayo.[21] Roman Catholic schools took nearly half of those enrolled, with most of the rest in Church of England or Baptist schools in equal proportions.[22] Difficulties faced by these primary schools and the church authorities that sponsored them included recruitment and retention of adequate teachers, roads that were often impassable for the scattered populations they served, and the multiplicity of languages spoken by pupils at home. Secondary education was only available to about 300 pupils attending privately endowed institutions.[23]

Public health was the responsibility of the Colonial Surgeon, who submitted a detailed report to the Governor each year. In 1899, with yellow fever outbreaks seemingly a thing of the past, there had been no 'rapidly fatal epidemic disease', and his main concern was whooping cough.[24] The following year, a bubonic plague scare having come to nothing, his attention shifted to the first recorded cases of diptheria.[25] The Colonial Surgeon was also responsible for the administration of the main hospital at Belize, the smaller district hospitals at Orange Walk and Corozal, the Poor

House, and, in 1901, almost as busy as the main hospital, the lunatic asylum.[26] Significantly he noted then that activity at Corozal hospital had declined owing to closure of many of the sugar estates in that district and emigration of the workers.

This downturn in the economy was the focus of attention of all the members of the Legislative Council. Inevitably the 'officials' and the 'unofficials' had very different views on what the government should do to meet it. The disagreement had started in 1898, when out-turn figures showed a deficit in public finances for the previous year. To cover it the Governor then persuaded the unofficial majority to accept a temporary export duty on shipments of mahogany and logwood. The following year saw a surplus, but in 1899, with the timber export duty still in force, the deficit returned.[27] When that prospect became clear towards the end of that year, feelings ran high. The unofficial members of the Legislative Council drew up a petition to the Secretary of State demanding an enquiry into 'the financial condition' of the colony. Their main specific complaint was that at this time of considerable economic difficulty, and with spending on public works falling, public expenditure on 'personal emoluments' was rising. This in their view was wrong and also unnecessary, because 'the Civil Establishment of the Colony is in the opinion of your petitioners in excess of its means and requirements'.[28] Their views were supported by a letter from London-based business interests led by the Belize Estates Company.

A fending-off of the enquiry proposal by the Secretary of State, on the grounds that it would not add to existing knowledge, returned the initiative to the Governor. He had a number of ideas for putting the government's revenue on a more stable basis, including a strengthening of land tax and the introduction of stamp duty. But having himself ruled out increasing excise duty because of difficulties already faced by the distilleries, all that he could get through the Council was a temporary increase in import duty. This he saw as counter-productive in the sense that it would unsettle both trade and development.[29]

Wilson's frustration now began to show in the way that Superintendents' feelings had surfaced seventy or eighty years before: he protested at his position of responsibility without power. In a strong letter to the Secretary of State he urged the abolition of the 'unofficial' majority on the Legislative Council, arguing that it was 'wrong in principle and in practice that in a Crown Colony the control of affairs should rest in the hands of a totally irresponsible unofficial majority'. He proposed to end it by appointing two more 'officials' to the Council, the Surveyor-General and the Colonial Auditor. The practical point he was referring to was the problem for British Honduras that to be eligible for a development loan under the Colonial

Loans Act the government of a territory had to have control of its public finances. Once again the argument was also made that it was in any case very difficult to nominate as 'unofficials' men of 'sufficient intelligence and education outside of the very small number of principal merchants, land-holders, and store keepers', with, implicitly, their vested interest in opposing some of the measures needed to open up the country.[30] The Governor's representations, as so often in the past, did not bear fruit.

It was his perception of the need for diversified development that drove most of what the Governor said and did about the colony's future in those first years of the new century. Central to his thinking in 1900 was the Belize–Peten railway project. While on leave in England that autumn he attended a conference promoting it. The next year he was still arguing that it was 'of vital importance to the future welfare – perhaps even to the existence – of this colony'.[31] He could see that in whatever way it was financed, some of the cost would fall on the colony. But he was convinced that this cost would be amply repaid by the prosperity that would flow from the railway, and that the increased taxation called for meanwhile would be a burden well worth bearing.[32] It was for this reason that he appointed a Commission of Enquiry 'into the existing mode and rate of taxation of land', to see how land tax might be 'remodelled' with a view to making it at the same time more equitable and more productive.[33]

Meanwhile a draft contract for the railway scheme drawn up by the Crown Agents continued to attract some serious, and some less serious, interest in both 1900 and 1901. But the sticking point remained, despite efforts by some interests to remove it,[34] that any contractor must have secured the necessary land concessions on the Guatemalan side of the border; as we have already noted, the Guatemalans had by this time lost interest. A combination of this difficulty, continuing Treasury opposition, and the suspect motives and also strength of the most recent approaches received caused Wilson to change direction in 1902. By July of that year he had come to the conclusion publicly that the railway scheme was impracticable.[35] In October he told the Secretary of State that he was glad to hear that the Crown Agents had withdrawn it from public competition, and that he was hoping to appoint an expert to explore development on 'other lines'. His new vision was of outside investment for smaller projects centred on swamp drainage, coastal pier improvement and the construction of local light railways like the one soon to be working at Stann Creek. He saw these schemes as precursors for the development of promising land in some of the river valleys in the south of the territory.[36]

The impetus for this energetic floating of ideas was the reversion of the economy once again to a timber near-monoculture. But the timber industry only employed about 3000 men.[37] In the north a mere 452 acres of land was planted with cane, and both there and in the southern district of Toledo sugar was only produced on a scale to meet local consumption.[38] Earnings from banana exports to the United States had been hit over the previous three years by competing low-cost production from Honduras and Guatemala, which was carried on the same United Fruit Company steamer service. As a result many smaller growers were giving up throughout the south, production had stopped altogether in the Mullins River area, and in Stann Creek the only significant export trade was in the hands of the British Honduras Syndicate's Melinda Estate.[39] Attempts were being made to interest the British shipping company Elders and Fyffes in the export of bananas to Britain, but prospects were very uncertain.[40] Meanwhile the colony's only substantial coffee estate, on the Sarstoon River, was, partly because of a labour shortage, still not paying.

Mahogany exports had begun to pick up in 1897 with the increase already referred to in demand in the United States, although the decline in the less important logwood shipments continued.[41] It was because of the comparative profitability then enjoyed by the timber producers that the Governor was able to introduce the export duty that brought the public finances almost back into balance. It was the same consideration that decided him to take steps to 'remodel' the land-tax so that the big land-owners paid a fairer share. But before his Commission of Enquiry could report, this brief mahogany boom had subsided. Production costs increased significantly as the woodcutters ventured into ever more remote areas in order to maintain supply; and at the same time, for external reasons, shipping costs also went up.[42] At the end of 1901, under pressure from the timber companies, the Legislative council halved export duty.[43] But the following year, with prices, though not volume, falling, a number of producers were still complaining that they were losing money on their shipments, and three companies had suspended production.[44] The Governor soon afterwards reported a 'severe depression' in timber as well as bananas.[45] His willingness up to that point to entertain almost any reasonably serious proposals for the Belize–Peten railway project, which would have both stimulated development and restored an entrepot trade, was thus understandable, as was his enthusiasm for 'other lines' of development when the railway scheme finally died.

Meanwhile the pattern of British Honduras' external trade remained unchanged. The two main trading partners were Britain and the United States. More exports went to Britain, but the major source of imports was the United States.[46] Most of the British trade was carried in sailing ships, most of the American trade in steamships. The other flag that appeared in Belize harbour most regularly was Norwegian.[47] The only regular passenger service was that run from New Orleans by the United Fruit Company, which called at Belize *en route* to Puerto Barrios in Guatemala and which also carried the colony's mail and bought its banana exports. That was put at risk in 1902 when the Legislative Council sought to reduce the government subsidy paid for the mail service.[48]

From this wider world, foreign government representation in the colony in 1900 consisted of consuls from the United States, Mexico, and, for no obvious reason, the Austro–Hungarian Empire. Apart from the steamer service to Puerto Barrios, the only significant more local connection seems to have been with the Yucatan, where local traders had switched from supplying the Santa Cruz Indians to supplying the Mexican army. In August 1900 the Governor, who had met the Mexican commander more than once, was unable to say when the long-delayed expedition to pacify the southern part of the region might set out, and could only refer to 'protracted preparation'.[49] The launch was eventually reported to him in March 1901 by the Mexican Consul in Belize, who also announced travel restrictions in the area and requested that Indians living in Corozal be kept under firm control.[50] The following month Wilson reported that Bacalar had been occupied without fighting and that the complementary expedition from the north was approaching the Santa Cruz headquarters.[51] By October there had still been no major actions, and he was optimistic that continuing operations would gradually reduce the Santa Cruz to 'submission' without serious loss on either side.[52] By August 1902 the District Commissioner in Corozal was able to report that trade across the border was slowly developing 'as the territory becomes settled'.[53]

Because it was taking place so close to British Honduras, the Mexican expedition in the Yucatan was the main object of local press interest outside the colony's borders. There was also excitement about the Panama Canal project and considerable coverage of the Boer War. Domestically press attention was focused on the government's inability to undertake more public works schemes and the failure of economic development initiatives. In the context of shortage of funds the *Clarion* newspaper criticised the award of a higher salary to the Chief Justice, arguing that restraint should start at the top.[54] As to development, there was considerable criticism of the Crown Agents for 'sloth', together with the suspicion that they were influenced by 'monopolists' who wished to see off the tax increases that infrastructure improvement would entail.[55] Unfavourable comparisons were also drawn in the press with the level of subvention offered by the French and German governments to their colonies.

At a more parochial level there was discussion of the case for a new district administration for the Monkey River area. Specific items of good news reported in 1900 and 1901 included the launch of the biggest-ever ship built locally, a 110-ton schooner,[56] and the success of a new training scheme for female nurses.[57] Bad news included an increased incidence of stabbing affrays in the northern districts[58] and the health hazard caused by the Belize rubbish dump.[59] But with legislation generally limited to amendment of existing laws, an absence of epidemics and hurricanes, and broadly settled relations with neighbouring states, the *Clarion*'s overall conclusion for the turn of the century was that it brought 'no great calamity and no ... great benefit'. A reasonable enough assessment for the year, even if the prevailing economic stagnation and the continuing consumption of finite resources raised more serious questions against a longer perspective.

Notes

1. Narda Dobson, *A History of Belize*, London (1973), 300.
2. Peter Ashdown, 'Sir Frederick Mackenzie Maxwell', *Belizean Studies*, Vol. 7 No. 3, (May 1979), 2.
3. Moloney/Knutsford, 15 March 1892, CO 123/198; and Peter Ashdown, 'The Colonial Administrators of Belize: Sir Alfred Moloney', *Belizean Studies*, Vol. 14 No. 2, (1986), 2.
4. Wilson/Chamberlain, 23 April 1902, CO 123/240.
5. Wilson/Chamberlain, 28 November 1900, CO 123/236.
6. Wilson/Chamberlain, 3 October 1901, CO 123/239.
7. Wilson/Chamberlain, 24 December 1901 and 3 October 1901, CO 123/239.
8. Nigel Bolland, *The Formation of a Colonial Society: Belize from Conquest to Crown Colony*, Baltimore and London (1977), 190.
9. Enc. to Wilson/Chamberlain, 7 August 1902, CO 123/241.
10. Wilson/Chamberlain, 13 November 1900, CO 123/236.
11. Enc to Wilson/Chamberlain, 2 August 1900, CO 123/236.
12. Enc to Wilson/Chamberlain, 15 August 1901, CO 123/239.
13. Enc to Wilson/Chamberlain 27 September 1900, CO 123/236.
14. Enc to Wilson/Chamberlain, 28 May 1901, CO 123/238.
15. Wilson/Chamberlain, 2 January 1902, CO 123/240. A further reason for the merger was that the Constabulary had never been popular, and in 1894 had mutinied when constables' pay, like other workers' wages, was in effect devalued in a change of local currency – see Peter Ashdown, 'The Labourers' Riot of 1894', *Belizean Studies*, Vol. 7 No. 6, (November 1979).
16. Wilson/Chamberlain, 21 November 1901, CO 123/239.
17. Wilson/Chamberlain, 28 March 1901, CO 123/238 and 27 March 1902, CO 123/240.
18. Wilson/Chamberlain, 25 July 1901, CO 123/239.
19. Enc. to Wilson/Chamberlain, 27 September 1900 op. cit. and enc. to Wilson/ Chamberlain, 3 October 1901 op. cit.
20. ibid.
21. Enc. to Wilson/Chamberlain, 15 August 1901, CO 123/239.
22. Enc. to Wilson/Chamberlain, 27 September 1900 op. cit. and enc. to Wilson/ Chamberlain, 3 October 1901, op. cit.
23. ibid.
24. Enc. to Wilson/Chamberlain, 5 July 1900, CO 123/236.
25. Enc. to Wilson/Chamberlain, 13 June 1901, CO 123/238.
26. ibid.

27. Enc. to Wilson/Chamberlain, 3 October 1901 op. cit.
28. Enc. to Wilson/Chamberlain, 23 May 1900, CO 123/235.
29. Wilson/Chamberlain, 27 June 1900, CO 123/235.
30. Wilson/Chamberlain, 11 July 1900, CO 123/236.
31. Wilson/Chamberlain, 25 July 1901, CO 123/239.
32. See for example speech to Legco dated 22 May 1900 enclosed with Wilson/Chamberlain, 23 May 1900, CO 123/235.
33. Wilson/Chamberlain, 25 June 1901, CO 123/238.
34. Wilson/Chamberlain, 3 September 1901, CO 123/239.
35. Enc. to Wilson/Chamberlain, 29 July 1902, CO 123/240.
36. Wilson/Chamberlain, 16 October 1902, CO 123/241.
37. Ashdown in *The Belizean Elite and its Power Base*, 34.
38. Enc. to Wilson/Chamberlain, 2 August 1900, op. cit., enc. to Wilson/Chamberlain, 3 October 1901 op. cit., and enc. to Wilson/Chamberlain, 7 August 1902, CO 123/241.
39. Wilson/Chamberlain, 27 May 1901, CO 123/238.
40. Wilson/Chamberlain, 11 September 1902, CO123/241.
41. Enc. to Wilson/Chamberlain, 27 September 1900 op. cit.; enc. to Wilson/Chamberlain, 3 October 1901 op. cit.; and enc. to Wilson/Chamberlain, 29 July 1902, CO 123/240.
42. Wilson/Chamberlain, 29 July 1902 op. cit.
43. Wilson/Chamberlain, 5 December 1901, CO 123/239.
44. Wilson/Chamberlain, 29 July 1902 op. cit.
45. Wilson/Chamberlain, 11 September 1902 op. cit.
46. Enc to Wilson/Chamberlain, 27 September 1900 op. cit.
47. Enc to Wilson/Chamberlain, 3 October 1901 op. cit.
48. Wilson/Chamberlain, 13 and 27 February 1902, CO 123/240.
49. Enc. to Wilson/Chamberlain, 2 August 1900 op. cit.
50. Enc. to Wilson/Chamberlain, 27 March 1901, CO123/238.
51. Wilson/Chamberlain, 13 April 1901, CO 123/238.
52. Enc. to Wilson/Chamberlain, 3 October 1901 op. cit.
53. Enc. to Wilson/Chamberlain, 7 August 1902 op. cit.
54. Clarion newspaper, January 1900, BA.
55. Clarion, February 1900, BA.
56. ibid.
57. Clarion, February 1901, BA.
58. Clarion, February 1900, BA.
59. Clarion, February 1901, BA.

12

Wars, a Hurricane and a Global Slump: The First Half of the Twentieth Century

The forty-five years after 1900, when British Honduras entered the twentieth century 'with no great calamity and no great benefit', were more eventful than the corresponding period beforehand. The re-enhancement of local political representation that had started in 1892 took only one significant further step forward and the colony's economic fortunes continued to fluctuate as they had throughout the nineteenth century. But British Honduras was also affected in this next phase of its life by external and local upheavals, in both cases on an unprecedented scale. Ironically the former, the two world wars, whilst cataclysmic in their impact on Europe, were comparatively mild disruptions in British Honduras; whereas the latter, the hurricane of 1931, was the greatest natural catastrophe the territory had known since the arrival of the white man three hundred years before. This disaster came, moreover, just after the beginning of the worst economic slump of modern times.

1905–18

By the outbreak of the first world war in 1914, the industry around which the colony's economy revolved had enjoyed some years of relative prosperity, with mahogany export prices firmer, and volume topping 10 million superficial feet, from 1907.[1] With exports at around half-a-million stems per annum, and now supported by a railway from the top of Stann Creek valley to a pier at Commerce Bight,[2] banana earnings were once again close to those of the mid-1890s. To these economic gains had been added a significant new industry, chicle, the resin extracted from the sapodilla tree that was used in the manufacture of chewing gum. This general upturn, from which only sugar was excluded, had enabled the Governor in 1911 to negotiate a capital works loan and thus at last to take forward a limited programme of infrastructure development. It had also encouraged the Royal Bank of Canada, with its solid asset base and wide branch network, to take over the fledgling Bank of British Honduras.

127

The outbreak of war in August 1914 inevitably disturbed this prospect of modest economic prosperity and stability. Within a month the Governor was reporting that it 'seemed to close down the (mahogany) export to England' and that because of that, and also because of falling prices in and rising shipping costs to the other main market, the US, some of the timber companies were laying off substantial numbers of workers.[3] There was also at the same time an 'unaccountable' reduction in US demand for bananas and a fall in the export market price for coconuts.[4] All this led for the first time for many years to a significant labour surplus, which the government mopped up, albeit at the lowest possible wage cost, by resort to corn 'plantations' on unused land leased from private owners.[5]

But on first receipt of the news of war, the colonial government's main priority was the security of the territory. In response to Colonial Office instructions to round up any German reservists, the Governor reported that there were no more than five residents in that category, four of whom lived in remote locations and were eventually paroled rather than detained. The only other Germans were two or three 'elderly drunken naturalised citizens of the US' who lived in Belize.[6] The second immediate conclusion the Governor came to was that neither the population of Belize town nor the stocks of materials held there could for practical purposes be moved into the interior away from the threat of seaborne invasion.[7]

As to more active steps to resist an enemy assault, the Volunteers, now renamed the Territorial Force and under the command of the Attorney General, started a programme of daily training. This lasted for three months, after which training musters were scaled back to three times a week. By then the force had built up to a strength of nearly 400.[8] Also by then the government had completed the installation of a wireless transmitting station to complement the receiving station opened at the outbreak of war.[9] This was badly needed because of constant disruption of the telegraph service to New Orleans via Mexico. The range of the wireless sets was short, but communication with Jamaica was possible via Swan Island, half-way between the coast of northern Honduras and the Cayman Islands.

The main threat during the early days was attack by any one of three German commerce-raiding cruisers that were at large in the Caribbean. When in early 1915 only one remained unaccounted for, the scale of the coastwatching system that had been instituted was reduced.[10] No new immediate threat emerged for over a year. Then in June 1916 news arrived of the takeover of a part of the Peten district of Guatemala by a large gang of Mexican adventurers, who proceeded to seize consignments of chicle belonging to British Honduras interests. There was concern that they

14 Harvesting bananas
(Belize Archives Department)

15 Harvesting chicle
(Belize Archives Department)

16 A Maya woman
(Belize Archives Department)

17 The Stann Creek Railway
(Belize Archives Department)

18 The Court House
(Belize Archives Department)

19 The market
(Belize Archives Department)

20 The hospital
(Belize Archives Department)

21 North Front Street
(Belize Archives Department)

22 The harbour entrance
(Belize Archives Department)

23 The Parade Ground
(Belize Archives Department)

24 The aftermath of the 1931 hurricane
(Belize Archives Department)

25 San Pedro town on Ambergris Cay
(Belize Archives Department)

26 Independence Plaza, Belmopan
(Belize Archives Department)

27 The Princess Hotel, Belize City
(Belize Archives Department)

28 Lobster smacks at the entrance to Haulover Creek, Belize City
(Belize Archives Department)

29 The lighthouse at Fort George, Belize City
(Belize Archives Department)

might have plans to carry the revolution they proclaimed into British Honduras. For some time the Guatemalan army remained inert, and indeed the only action they undertook was to ambush a British Honduras police patrol that had strayed across the border, killing the corporal in charge. In the event, and possibly because of the dispatch to the Cayo district of a strong detachment of the Territorial Force, there was no violation of the border by the 'revolutionists', and indeed after the end of the chicle season in the autumn they returned to Mexico.[11]

The next alarm came another year later, when, in May 1917, a British Army colonel visiting the Territorial Force from Jamaica reported the possibility of a direct attack by a band raised and led by German settlers and agents resident in the Yucatan. The acting Governor, whilst acknowledging the Mexican government's lack of effective control of the region, believed that there was unlikely to be support for such an enterprise from Mexico City, and did not agree that the colonel's recommendation for the dispatch of 250 regular troops from Jamaica was justified. This was partly because he thought any Mexican 'freebooting' party was unlikely to attract the sympathy of the Indians, partly because of what he saw as the 'salutary effect' of US naval patrols in the Gulf of Mexico, but above all because he believed that the renamed Volunteers, now 800 strong and with 150 men at Corozal, were a more effective force than the colonel allowed.[12]

As to a more direct contribution to Britain's war effort, the Governor declined a request for men for a labour battalion for railway construction in France, partly on grounds of the climate there.[13] But remarkably for a colonial territory with a population of only 40,000, British Honduras, besides raising a Territorial Force of 800 for home defence, had already also raised two contingents of men, all volunteers, for active service with the British West Indies Regiment in the Middle East. The first of these, mustering 128 men under the command of the Registrar General, had left the colony in November 1915; the second, with 410 officers and men, in August 1916.[14] Both served with distinction in the ill-starred Mesopotamian campaign.

British Honduras was able to sustain most of the cost of the Territorial Force and some of the cost of the British West Indies Regiment contingents because the economy, after the initial downturn, became stronger as the war progressed. This was brought about first by the firming of timber prices in the American market as the US began to move towards entry into the war[15] and then, from 1916, by the negotiation of a contract to supply large volumes of mahogany to the British Admiralty mainly for aircraft propellers for the rapidly expanding Royal Naval Air Service.[16]

1919–31

Inevitably things changed when the war came to an end in late 1918. The lucrative Admiralty mahogany contract, which had led to buoyant wage levels, was swiftly terminated.[17] In the middle of the following year men who had served overseas came home to a much slacker labour market, supply shortages and price inflation. This and resentment at the treatment they had received while in uniform caused serious rioting and looting in Belize in July 1919.[18] This hastened a government decision to institute a system of land grants for ex-servicemen.[19] But despite this and the programme of public works funded by a second substantial development loan raised in 1921,[20] the difficulties the colony faced were fundamental. Sugar production around Corozal and in Toledo, at 1500 tons a year in the early 1920s, remained insufficient even to meet local demand,[21] and soon ceased altogether in Toledo.[22] The banana industry at Stann Creek was 'practically ruined' by Panama Disease.[23] Exports from there and Toledo had declined to 332,000 bunches by 1923 and the decline was continuing rapidly[24] Of longer-term concern, timber resources were much depleted as a result of war-time extraction. This had already prompted the Governor to ask for a visit by an expert as soon as the war ended to make recommendations on the establishment of an Agriculture Department.[25] That step, finally achieved in 1928, was intended to reinforce the somewhat random attempts at economic diversification of the late nineteenth and early twentieth centuries.

A slightly earlier request, linked more directly to timber sustainability worries,[26] led to the formation of a Forestry Department in 1922. The Governor claimed as early as the following year that the territory's timber resources were already being brought under 'proper forest management with a view to exploiting these forests more systematically and profitably'.[27] It was nonetheless another eleven years before the new department was able to publish the colony's first comprehensive forestry management policy.[28] Meanwhile the introduction of powered machinery to reach less accessible timber, and then to extract it more efficiently, helped maintain mahogany exports at the wartime annual average of nearly 10 million superficial feet in the first half of the 1920s and increase them to about 17 million in the second half.[29] Notwithstanding the Governor's assurances, this raised even more questions about sustainability while doing little for employment; and it was probably those concerns which led at that time to initial steps to exploit the colony's pine resources.[30] But all this, together with the beginnings of a citrus export trade in 1925 plus the export tax revenues from a substantial boot-legging industry during US prohibition,[31] enabled the administration of British Honduras to remain financially self-sufficient until the onset of the world-wide slump that followed the Wall Street crash of 1929.[32]

That depression was quick to make itself felt. Exports in all sectors plummeted, and by June 1931 the government had to resort to relief work for the unemployed.[33] The effects of the slump were then shatteringly compounded for the colony by the devastating hurricane of 10 September 1931. Ironically that struck during the annual celebrations commemorating the Battle of St George's Cay of 1798. The next day the Colonial Office in London received a laconic telegram from the Governor, Sir John Burdon: 'Much regret very severe hurricane struck colony 2 p.m. September 10. Seventy per cent of Belize destroyed and damage estimated over $1 million'.[34] The wind had reached over 100 mph, and even worse damage had been done by a tidal surge that flooded the town to a depth in places of 15ft.[35] The first outside help to arrive was from two US warships, followed on 16 September by the British cruiser HMS *Danae* with relief supplies from Jamaica.

Initial steps to bring the situation under control were reasonably effective. On 18 September the Governor was able to report that the dead had been disposed of, either by burial or by burning inside the wreckage where they lay; that with the canals and drains cleared there was no immediate fear of an epidemic; and that food stocks were ample.[36] By 24 September, with some power and telephone links restored, the scale of the disaster was more quantifiable. The Governor having left due to illness, his acting replacement, the Colonial Secretary, reported that three-quarters of Belize's 4000 houses, 14 of its schools, and 5 of its 7 churches would need to be rebuilt. He also put the figure for deaths, later reduced to 693, at just over 1000.[37] It was not therefore surprising that on 30 September, as the size of the reconstruction task sank in, he should report in a telegram that 'dull despair has settled on population appalled at magnitude of disaster'.[38]

Some financial and material assistance was arranged very quickly: £5000 from the British government, £3000 from public and voluntary funds in Jamaica, and a substantial gift of roofing material from Canada.[39] But although the acting Governor was able to close the last soup kitchen on 7 November, and on 3 December to report surprising progress with the rebuilding of private housing, a more systematic reconstruction of the town, including refilling of former swamp land, clearly called for much larger-scale external funding. This was under consideration by the British Treasury as early as 1 October.[40] One issue, which the Treasury ruled against, was compensation for houses burnt by the authorities because of the need to dispose rapidly of corpses underneath them. Negotiations with the Colonial Office on a government guarantee of a $1 million loan continued into the new year. The last condition to be agreed was Treasury insistence that steps be taken to give them 'effective control of the colony's finances'.[41] This meant that the colony's annual budget had to be submitted to the Treasury for approval before being presented to the Legislative Council. The acting Governor, acknowledging agreement on the loan and associated guarantee on 12 January 1932, then proposed first drawing down a more favourable $500,000 overdraft facility with the Royal Bank of Canada, arranged mainly but not only for the repair of public buildings. In his list of overall needs, the main items were $430,000 for lending for rebuilding of private housing, $225,000 for public works and $200,000 for agricultural resettlement.[42]

1932–38

This last scheme, because of the general dislocation now much more urgent, had been under consideration for some time, and indeed had been the first aspiration of the new Agriculture Department. The first application for development aid made by British Honduras under the Colonial Development Act of 1929 had been for a grant for the building of a road from Belize to Cayo, the western district, to enable the opening up of that area for such settlement.[43] That bid had been turned down. But after the 1931 hurricane the Colony was more successful. By October 1935 the Colonial Development and Welfare Fund was supporting eleven infrastructure and development projects, including the paving of the roads between Belize and Orange Walk and Orange Walk and Corozal, drainage and reclamation in Belize, installation of a grain drying kiln in the Northern District, and a pilot project for a sponge fishery in the Turneffe Islands.[44] By the end of 1936 the sum allocated to the territory by the Fund was £184,330.[45]

Despite this injection of resources, and despite in particular an expansion of the all-weather road system from 27 to 250 miles between 1934 and 1940,[46] the performance of the economy remained weak. In 1932 export volume was a quarter of the 1930 level and mahogany cutting was at a standstill.[47] The depression had defeated an attempt to establish an industry in the south to extract oil from cohune nuts.[48] Chicle entered a decline as the American purchasing companies, having combined under the leadership of Wrigleys, drove prices down throughout Central America to a level 'where legitimate collection hardly pays'.[49] The agricultural settlements, designed to produce staple food crops, languished despite the establishment of supporting district agricultural centres in 1933. This was due partly to inadequate transport and marketing facilities and partly to lack of the basic services needed for the settlers' families to accompany them.[50]

Citrus exports continued on a modest scale. A visiting official in 1932 identified the lack of a centralised grading, packing and marketing system as an obstacle to substantial further growth.[51] There was a first step towards meeting that recommendation the following year with the opening of a packing plant at Stann Creek, and further progress in 1935 when a factory to can fruit slices was established nearby.[52] Meanwhile acreage under citrus cultivation expanded gradually over the decade from 400 to 800 acres. Export volume consequently continued to increase slowly during the 1930s, but it was not until 1945, with the completion of a larger-scale canning plant started in 1939, that the industry was able to reap the benefit of more substantial local processing.[53] Meanwhile the fortunes of the banana industry fluctuated but failed to settle in a favourable direction. The Stann Creek area remained blighted by Panama Disease and a further infection, sygatoca. In 1932 the Governor considered that 'the Colony appears to be generally unsuitable for the large-scale cultivation of bananas'.[54] Two years later he reported that recently 'quite a promising export trade has developed in Toledo District'.[55] Exports then briefly exceeded the generally agreed threshold for an established trade of half a million stems. But by 1937 Toledo had also succumbed to disease, and the Agriculture Department was looking, as it turned out in vain, to new planting in Cayo District.[56]

As an export crop, sugar was in this period an equally disappointing proposition, although in this case for management and world market rather than investment or natural reasons. Local consumption in the early 1930s was about 1500 tons per annum, of which about half was imported and the other half processed near Corozal in a small, inefficient, and very out-of-date mill.[57] A group of promoters, having been told that a new 1500-ton mill would not be viable, put forward a plan in 1934 for a plant in which production would build up to 2000 tons over four years (a planning figure subsequently increased to 2500 tons), thus eventually producing an export surplus.[58] The Treasury, who were consulted because a third of the necessary capital was to be from British government debentures, dragged their feet partly because they were very reluctant to see world sugar exports increased with the market already well supplied. The project was finally agreed in 1936, and an annual export quota of 1000 tons granted under the International Sugar Agreement the following year, when the factory opened.[59] Although it was soon able to meet a good part of local demand, production build-up then fell behind schedule for local reasons, and the beginnings of an export trade were only achieved sixteen years later.[60]

Thus from an overall economic perspective, with only a slow recovery in mahogany exports between 1935 and 1938.[61] and the new twin burden of reconstruction and debt service, there was no prospect of the colony's government regaining financial self-sufficiency. The need for British government grants-in-aid to balance the budget remained despite a substantial programme of retrenchment in the apparatus of government agreed in 1934.[62] As a result, Treasury control of British Honduras's public finances continued for a further eighteen years.[63]

To give effect to this locally the Governor's reserve powers had to be extended. Although this was much resented in British Honduras at the time, it had in a sense one constructive result. It made it easier for the Colonial Office to agree in 1935 to the reinstitution in the legislature of elected members. This had been a bone of contention since the abolition of the old elected Legislative Assembly in 1871, and one that had been resurrected actively in 1921 in the wake of the post-war riots. Twelve years later the balance of power and the nature of representation in the nominated Legislative Council remained as it had been since 1892, when an 'unofficial' majority, albeit still nominated, had been agreed. The only change of detail had been that made in 1912, when, in order to balance an increase in the number of 'officials' from three to five, the number of 'unofficials', still all nominated, had been augmented to seven. Under the further, and much more significant, change of 1935, five of these seven 'unofficials' were to be elected.[64] The new council met for the first time on 12 March 1936.

1939–45

Such were the economic and political circumstances of British Honduras when the second world war broke out in September 1939. The resumption of war had been foreshadowed early that year with the arrival of small groups of Jewish refugees fleeing persecution in Nazi Germany. This led to concern in the colonial government because of doubts about the refugees' ability to make a living in the local environment. The Governor reported in mid-January 1939 that 30 had landed in the previous few days alone.[65] Ten days later he reported that he had refused permission for a larger group of 83 to enter the colony.[66] The following month he proposed both a substantial increase in the financial deposit required of new arrivals and powers to prohibit immigration in certain cases altogether.[67] Although efforts on their behalf came to nothing, the refugees were not without their supporters. In March and April there were at least three letters in the London *Times* suggesting that the southwestern highlands of British Honduras might be opened up by a community of 40,000 Jewish pioneers on the lines of what had been done in Palestine.

But as in 1914 the priorities for the colonial government when war broke out six months later were the defence and economic stability of the territory. Because the German presence in the Caribbean was smaller, Mexican control of the Yucatan greater, and communications better, security was the simpler matter. As before, the local militia, now called the British Honduras Defence Force, was increased in strength (from 105 to 207 officers and men), and the movements of 'enemy aliens' were restricted.[68] A new threat to stability was perceived in 1940 with the formation of an anti-British radical black nationalist movement, the leaders of which were detained for five months in the autumn and winter of 1941–2.[69] The only other significant security measure came half-way through the war, when the Governor sought and obtained Colonial Office agreement to legislation banning strikes in very broadly defined essential services. Covering all the important areas of economic activity in both the public and private sectors, these included public transport, utilities, rubbish collection, communications, services to ships, mahogany extraction, saw-milling and sugar manufacture.[70]

For the economy, British Honduras was fortunate in 1939 that the Colonial Development and Welfare Fund capital works programme started after the 1931 hurricane had, with the exception of the dredging of the Belize River, been completed.[71] Nor, with the experience of the first world war, was there so much concern for the war-time market for the colony's main export commodity, which, unlike fruit exports, held up reasonably well at 5–800,000 cubic (as distinct from the earlier measure of 'superficial') feet of mahogany.[72] There were worries that shortage of shipping might interrupt the supply of imported foodstuffs; and for that reason efforts were made to increase local food self-sufficiency by means of land grants for small-holders coupled with a system of demonstration farms set up by the Agriculture Department.[73] But the greater anxiety was the possibility of reduction or even termination of the direct fiscal support from the British Treasury that British Honduras had come to depend on in the 1930s. Even after the introduction of a war-time surtax on the incomes of higher earners and of an increase in import duty on wines, spirits, tobacco, and 'other luxuries', the acting Governor believed that without Treasury support proper public administration might become an impossibility.[74] In the event, the British government agreed to continue their subventions, although on condition that the colonial government would impose 'taxation on a scale comparable (after taking account of local conditions) with that which has had to be imposed in this country'.[75]

The anti-strike legislation of 1943 was prompted by a labour market that had tightened very considerably as the war progressed. This was the result of both a further public works programme funded by the Colonial

Development and Welfare Fund (the new Belize–Cayo highway and new airfield runways) and a direct British Honduras contribution to the war effort in three main forms: the dispatch to Scotland of a 900-strong Forestry Unit in two contingents in late 1941 and late 1942;[76] the movement during the next two years of over 1000 labourers to work in the rapidly expanding United States base in the Panama Canal Zone; and finally, in 1944, the recruitment by the US Government of 1200 workers returning from Scotland and Panama for forestry work in the southern states in place of Americans drafted into the armed forces.[77]

As the prospect of victory came in sight, the Colonial Office began to consider how to avoid a repetition of the trouble encountered when British Honduran soldiers and war workers came home in 1919. Concern was reinforced by at least one question in Parliament in London.[78] As early as August 1944, therefore, the Governor was instructed to forward plans to reabsorb up to 2000 such people possibly returning in as little as six months time.[79] The reply envisaged 100 jobs in mahogany, 125 in agriculture, 925 in public works and 850 in forestry regeneration.[80] But employment creation on that scale called for the importation of not only machinery and plant, but also supervisory expertise that was simply not available in wartime conditions.[81] Much of the programme had therefore to wait until the end of the war. There is no doubt, however, that the programme of more substantial economic development gradually consolidated after the peace, badly delayed though it was, had its roots in, and was impelled by, the employment considerations identified in 1944.

Notes

1. Blue Books for 1907–11, BA (Blue Books) and table in C. H. Grant, *The Making of Modern Belize*, Cambridge (1976), 39.
2. Departments of Archaeology, Archives, and Museums, *Moments in the History of Belize*, Belize (1990), 22. The railway was completed in 1908.
3. Collett/Harcourt, 27 August 1914, CO 123/279.
4. Collett/Harcourt, 3 September 1914, CO 123/279.
5. ibid.
6. Collett/Harcourt, 13 August 1914, CO 123/279.
7. Collett/Harcourt, 13 August 1914, CO 123/279 (second letter).
8. Collett/Harcourt, 12 November 1914, CO 123/279.
9. Collett/Harcourt, 2 September 1914, CO 123/279.
10. Collett/Harcourt, 25 March 1915, CO 123/281.
11. Collett/Bonar Law, 29 June and 24 August 1916, CO 123/285.
12. Walter/Long, 8 May and 20 June 1917, CO 123/288.
13. Collett/Bonar Law, 10 October 1916, CO 123/285.
14. Collett/Bonar Law, 3 August 1916 and enc. to 23 November 1916, CO 123/285. Most of the troops served in the lines of communication, particularly water transport, for the campaign to capture Baghdad. Their work was highly commended – see Brigadier General Hughes/Commanding Officer British Honduras Territorial Force, 24 February 1919, BA (MP 1214–19). The war memorial in Belize City lists the names of 29 members of the two contingents who died on active service.

15. First reported as early as March 1915: see Collett/Harcourt 19 March 1915, CO 123/281.
16. Collett/Bonar Law, 19 October 1916, CO 123/285.
17. Walter/Long, 12 December 1918, CO 123/292.
18. Peter Ashdown, 'Race Riot, Class Warfare, and Coup d'Etat: the Ex-servicemen's Riot of July 1919', *Journal of Belizean Affairs*, Vol. 3 No. 1 (June 1986).
19. Acting Colonial Secretary/Hon. Sec. Returned Soldiers' Welfare Committee, 4 August 1919, BA (MPP 344–18).
20. Hutson/Duke of Devonshire, 29 February 1924, CO 123/317.
21. M. S. Metzgen and H. E. C. Cain, *A Handbook of British Honduras*, London (1925), 177–8.
22. Belize Sugar Industry Ltd., *A Brief History of Sugar in Belize*, Belize (1989).
23. Hutson/Duke of Devonshire, 11 October 1923, CO 123/315.
24. Metzgen and Cain, 176–7.
25. Hart Bennett/Long, 8 July 1918, CO 123/291.
26. Walter/Long, 27 March 1918, CO 123/290.
27. Hutson/Duke of Devonshire, 11 October 1923, CO 123/315.
28. Narda Dobson, *A History of Belize*, London (1973), 261–2.
29. Grant, *The Making of Modern Belize*, 39.
30. Hutson/Duke of Devonshire, 29 July 1924, CO 123/318.
31. Peter Ashdown, 'Bootlegging in Belize 1920–33', *Belizean Studies*, Vol. 8 No. 5, (September 1980), 15–16.
32. D. A. G. Waddell, *British Honduras: a Historical and Contemporary Survey*, London (1961), 100.
33. O. N. Bolland, *Colonialism and Resistance in Belize*, Belize (1988), 169.
34. Telegram Governor/Secretary of State, 11 September 1931, CO 123/335/1.
35. E. E. Cane, *Cyclone: the City of Belize 1931*, London (1932).
36. Telegram Governor/Secretary of State, 18 September 1931, CO 123/335/1.
37. Pilling/Thomas, 24 September 1931, CO 123/335/1.
38. Telegram acting Governor/Secretary of State, 30 September 1931, CO 123/335/1.
39. Secretary, Treasury/Under Secretary of State, Colonial Office, 22 October 1931 and Stubbs/Thomas, 7 October 1931, both CO 123/335/1; Pilling/Thomas 3 December 1931, CO 123/335/9.
40. Treasury/Colonial Office, 1 October 1931, CO 123/335/1.
41. Skevington/Beckett, 6 January 1932, CO 123/335/9.
42. Telegram acting Governor/Secretary of State, 12 January 1932, CO 123/335/9.
43. Burdon/Secretary of State, 5 September 1929, CO 123/331/6.
44. Burns/Secretary of State, 8 October 1935, CO 123/352/14.
45. Colonial Office note in CO 123/356/10.
46. Assad Shoman, *Thirteen Chapters of a History of Belize*, Belize (1994), 158.
47. Bolland, 169.
48. Departments of Archaeology etc., *Moments in the History of Belize*, 25.
49. Pilling/Secretary of State, 20 September 1933, CO 123/341/7; and table for 1935–9 production in Waddell, 87.
50. Grant, 72.
51. Stockdale/Hibbert, 14 April 1932, CO 123/339/2.
52. W. A. J. Bowman, *Citrus Culture in British Honduras*, Belize (1955).
53. Waddell, 90.
54. Kittermaster/Secretary of State, 28 June 1932, CO 123/336/9.
55. Kittermaster/Secretary of State, 2 April 1934, CO 123/347/3.
56. Encs. to Burns/Secretary of State, 20 February 1937, CO 123/362/10, and 17 November 1938, CO 123/368/11.
57. Stockdale/Hibbert, 14 April 1932, CO 123/338/8.
58. Campbell (Colonial Office)/Ryan (Treasury), 25 April 1934, CO 123/347/2.

59. Dobson, 270 and Burns/Secretary of State, 20 February 1937, CO 123/362/10.
60. Waddell, 90.
61. Table of Principal Exports 1935–45, CO 123/395/3. Shipments then fell back a little for the duration of the war.
62. See report by Sir A. Pim, agreed in Hopkins (Treasury)/Campbell (Colonial Office), 19 July 1934, CO 123/345/13.
63. For correspondence on termination of Treasury control of British Honduras' public finances in 1952, see CO 1031/40.
64. Dobson, 302–5. With an extremely limited franchise, however, the number of voters at the 1936 election represented less than 2 per cent of the population.
65. Telegram Governor/Sectretary of State, 14 January 1939, CO 123/376 /6.
66. Telegram Governor/Secretary of State, 23 January 1939, CO 123/376/6.
67. Burns/Macdonald, 28 February 1939, CO 123/376/6.
68. Burns/Macdonald, 4 April 1939, CO 123/375/3; and Johnston/Macdonald, 29 January 1940, CO 123/379/19. In terms of military capacity, defence measures taken in the Second World War seem to have been very limited. A letter from the Governor in late 1942 indicates that were only 16 British Army personnel in the colony, mostly on the staff of the government's Defence Security Officer – see Hunter/Stanley, 10 December 1942, BA (Outward Dispatches 1942 D187).
69. Bolland, 179.
70. Turnbull/Secretary of State, 13 May 1943, CO 123/384/15.
71. Telegram Governor/Secretary of State, 17 September 1939, CO 123/373/12.
72. See table of exports for 1935–45 in CO 123/395/3.
73. Officer Administering Government/Secretary of State, 9 February 1940, BA (Outward Dispatches 1940, D 41).
74. Agreement on the tax increases had been reported in a telegram dated 27 September 1939 from the Governor to the Secretary of State – see CO 123/373/12.
75. Telegram Secretary of State/Governor, 12 October 1939, CO 123/373/12. Even with continuing Treasury subvention, the Governor complained in late 1940 that the obligation 'to make as few calls on H. M. Treasury as is humanly possible' had made it necessary to reduce some government departments where 'the provision made ... was already so inadequate as to militate against their efficiency' – see Hunter/Lloyd 30 September 1940, BA (Outward Dispatches 1940, D175).
76. see Marika Sherwood, *The British Honduras Forestry Unit in Scotland 1941–3*, Belize (1982). The unit's reception in Scotland seems to have been badly mismanaged. There were complaints, upheld by the Colonial Office, of primitive accommodation, inadequate clothing, inappropriate food, and, though not universally, racial hostility.
77. See correspondence between January and August 1944 on file CO 123/388/3.
78. Telegram Secretary of State/Governor, 28 January 1944, CO 123/388/3.
79. Hunter (on leave)/Wolfson, 3 August 1944, CO 123/388/3.
80. Wolfson/Stanley, 17 August 1944, CO 123/388/3.
81. Telegram Secretary of State/Governor, 14 November 1944, CO 123/388/3.

13

The Economy after the Second World War

The sustainable diversification of the economy that eventually took place after the second world war had its roots in initial progress in the 1930s in two areas: the slow development of an alternative export crop (citrus), and the equally gradual development of a road system (linking Belize and the northern and western towns) to enable the opening up of parts of the interior to settlement and agriculture. In both cases there was a deceleration during the war years, and, ultimately, a significant resumption thereafter.

Post-war development was more wide-ranging, and on a significantly larger scale, than the pre-war programme launched after the 1931 hurricane. It was initially driven both by the employment considerations at last fully recognised towards the end of the war and by the much older concern about exhaustion of timber resources. As before it was led by public investment through the Colonial Development and Welfare Fund. That investment amounted over the fifteen years from 1945 to $20 million (£4 million) allocated in three phases.[1] It was directed at most elements of the economic infrastructure, from the road network (once again the priority in the early years) and rural water supplies to forestry regeneration and agricultural extension services. Increasing importance was attached to this last as development progressed, because of the steady growth of a population who lacked any tradition or knowledge of cereal cultivation or livestock rearing except on the smallest scale. But as early as 1946 it was decided to drop the pre-war formula of government-sponsored agricultural settlement, for which 'no activity in British Honduras has a more depressing history of failure and frustration',[2] and rather to adopt, as the appropriate role for government, support for private investment. That support was to take the form of experimental work and extension services, in both crops and livestock. It was based at the government's new (and today still active) Central Farm, set up in 1948 to replace the district agricultural centres established in 1933.

Planning for the first phase, 1948–52

The lack of agricultural experience was highlighted in both the two reports on the economic future of British Honduras that were compiled by outside experts in 1947. Both concluded that the solution lay in the importation of the necessary skills from the overcrowded West Indian islands. They also took the view that if the colony's full agricultural potential was to be realised, there would in addition be a need for a substantial injection of labour from other Caribbean territories. Both reports called too for a considerable strengthening of the local administration. The first report, by Professor C. G. Beasley, drew attention moreover to the lack of action on recommendations for agricultural development contained in no less than three similar reports commissioned during the 1920s and 1930s.[3] The second and fuller 1947 report was by a team of three led by Sir Geoffrey Evans. Evans, who saw the slowly but steadily growing citrus industry as the colony's only current economic success, went further. In his preliminary findings, which formed the basis of his report, he recommended that food production be focused on the western district of Cayo, where he thought there was ample suitable land for development of modern livestock and arable farming. But to meet both future employment demands and the need for new export earnings, he also recommended large-scale expansion of the sugar industry in the northern districts. This scheme would be based on replacement of the 1937 mill, which, post-war, had the notional capacity to produce about 4000 tons of sugar per season, by a new plant to produce four or even six times that amount, together with the clearing of several thousand acres of land for new cane to help feed it.[4]

The Evans report, after what seemed to the Governor to be interminable delays,[5] eventually led to the addition of £800,000 from the Colonial Development and Welfare Fund to the £600,000 that had been allocated by the Fund immediately after the war. The combined sum financed the first phase of the post-war development programme, from 1948 to 1952. But because the territory's transport infrastructure was still, despite the work undertaken in the 1930s, so inadequate for agricultural development of any kind, no less than 74 per cent of this initial funding went on roads, principally the new highway connecting Stann Creek to the Belize–Cayo road (the Hummingbird Highway – another Evans recommendation) and feeder roads off the other main highways that had already been built.[6] The sugar industry had to wait.

The building of the mountain road from Cayo to Stann Creek finally provided a land link between the north and west of the territory and the nearer part of the south. It was the Stann Creek valley in the south and the Corozal and Orange Walk districts of the north that were the focal points of the private sector investment stimulated by the Colonial Office's infra-structure development programme; and it was that private sector invest-ment, albeit government-aided in the north, that at last brought about for the first time, with the development of substantial new export industries, a lasting diversification of the British Honduras economy.

Timber 1945–60

Inevitably the post-war programme did not show great progress towards this goal for some years. It was not until 1953 and the beginning of a sugar export trade that the colony's dependence on timber began to fall below the traditional 80–85 per cent of overall export earnings.[7] That was because citrus export growth was matched in the early years after the war by a growing export trade in a new timber product, pine lumber, while mahogany exports maintained the level of 5–700,000 thousand cubic (as distinct from the earlier measure of 'superficial') feet per annum recorded in most years since the mid-1930s. In the post-1945 period there were high hopes for a stable future for pine extraction. Natural regeneration of this wood was considerably faster than for mahogany, where production was only being sustained by the traditional and inevitably term-limited method of penetrating ever more remote areas. But it was then found that regener-ation of pine was not as straightforward as had been thought because of the vulnerability of young trees to fire. Pine lumber exports consequently declined, albeit slowly, during the 1950s.[8]

All pine extracted was exported as lumber, having been processed by small mobile milling machines. For mahogany, lumber exports had begun in the 1930s following the opening in 1933 of the colony's first substantial saw-mill. This had been established by the Belize Estate and Produce Company with the assistance of a controversial loan drawn from the British government-backed facility set up after the 1931 hurricane. Encouraged by the removal of export tax on sawn, but not unsawn, logs, the proportion of mahogany exported as lumber increased steadily. It was not until just after the war that the balance shifted finally in favour of processed timber.

By the end of the 1950s more than 90 per cent of mahogany exports were in the form of lumber, the 'value addition' of the milling process use-fully enhancing earnings.[9] But by that time mahogany extraction was in significant, and this time permanent, decline. In 1959 the volume extracted was half the figure for 1951,[10] bearing out a 1950 estimate of stocks lasting no longer than 20 years on Belize Estate and Produce Company land and less than 10 years elsewhere.[11]

The third forest product, chicle, continued the steady decline begun in the 1930s. The problem for that industry now was the development of synthetic alternatives for the production of chewing gum.[12] The effect was a further 25 per cent fall in exports by the end of the 1950s below the already reduced levels recorded in the late 1930s.[13] In the next five years export volume halved again.[14] In 1961, due to both forestry decline and growth in other sectors, forest products accounted for no more than 43 per cent of overall export earnings.[15]

Citrus, sugar and other projects, 1945–60

Of the non-forest products, citrus led the way until the end of the 1950s. Export growth was boosted, as mentioned in the last chapter, by the completion in 1945 of a modern plant, started in 1939, to undertake the canning of grapefruit sections on a substantial scale. This factory, at Pomona in the Stann Creek valley, was complemented in 1952 by the installation of a second factory, also at Pomona, to produce juice concentrate from the newer orange plantations.[16] Again the economic benefits of local processing were quickly felt and further growth stimulated. Thus the 900 acres under cultivation of citrus in 1950 had grown ten years later to 5000 acres.[17] The statistics for export earnings are even more striking. Whereas the figure for 1946 was $344,000, by 1951 increased acreage had increased earnings to $731,000. The addition of the juicing plant then raised that figure to over $1 million for the first time in 1954, and by 1956 to over $2 million. The same statistics, confirming the case for local 'value addition', show that pound for pound weight, the processed product was worth nearly three times the unprocessed fruit.[18]

It was in sugar production and exports where growth was even more dramatic once it got going. But that did not start until after both the award of a more substantial export quota in 1950, when there were only 2000 acres under cultivation,[19] and the subsequent expansion of the Corozal mill. The new quota was set, under the Commonwealth Sugar Agreement, at 5000 tons, with a provision for an increase over time to 25,000 tons. This had already led to plans for a mill that would in due course fill that longer-term quota, as envisaged by Evans. The replacement of the 1937 mill, which in 1950 was still only producing 1200 tons of sugar (all for local consumption) was a longer story than the securing of the quota. The administration's initial hope was that the whole enterprise would be led by the Colonial Development Corporation (CDC), a British government-owned company set up after the war to lead investment in businesses that could be developed on commercial lines in partnership with or for later transfer to private companies. CDC had already embarked on three such projects in British Honduras: livestock rearing on the Mountain Pine Ridge (soon abandoned), banana cultivation in the Stann Creek valley (abandoned after three years), and the building of the Fort George Hotel in Belize (CDC's main legacy from this period).[20]

Discouraged by difficulties with two of their first three projects in British Honduras, CDC were naturally cautious about the technical challenge and the commercial risk of a new industry where international market supply was already plentiful. In their discussions with the Colonial Office they insisted on two conditions: first, freedom to bring in outside expertise and, as they thought would eventually be necessary, labour; second, because of high production costs, a guaranteed premium price for the exported sugar on the UK market.[21] The former demand presented no problem. Indeed from a British government policy point of view, 'finding settlement opportunities for West Indians' was 'one objective among other important ones in the development of British Honduras'.[22] The second condition was much more difficult and indeed was the rock on which CDC involvement, and therefore the whole scheme, foundered in early 1951.[23] It was also the issue which lay behind the breakdown of further negotiations in 1952 and 1953 for CDC to join a subsequent project for a much more limited expansion of the plant, to provide a production capacity of 7000 tons of sugar and thus an export surplus of 4000 tons.[24]

The 1950s expansion of the Corozal sugar factory was finally brought about in 1954 through a combination of local, British government and Jamaican capital. A new mill was bought with a capacity to produce 14,000 tons of sugar and a start was made with clearing land for new cane plantations.[25] At that stage the new acreage was largely cultivated by a rapidly increasing number of small farmers competing with the bigger growers who had monopolised the industry until the late 1940s.[26]

Driven largely by Jamaican management and expertise, around 2000 tons of sugar was exported from the new plant in 1955 and 1956.[27] It was then that discussions started on the possibility of establishing a second mill, with similar capacity, in the Orange Walk district so that the territory's full 25,000 export quota might be taken up.[28] The second factory was not, in the event, opened until 1966. But production from the Corozal mill continued to grow rapidly. By 1957 exports, at 6028 tons, exceeded the initial quota.[29] Following a substantial expansion of the factory that year, exports then surged, so that by 1961 they filled the original longer-term provision of 25,000 tons.[30] The rapid increase in supply of the necessary cane was achieved partly by increased acreage, partly by a slow increase in the yield per acre. From 1957 the new plantations included a significant amount of land bought and cultivated by a subsidiary of the company that owned the mill. Local opposition to this led to a radicalisation of the smaller cane farmers and to a difficult relationship between them and the company which continued as the industry grew.

During this period there was no significant revival of the banana industry. Following the blighting by Panama Disease of both the Stann Creek and Toledo plantations in the 1920s and 1930s, some attempt had been made before the war to develop banana cultivation in the western (or Cayo) district. This had not been successful. An attempt to interest the Barclays Overseas Development Corporation in a substantial banana scheme in that district in 1950 came to nothing because the patches of land offering suitable soil were too scattered.[31] As already mentioned, the Colonial Development Corporation had introduced the year before, in an experimental plantation of 1800 acres in the Stann Creek valley, a strain of banana resistant to Panama Disease, although there were doubts about its marketability. But by 1952 leafspot had developed in the new plantation to such an extent that the project was abandoned. Some shifting cultivation continued as in the 1930s. But the original market, the US, was now well supplied from the huge plantations managed by American companies in Guatemala and Honduras. A systematic effort to put the industry back on its feet had therefore to await an agreement in 1970 with the British company Fyffes, who were active in the industry elsewhere in the Caribbean. They were able both to buy and develop new land for plantations and to help negotiate the opening of a preferential market in the European Economic Community.

What was established in the late 1950s, on the other hand, was a dairy industry, thanks to the arrival of the first Menonites from the United States,[32] who contributed substantially to the doubling of the colony's cattle herd between 1955 and 1965.[33]

Trade patterns

The eventual shift in the marketplace for the banana industry was part of a wider pattern that had already emerged. In the 1920s the US accounted for some 80 per cent of British Honduras' exports, and in the 1930s the figure was still 60–70 per cent.[34] But from the mid-1950s, with the institution of a direct shipping service, the United Kingdom, which had previously only taken some mahogany lumber and a small proportion of chicle exports, became the main destination. This was because the new export commodities, processed citrus and sugar, were sold at that stage exclusively to Britain. The other important market which opened up post-war was the West Indies (principally Jamaica), which bought almost all of the pine lumber now being exported and also most of the more traditional secondary hardwoods such as cedar.[35] Thus the diversification of the colony's export industries brought in its train a significant widening of trading connections.

For other reasons something of the same happened with the pattern of imports. Again the US was in the 1920s the dominant supplier by a wide margin, in this case with a 60 per cent share. The United Kingdom, with a 17.5 per cent share, was the only other single significant supplier. That balance began to change after the 1931 hurricane. Britain never overtook the US. But by the 1950s about a third of the colony's imports were British, and the American share had declined to around 40 per cent. Imports from other countries remained at the 1920s level of about a quarter of the total.[36]

One of the striking features of the pattern of British Honduras imports is the proportion accounted for during this period by foodstuffs. For the years 1953–6 this was as much as a third of overall imports, despite the admittedly limited expansion of farming brought about by early post-war development. By the mid-1950s agricultural expansion had brought about self-sufficiency in maize and beans, but not for rice, meat, milk, or even vegetables.[37] The continuing high level of import dependency accounted for the substantial trade deficits recorded by the colony, deficits which in some years equalled the total value of exports and which were in no single year in the 1950s less than 60 per cent of export earnings.[38] As the population increased, this dependency, which hobbled the colony's economy, became an increasingly important factor in government planning.

Planning, 1952–64

Transport infrastructure, however, remained the first priority in the second (1952–6) as well as the first phase of the 1948–60 development plan, although the proportion of capital funds devoted to it fell sharply, to 39 per cent.[39] But it was natural for what slack there was to be taken up by agriculture, the sector of the economy that the new roads were designed to serve. This would now account for 35 per cent of the overall budget, once again £1.4 million. The aim was to both increase exports and reduce imports. In the words of the plan document, the time had come 'to ensure that areas opened up are put into the most effective use'.[40] Funding for agricultural development was to be provided almost entirely, in nearly equal proportions, by a Colonial Development and Welfare Fund grant and a British government-backed loan. The principal items were a strengthened Agriculture Department, expansion of the trials and training programme at the administration's Central Farm, resurrection of the district agricultural centres for extension services, and provision of land-clearing units, marketing subsidies and credit facilities.[41]

For the final (1956–60) four-year phase of the 1948–60 development plan, there were reductions in the shares of both infrastructure and, surprisingly, agriculture in order to make way for a significant increase in capital spending on forestry.[42] But that adjustment was reversed after 1960 in a significant change in policy. A further four-year plan was launched then with applications the following year for Colonial Development and Welfare grants for, principally, a new road to link the two southern coastal towns of Stann Creek and Punta Gorda, further feeder roads, agriculture, some forestry and education. Details of the plan were published in May 1961. It was based on recommendations, made in late 1959 and broadly accepted by the Colonial Office, by a senior economic adviser at the British Treasury. In resurrecting the 1947 notion of large-scale immigration to support agricultural investment by big companies, Jack Downie had insisted on the need for a prior further development of British Honduras' road network and social infrastructure. He had also for the first time argued that public funding for the forestry sector should be devoted almost entirely to the colony's quicker-regenerating pine resources (both timber and resin), rather than to the much longer-term effort to rehabilitate mahogany that was being pursued under previous plans. This reorientation of forestry became another of the main components of the 1961 plan. Other elements included the further expansion, with some subsidisation, of the cattle industry, aimed at both import substitution and new export earnings; and assistance to both cane and citrus growers with improvement of currently low yields.[43]

A bone of contention between the colony's government and the British Treasury was whether the $8 million (£2.4 million) balance of capital funding called for by Downie beyond what was available in agreed grants might be provided by loans. In the end, at the expense particularly of the road programmes, it was ruled that loan finance could only be used to fund revenue-generating projects.[44] Another difficulty during this period was the need from 1957 for a resumption of grants-in-aid to balance the administration's recurrent budget. From 1960 these took the form of a four-year and then a tapering three-year block grant. But inevitably they led to Treasury insistence on closer consultation in the preparation of the annual estimates than the Legislative Council had grown used to in the mid-1950s, though not to the full formal approval process of the 1930s.[45] A much more clear-cut case then arose early in the 1960–4 plan period for substantial further British government financial assistance: the destruction caused to

Belize and the southern half of the country by another severe hurricane, the so-called Hurricane Hattie of 1961.

The 1961 hurricane and its aftermath

For Hattie, with the improved forecasting methods developed during the war including the use of radar, the US Weather Bureau at Miami was able to give warning of the hurricane's coming nearly 24 hours before it was expected. This was thought to be the morning of 31 October. That estimate was not significantly modified in the second warning issued at midnight on 30/31 October. It was then that the broadcasting station announced that there would be a final warning issued at 4 a.m. Unfortunately the hurricane hit Belize at 1 a.m., only an hour after the midnight announcement. This forecasting error undoubtedly increased the number of fatal casualties in the two towns struck by the hurricane. In Belize, 147 people died and in Stann Creek, 114.[46]

The pattern of the hurricane was familiar: winds up to 150 miles an hour, first from the southwest, then from the northeast; very heavy rain for 8–9 hours; and a tidal surge estimated at 15 feet. The flooding lasted for days, the mud for weeks. The Colonial Office said that Hattie was the worst storm ever to hit a Commonwealth territory. The damage to the fabric of Belize was once again massive: a third of the buildings were destroyed, another third heavily damaged.[47] The devastation of the productive economy was worse than in 1931, because the economy was more developed. Worst hit in that respect was the Stann Creek valley, where 95 per cent of the citrus crop was wiped out. Indicative of the wider destruction was the estimate of the Belize Estate and Produce Company, whose interests were elsewhere in the colony, of damage to their assets of $1 million.[48]

Initial Treasury authority enabled the Colonial Office to reimburse £200,000 of the cost of emergency relief provided from Jamaica, the US, and Mexico.[49] Other immediate relief was mounted, at an estimated cost of £344,000, by the British armed forces.[50] Local government expenditure on emergency work in the three months which followed the hurricane was close to $1 million (£300,000).[51] But none of this began to cover the cost of reconstruction. For that an expert mission visited the territory at the beginning of 1962. Their report put the bill at £3.1 million for making good damage to housing, public buildings, utilities, medical facilities, roads, forestry infrastructure and citrus crops; £1 million for a new airport or at least runway; and £3 million for a new capital town to be sited at a safer distance inland.[52] After three months deliberation, the British government, which had doubts about the absorptive capacity of the local administration, agreed to make available £2.5 million for reconstruction (with the possibility of another £0.75 million if the case could be made), and £1.5 million towards the cost of the new capital that had by then been decided upon.[53]

This project for a new capital, Belmopan as it was to become, was the result of studies undertaken by a local committee set up within two weeks of the hurricane.[54] Their case that Belize was both overcrowded and unduly vulnerable to hurricane damage was accepted by the British government. The committee favoured a location on the Western Highway 31 miles inland, where there was already a small settlement.[55] A second expert mission from Britain disagreed on the grounds of liability to flooding, and settled for an alternative site identified by the local committee a further 20 miles up the road close to the existing village of Roaring Creek. Here there was a limestone sub-stratum, good natural drainage, and no shallow water-table.[56] Construction of the new capital began at last in 1966,[57] and it formally became the seat of government five years later.[58]

The 1964–70 plan

Meanwhile the next overall development plan, that for 1964–70, was prepared by a team of experts from the United Nations and accepted in late 1964 by the Colonial Office subject to some re-phasing.[59] It had to take account of the disaster of Hurricane Hattie as well as the more familiar factors behind earlier plans. Of these, the need to increase food production was given a further increase in priority. This affected more substantially than before the country's traditional mainstay, forestry. Whereas in 1947 Sir Geoffrey Evans had advised that agricultural development should not be at the expense of forestry, in 1964 there was a conscious decision to down-grade the place of the forestry sector in economic planning considerably further than had been agreed in 1960/1 following the Downie report. This was seen as 'in keeping with the relative importance to the country's economy'.[60] Thus the Forestry Department's staff was to be cut back as the steady expansion of their network of vehicle tracks was ended and as management and reforestation activity was curtailed to a minimal level. Resources saved were to be switched to agriculture. For food products the objectives were to achieve self-sufficiency in meat and rice and to establish export industries in cattle and cocoa. The means to those ends were to be land clearance by the government's specialist units, an agricultural education programme based at the Central Farm, increased credit facilities from a new Development Finance Corporation, and help with marketing by a new Central Marketing Agency.[61]

Besides increased food production, the accelerated expansion of the agricultural sector that the government was now seeking was once again aimed, for 1964–70, at citrus and sugar. These industries were now much more significant components of the economy. Earnings from timber exports had fallen below $3 million for the first time in 1958,[62] and extraction continued to decline in the 1960s.[63] By 1961, the value of citrus and of sugar exports for the first time in each case exceeded the figure for timber.[64] Diversification had thus been achieved. But because import substitution through greater local food production was necessarily a long-term aim, the trade deficit could only be narrowed in the shorter term by further increases in these export earnings. To that end the plan envisaged a further 50 per cent enlargement of citrus acreage, from 7000 acres to 10,500 acres, so as to take up new export opportunities in the United States and Canada.[65] For sugar, for which there was 15,000 acres under cultivation, there was to be a further increase in the Corozal factory's annual production capacity from 30,000 tons, to which it was already working, to 40,000 tons, in order to take full advantage of a new 10,000 ton export quota for the US.[66] Funding for the overall plan was to be centred on but by no means restricted to a £2.2 million Colonial Development and Welfare grant agreed for the years 1965–8.[67]

The transformation of the sugar industry

In the event the expansion of the sugar industry was to be more massive than the UN planners envisaged. During his visit to Britain in mid-1963 for the constitutional conference that was to lead to full internal self-government under his leadership, First Minister George Price met with the UK sugar company Tate and Lyle. Against a background of a dramatic rise in world sugar prices,[68] Tates expressed serious interest in the colony, the first major overseas company to do so since the war. Following their visit later that year and subsequent negotiations, Price was able to announce in July 1964 an investment programme that was to transform the industry. Tate and Lyle had agreed to buy the Corozal factory, to spend $3 million on it, and to build, at a cost of $14 million, a new plant with a capacity of 40,000 tons at Tower Hill near Orange Walk.[69] They were also prepared to invest substantially in the purchase and clearance of further land, particularly in the Orange Walk district, to add to the company-owned plantations taken over with the Corozal mill. This ultimately gave them enough cane production capacity to supply no less than half the feedstock of the two mills.[70]

Thus was at last achieved the twin aim of mills to serve both sugar producing districts and a scale of production that would make British

Honduras a substantial sugar exporter to Europe and North America. Tate and Lyle's two factories effectively reached their full production capacity in 1970, the last year of the 1964 development plan period.[71] Two years later, sugar for the first time accounted for more than 50 per cent of export earnings. By then there were 40,000 acres under cultivation.[72] The same year, with cane production consolidated and following considerable organised agitation by local farmers (the caneros), Tate and Lyle agreed with the government to sell its company plantations, a third of the total acreage, to indigenous growers.[73]

This large-scale development of the sugar industry did not in the event call for the substantial immigration from the Caribbean islands envisaged by Evans and Downie, because British Honduras was by then already attracting immigrant workers from the neighbouring republics. But together with further growth of citrus production and processing, and the redevelopment of the banana industry under the 1970 agreement with Fyffes, the scheme led by Tate and Lyle laid the basis of the modern economy of first the autonomous territory, then the fully independent state, of Belize.

Notes

1. D. A. G. Waddell, *British Honduras: A Historical and Contemporary Survey*, London (1961), 102. The Belize dollar enjoyed parity with the US dollar until the 1949 devaluation, after which it traded at US $ 1.00/Bz $ 1.4 throughout the 1950s. Since the 1970s the rate has been fixed at US $ 1.00/Bz $ 2.00.
2. Report of Development Planning Committee, 11 January 1946, paragraph 43, CO 123/398/3.
3. Enc. to Macpherson/Hawkesworth, 15 August 1947, CO 123/398/3.
4. Evans/Swiredale, 28 November 1947, and subsequent undated note, CO 123/398 /3.
5. C. H. Grant, *The Making of Modern Belize*, Cambridge (1976), 74.
6. Enc to Hone/Lyttleton, 14 February 1952, CO 1031/507. It seems from a letter from the Governor in 1942 that the roads built in the 1930s had not lasted well, suffering from 'poor materials and unsound construction' – see Hunter/Cranborne, 7 September 1942, BA (Outward Dispatches 1942, D130).
7. Waddell, 83.
8. *The Economy of British Honduras*, IBRD (April 1962). The earlier attempts to establish a pine industry in the 1920s had not been successful, and when the post-1945 programme was first mooted in 1942 there was local resistance to proposals for government backing – see Hunter/Lloyd, 23 February 1942, BA (Outward Dispatches 1942, D38).
9. Waddell, 84.
10. *The Economy of British Honduras*, IBRD (April 1962).
11. Report by W. A. Robertson, 30 May 1950, CO 123/407/3.
12. Note of Colonial Office meeting, 11 September 1947, CO 123/398/3.
13. Waddell, 87.
14. Narda Dobson, *A History of Belize*, London (1973), 265.
15. *The Economy of British Honduras*, IBRD (April 1962).
16. Enc. to Hone/Lyttleton,14 February 1952, CO 1031/507.

17. British Honduras Ministry of Finance, Development Policy and Interim Expenditure Programme, May 1961, CO 1031/3524.
18. Waddell, 92.
19. P. A. Furley and A. J. Crosbie, *The Geography of Belize*, London (1974), 36.
20. Marnham/Beasley, 2 June 1949, CO 123/398/5.
21. Trefgarne/Griffiths, 19 July 1950, CO 123/409/6.
22. Marnham/Garvey, 14 September 1949, CO 123/398/5.
23. Telegram, Governor/Secretary of State, 24 February 1951, CO 123/408/4 and enc. to letter Mayle/Cable 30 March 1951, CO 123/409/7.
24. Telegram Governor/Secretary of State, 23 February 1952 and letter Rendell/Melville, 9 March 1953, CO 1031/66.
25. Telegram, Governor/Secretary of State, 12 August 1953, CO 1031/66, reporting the order for the new mill.
26. Assad Shoman, *Thirteen Chapters of a History of Belize*, Belize (1994), 192.
27. Unsigned Colonial Office letter of 1 October 1956 to the Governor (Thornley), CO 1031/1445.
28. Thornley/Kennedy, 25 March 1956, CO 1031/1445.
29. Waddell, 91.
30 British Honduras Ministry of Finance, Development Policy and Interim Expenditure Programme, May 1961, CO 1031/3524.
31. Telegram, Governor/Secretary of State, 29 March 1950, CO 123/409/5.
32. Paul Martin, The Menonites of Belize (Belizean Studies Vol. 1 No. 3, May 1973), 12–13.
33. Edward G. Benya, 'The Cattle Industry of Belize', *Belizean Studies*, Vol. 4 No. 5, September 1976), 24 and 26.
34. Waddell, 94.
35. ibid.
36. Waddell, 96-7.
37. Waddell, 89.
38. Waddell, 98.
39. *The Economy of British Honduras*, IBRD (April 1962).
40. Enc. to Hone/Lyttleton, 14 February, 1952, CO 1031/507.
41. ibid.
42. The Economy of British Honduras IBRD (April 1962).
43. British Honduras Ministry of Finance, Development Policy and Interim Expenditure Programme, May 1961, CO 1031/3524.
44. Thomas/Thornley, 19 April 1962, and Baker/Burnett 21 April 1961, CO 1031/3565.
45. Baker/Lee, 27 January 1960 and Lee/Baker, 12 February 1960, CO 1031/3526.
46. E. E. Cain, *Cyclone: Hattie 1961*, Ilfracombe (1963).
47. John C. Everitt, 'The Growth and Development of Belize City', *Belizean Studies*, Vol. 14 No. 1(1986), 30.
48. ibid. This marked the end of a reforestation programme the company had begun in 1958.
49. Burrett/Kirkness, 10 November 1961, CO 1031/4136.
50. Barker/Wooton, 31 January 1962, CO 1031/4136.
51. Telegram Governor/Secretary of State, 30 January 1962, CO 1031/4136.
52. Enc. to Barker/Piper, 6 February 1962, CO 1031/4136.
53. Telegram Secretary of State/Governor, 2 May 1962, CO 1031/4136.
54. Telegram Governor/Secretary of State, 15 November 1961, CO 1031/4132.
55. ibid.
56. Enc. to Ward/Piper, 16 March 1962, CO 1031/4132.
57. Everitt, 30.
58. Dobson, 284.

59. Woods/Beazley, 29 October 1964, CO 1031/4675.
60. British Honduras 1964–70 Development Plan, CO 1031/4674.
61. ibid.
62. Waddell, 85.
63. Edward Benya, 'Forestry in Belize: Modern Times and Transition', *Belizean Studies*, Vol. 7 No. 3 (May 1979), table at 26.
64. Dobson, 265.
65. British Honduras 1964–70 Development Plan, CO 1031/4674.
66. ibid.
67. Carter/Slater, 12 October 1965, CO 1031/4675.
68. Belize Sugar Industries Ltd., *A Brief History of Sugar in Belize*, Belize (1989).
69. *Belize Times*, 5 July 1964.
70. Shoman,198.
71. Dobson, 270.
72. Furley and Crosbie, 36.
73. Shoman, 200.

14

The Road towards Independence

Representative politics, albeit once again on a minimal basis, returned to British Honduras with the 1935 constitution. In the early years of the twentieth century the only elective body had been, from 1911, the Belize Town Board, where efforts had been made from time to time to devise common positions among members. But Town Board groupings such as the Progressive Movement had made little impact beyond the scope of municipal administration. The result of the introduction of an elective element – five seats out of twelve – into the Legislative Council began to address this democratic void, but only on behalf of a very small section of the community. For the franchise on which representation was re-introduced into the wider conduct of affairs in 1935, and the qualifications for candidacy, were as restrictive as they had been in the days of the nineteenth-century Public Meeting. Eligibility for the vote required an income of $300 per annum, or ownership of real property worth $500, or payment of rent of at least $96 per annum. To qualify to run for election, a candidate needed to have an even larger income, $1000 per annum, or, again, real property worth $500. In the distressed economic circumstances of British Honduras in the 1930s, the result was inevitable: in the first elections under the new constitution in 1936, the number of voters, at 1035, accounted for precisely 1.8 per cent of the population.

The early labour movement

It was then because of a combination of this economic distress and this political exclusion that British Honduras saw the emergence of a labour movement to take up the real grievances of the mass of the working population, who were suffering from the economic and social dislocation left by the recent hurricane and the continuing slump. For it was clear to the leaders who emerged to make this case that the newly elected representatives of the elite, largely merchants but also local professionals, would be taken up first with their own priorities and those of their relatively wealthy voters, rather than with the much more basic concerns of the mass of the people. In a broad sense, political life would run on this dual track for thirteen years until the labour movement was taken over by a new generation of politicians; and until the British government's handling of the colony's finances and management of a further economic crisis brought the interests of those new politicians and at least the merchant element of the old elite together.

British Honduras was not new to labour unrest. There had been a mutiny of the British Honduras Constabulary in November 1894 followed by serious rioting by mahogany workers the following month, both sparked by a devaluation of purchasing power when the silver dollar was replaced by the gold standard; and again in 1919, when post-war unemployment hit the colony just as considerable numbers of wartime soldiers were returning from active service. But a demonstration in February 1934 by a large group of former workers calling themselves the Unemployed Brigade fed an appetite for continued protest at the plight of both unemployed and employed. This led to the formation the following month of the territory's first organised labour movement, the Labourers' and Unemployed Association (LUA), under the leadership of Antonio Soberanis Gomez.

Soberanis' strength lay in his ability as a public speaker. The LUA's main activity was public meetings at which workers and unemployed were mobilised for demonstrations, strikes and boycotts. Their campaign was limited to labour issues: a minimum wage, an eight-hour day, and work for the unemployed. Petitions to the Governor were initially couched as appeals rather than threats. But when they failed to bear fruit, Soberanis revealed another talent, for organisation and action. Within a surprisingly short time he had extended the reach of the LUA into the districts, and was able to mount strikes in September and October 1934 at Stann Creek and at the Belize Estate and Produce Company's sawmill. The undoubted success of the LUA was, however, short-lived. After further incidents in Belize town in 1935, a combination of internal dissension within the movement, emergency public-order legislation brought in by the Governor, the introduction of relief programmes, and a slowly improving economy, caused it to fade as force in the life of the colony.

The lack of a voice for ordinary workers even in labour affairs contin-ued, however, to be felt, and led in due course, in 1939, to the formation of a successor movement, the British Honduras Workers and Tradesmen's Union. Co-founded by Soberanis and R. T. Meighan, it was led by the latter after the former's departure for Panama early in the war. With a doubtful status in law until trades unions were legalised in 1941, it was even then hamstrung in its scope for activity by the Legislative Council's reluctance to remove breach of labour contract from the criminal code;

and even when that was achieved in 1943, wartime emergency legislation maintained much the same effect. Nonetheless, renamed the General Workers Union, the movement continued to organise both in Belize City and in the districts, despite considerable opposition particularly from the Belize Estate and Produce Company. As a result it was able to make a considerable mark with industrial action in the difficult years after the second world war, when the colony once again faced a depressed export trade and large-scale unemployment; and by 1949, with that record and a membership that had grown to three thousand, it was ripe to become an alternative pole for wider political activity to compete with the still very narrowly based Legislative Council.

Unrest in the Legislative Council

The focus of attention of the Legislative Council's elected 'unofficials' during the second half of the 1930s and throughout the 1940s was the degree of control they could exercise over the colony's affairs. This was heavily circumscribed by the British Treasury's direct control of British Honduras' public finances, and by the institution of certain reserve powers for the Governor. Both had been introduced in 1935, the first as a condition of the Hurricane Reconstruction Loan, the second as a condition of the British government's agreement to an elected element in the Council. Both had been accepted most reluctantly. Of the two the former was the more sensitive. Management of this sensitivity was then made more difficult by the narrow interpretation of the principle of Treasury control taken by successive governors, leading elected Legislative Councillors to feel that they were even more emasculated than they need be. They felt the more justified in their complaints in view of the administrative delays caused by constant reference to London on the smallest details of public expenditure even when the colony was still struggling to recover from the effects of the 1931 hurricane and slump. If Treasury control curbed the ability of the elected members to manipulate the public finances in the interest of the section of the population they represented, it also led to a degree of alienation amongst a class whose support the colonial government needed.

To the British government, however, there could be no question of lifting Treasury control until the territory could generate a balanced recurrent budget. But in November 1945 the elected unofficial members of the Legislative Council felt strongly enough to complain that the opinions they expressed on financial matters were ignored. Matters were brought to a head in June 1946, when they walked out of a Council meeting in protest at the Governor's use of his reserve powers to impose a tax increase. Tensions were then eased with agreement on the establishment of a joint fiscal review committee, and with a successful visit to London by a delegation of 'unofficials' to persuade the Colonial Office to remit the balance of the Hurricane Reconstruction Loan.

The same visit to London, in 1947, had a further-reaching result. The Colonial Office agreed that the Governor should set up a local commission to consider ideas for constitutional reform. These included universal adult suffrage, a Legislative Council with twelve elected and only four nominated members, and an Executive Council based on a quasi-ministerial structure. But the aim of this agenda, formulated by the Creole elite represented in the Legislative Council, was greater local autonomy rather than independence. Indeed, despite the strong resentment throughout this colonial society at the economic dominance of the London-owned Belize Estate and Produce Company, the Council went so far as to pass a resolution in March 1948 declaring loyalty to the Crown.

The Open Forum and the People's Committee

That this did not reflect the whole spectrum of public opinion is confirmed by the launch at about the same time of the colony's first overtly political (and moreover nationalist) movement outside the structure of colonial administration. The Open Forum, organised by Luke Dinsdale Kemp and Antonio Soberanis, capitalised on widespread opposition to British proposals to include British Honduras in an autonomous West Indies Federation, and proclaimed instead a Central American destiny for the territory. Drawing on the same unenfranchised working-class support, the General Workers' Union was a natural ally and the two movements found a ready public voice in a recently founded radical newspaper, the *Belize Billboard*. A new generation of politically inclined young men, educated at the colony's leading secondary school, was emerging, and in 1947 some of them were elected to the Belize Town Board. They recognised the opening these various entities offered them to attack the administrative stranglehold of the imperial government and the electoral stranglehold of the local commercial elite.

The climate for this kind of radicalism was right: 1949 was altogether a disastrous year for British Honduras. Mahogany and chicle exports slumped, and a serious drought caused a crop failure. With little action on recent recommendations on economic development, unemployment surged. But the main catalyst for a political upheaval was the decision of the British government in September of that year, under international pressure, to devalue sterling against the US dollar. That had an immediate effect on the viability of British Honduras exports of citrus to Britain and on the attitude of potential British investors in all sectors of the economy. Moreover, although the value of the local currency against the US dollar remained for the time being unchanged at parity, there was great uncertainty about its stability despite assurances from British ministers. This prompted merchants to stock up with imports from their US suppliers at a favourable cost while the going was good. When devaluation of the British Honduras dollar (from parity to $1.40) did come in the December, prices in shops and markets duly rose, and there was widespread recrimination about profiteering.

In the interval between sterling and Belize dollar devaluation, the moment was ripe for the formation of a united front that could claim to speak for the wider community. Established as the People's Committee, it was led by John Smith, a dissenting Legislative Councillor, as chairman, and George Price, a politically active member of the Town Board, as secretary. It seems to have been largely funded by another 'Legco' dissident, R. S. Turton, a successful businessman with US connections who, because of lack of formal education, had never been wholly accepted by the local elite. The immediate issue became Belize dollar devaluation, forced upon the colony against its wishes and despite hollow assurances. The new body's more general rallying cry was national unity against both foreign and domestic exploitation of the working class. As it mobilised the widespread support it attracted, it turned to mass demonstrations, sometimes violent, to promote a campaign for constitutional reform and improved labour conditions. For the first time in British Honduras there was a strong and explicit anti-British sentiment in the air. Comparisons were drawn between US investors and the detested Belize Estate and Produce Company. The notion of a Central American identity was developed further, and there was talk of accommodation with Guatemala. This was anathema to the British government because of strong suspicions that the President there was under Communist influence.

Smith and Price (who was also Turton's secretary) had been careful to include the president of the General Workers Union (GWU), Clifford Betson, in the leadership of the People's Committee. But he was an old-fashioned labour leader who belonged to a very different generation from their own. It came therefore as no surprise when they contrived Betson's replacement by Nicholas Pollard, the younger and more dynamic leader of a newer and smaller union, by the simple device of a merger between that and the GWU. This enabled the People's Committee to make more effective use of the GWU's branch network in the districts as it sought to become a genuinely national movement. That delivered the support of the urban working class throughout the colony. Similarly the rural population, who had never before actively engaged in politics, were attracted by the Committee leadership's strong connection with the Roman Catholic Church, the denomination of the great majority of the mestizo and Garifuna populations and the church with the fewest links with the local elite, the colonial administration, and indeed Britain. At the same time the *Belize Billboard* newspaper, edited by Philip Goldson, evolved as essentially an organ of the People's Committee rather than a sympathetic but independent broadsheet. Finally, though not so successful in interesting the professional element of the elite, the Committee was able to attract the support of most of the merchant class, who dominated the Legislative Council, as a result of the Governor's decision to introduce price controls rather than the wage increases both wanted. The Committee thus at last had the mass political awareness, the wide support, and the solid apparatus it needed to transform itself into British Honduras' first political party.

The formation of the People's United Party and the National Party

There were a number of factors propelling such a metamorphosis of the People's Committee. Foremost perhaps was the imminence in mid-1950 of the Belize Town Board elections, plus the chances that the constitutional deliberations started in 1948 would lead to universal suffrage for the Legislative Council elections due in 1951. Inevitably there were also personality considerations. Some members of the Committee were dissatisfied with the dominance that George Price, always the movement's moving spirit, had built up over the nine months of its life. They therefore favoured an organisation that was more formally constituted than the ad hoc body created in reaction to the devaluation crisis the year before. Others simply wanted an expansion of the leadership and an entity that would have a more permanent character. For all these reasons, the People's Committee was dissolved in September 1950 and reincarnated as the People's United Party (PUP), with Smith as leader, Leigh Richardson (news editor of the *Belize Billboard*) as chairman, Price as secretary and Goldson as the assistant secretary. What had begun as a workers movement was ready for the inauguration of democratic politics in British Honduras, even if that process was to be confined to domestic affairs and subject to the continuing veto, on certain key issues, of the colony's Governor.

The PUP's first success was to win five out of six seats in the November 1950 elections for the Belize City Council as the Town Board had been renamed. But there were in the event no Legislative Council elections in 1951 in which the PUP could show its wider strength. The colonial government decided instead to postpone the poll until the new constitution, already under discussion for three years, was agreed and adopted. The constitutional commission's report was delivered in April 1951, but not approved by the Legislative Council until the following year. It was then another two years before the ratification process had been completed and the necessary preparations laid for elections on an altogether new basis. An undeclared reason why these formalities took so long, and why elections were so long delayed, was that the British authorities both in London and in Belize City were wedded to the idea of a two-party system; and it was only in August 1951 that a second political party, the National Party (NP), emerged to provide voters with an alternative to the PUP. Led by Herbert Fuller, a Legislative Councillor and former member of the Belize Town Board, and with the strong support of the chairman of the constitutional commission, the prominent local lawyer W. H. Courtenay, the NP was seen primarily as the party of the Creole professional and administrative elite. But with the support of the Anglican and Methodist churches, it also proved a home for others who had doubts about both the PUP's strident anti-British line and the personal power of George Price.

The 1954 constitution and elections

The constitution under which the Legislative Council elections were finally held in 1954 offered a major advance in representation, but less towards the PUP's goal of self-government. This was justified in a long section in the commission's report on the benefits that British rule was perceived to have brought to the territory. It also reflected the commissioners' more general concern for stability. As to representation, the elected element of the Legislative Assembly, as the Council was renamed, was indeed to be found by universal adult suffrage, as were, with the exception of the District Commissioners, all members of the District Town Boards that had been established as nominated bodies in 1938. The number of elected members of the Assembly was increased to nine (each to represent a single-seat geographical constituency), to provide a majority against three nominated 'unofficial' and three official members. Consistent with this change, the Executive Council, which had always been an advisory body, became responsible for the conduct of government. The Governor was to chair the Executive Council, but he was obliged both to consult and to act on the advice of the councillors, six out of the nine members of which were to be 'unofficial' Legislative Assemblymen. But only four of those, i.e. an overall minority, were to be elected members; and the Governor in any case retained his reserve powers and his exclusive right to introduce financial measures in the Assembly. Neither of these constraints changed when a 'quasi-ministerial' system was adopted for the Executive Council in January 1955, with three elected 'unofficials' each taking responsibility for a particular portfolio.

In the elections themselves the PUP were able to point to this negative approach to self-government, to identify their National Party opponents with it, and thus to portray them as stooges of the real enemy, the colonial government. The latter had already given the PUP, in the first year of its life, an opening in this sense by dissolving the Belize City Council in a dispute about displaying the King's portrait and by arresting Goldson and Richardson, of the *Belize Billboard*, on charges of sedition. With the wide range of support the PUP had mobilised and retained in both town and country, the poll result in 1954 was, at least with hindsight, a foregone conclusion: with their General Workers Union allies, they swept the board, with 66 per cent of the votes cast and eight of the nine seats up for election. The ninth seat, moreover, went to an independent rather than an NP candidate. All this emboldened Price to maintain the collision course he had already set with the Governor and his officials.

Dissension in the PUP and consolidation of the opposition

Price's refusal to change this stance continued, despite a declared intention on the part of the colonial administration to co-operate with the newly elected PUP representation in view of the support they had mustered in the recent poll. Price's line was one that a number of prominent figures in the party felt unable to follow. John Smith had resigned as early as 1951 on the question of the party's Central American orientation. Cooperation with the Governor then emerged as a public issue in 1955 when Goldson and Richardson, who with Price still formed the party leadership, accepted portfolios of responsibility in the Executive Council, and Price refused to do so. This, and their by now more positive attitude towards relations with the West Indies, led the next year to the resignation from the party of both Goldson and Richardson and ten other senior members. Price, who clearly commanded the support of the rank and file, was able to keep the loyalty of the PUP as a body, but lost control of the General Workers Union. He attempted to finesse that with the formation by his ally Pollard of a rival union linked to the PUP, the Christian Democratic Union. The result was a split labour movement. That split, and the eclipse of labour issues by the larger question of national destiny, had the effect of diminishing the whole place of trades unions in the colony's political life. The split in the PUP's leadership, meanwhile, led within six months to the emergence of a third party, the Honduras Independence Party (HIP) under Goldson and Richardson. Although they were able to secure significantly more of the votes cast in the 1957 general election than the National Party (17.7 per cent as against 12.5 per cent), the further overwhelming PUP victory (59 per cent of votes cast and all nine elected seats in the Assembly) made it clear that there was only room for one opposition party in the newly emancipated British Honduras. The merger in July 1958 of the NP and HIP to form the National Independence Party (NIP) under the leadership of Herbert Fuller was thus a natural progression.

George Price and the colonial administration

Meanwhile George Price, especially after Pollard fell out with him in early 1958, enjoyed almost total control of the PUP. This gave him the power to remain a thorn in the side of the British both publicly and privately. One bone of contention was his continuing, and sometimes clandestine, contact with Guatemala. This was of course in line with his view, endorsed by the electorate, that there was a brighter future for the territory in the Organisation of Central American States (ODECA) – which Guatemala had joined in 1954 – than in the West Indies Federation. Already before the 1957 election the Governor had dismissed him from the Executive Council because of unauthorised discussions about some form of association that he had held with the Guatemalan Minister in London during an official visit there. The following year Price was actually, though unsuccessfully, charged with sedition. None of this seemed to make any difference to his popularity outside the small middle class. Although he remained banned from the Executive Council, and although the defection of two former PUP members put the party in an overall minority in the Legislative Assembly, he was still by far the most formidable politician in the colony. His position was moreover reinforced when he became Mayor of Belize after the City Council elections of November 1958. Labelled a communist, he was nothing of the sort, as his promotion of US investment and his strong ties to the Roman Catholic Church both showed, and as his later opposition to more extreme left-wing organisations such as the Revolitical (sic) Action Movement (RAM) were to confirm. But he was a resolute opponent of the colonial government. His constant demand throughout the 1950s was self-government. It was only after the British government proposed a further step in this direction, and Price realised that in due course he would need the skills of the professional elite still opposed to him, that he began to compromise.

The 1960 constitution and the Guatemala issue

The short-lived 1960 constitution was the work of Sir Hilary Blood. He was specifically invited to address the question of self-government, now favoured in principle by both established political parties. In the event he came down against more than a modest move towards it. He argued that the combination of the weakness of the second political party, the shortage of trained manpower, and the complications of grant-in-aid status and the Guatemalan claim counted decisively against further movement at that stage. What emerged from a constitutional conference to consider his proposals was principally an expansion of both the legislature and the system of portfolios of responsibility in the executive: a Legislative Assembly, with a life of four rather than three years, enlarged to eighteen elected, five nominated, but only two 'ex-officio' members; and an Executive Council still chaired by the Governor but with, besides the same two 'officials', six unofficial members each with a 'ministerial' brief. But where a temporary united front between the PUP and the NIP persuaded the Colonial Office to go further than Blood was in that five of these ministers were to be elected by the Assembly and the sixth, the leader of the largest party there, appointed as First Minister. Moreover one of them was to be a Finance Minister, replacing the Financial Secretary. This left only the Chief Secretary and the Attorney General as 'official' members in both the Assembly and the Council.

Sir Hilary Blood's assessment of the weakness of the second political party was borne out in the polls that followed agreement on the new constitution. The three-year-old National Independence Party, under the influence of a number of former PUP members and as its name implied, purported to be a nationalist party, aiming at independence for British Honduras. But this was to be within the Commonwealth rather than in a Central American framework. Such, however, was its credibility at that stage that it failed to secure a single seat in the 1961 election, leaving the PUP to net 63.5 per cent of the votes cast in an 80 per cent turnout of voters. Thereafter the NIP, now under the leadership of Philip Goldson, decided to distinguish itself from its opponents on one main issue, the Guatemalan claim. For years to come it would cast the PUP in the light of a party that was soft on the territorial ambitions regularly voiced in Guatemala City. But if some of the PUP's statements fed this characterisation, the NIP was as vulnerable in another sense. For the argument that there could be no compromise with Guatemala implied a corollary: independence could only come when the security of a British defence presence was no longer needed, that is with a lifting of the Guatemalan threat. That in turn enabled the PUP just as consistently to label their opponents as playing into the hands of the colonial power. The electorate thus separated into two fundamentally divided camps. The net disadvantage lay with the NIP, because their focus on Guatemala was at the expense of attention to social and economic issues, which Price linked to independence. But their strongly articulated opposition to the PUP rendered a service to the society in the longer run by nurturing the tradition of a two-party system in an era when one-party states had a considerable appeal to leaders of countries emerging from colonial tutelage.

Full internal self-government

Meanwhile British Honduras was approaching yet another, and more decisive, constitutional conference. The British government had accepted that the territory should proceed in stages to independence. This was a consequence of Prime Minister Harold Macmillan's 'Wind of Change' speech on colonial policy in Africa 1960 and, for the Caribbean, the collapse of the West Indies Federation (which Price had succeeded in keeping British Honduras out of) the following year. The next step was to be full internal self-government. It was decided in 1963 to bring this forward on the basis of proposals formulated by the PUP. As already indicated, the relationship between that party and the colonial government was now, in broad terms, one of co-operation rather than antagonism. The principle of independence was no longer an issue; the Governor had come to accept the overwhelming support enjoyed by the PUP; PUP Ministers had taken on substantive administrative responsibilities including reconstruction after Hurricane Hattie; and their attempt to replace the British economic link with US investment and development aid had proved disappointing. It was rather the opposition party, the NIP, which now questioned the imperial government's plans. Marginalised as they were, with only a single nominated member in the Assembly, they had to accept minimal representation at the conference and, with the increased powers likely to be given to PUP ministers, the prospect of even less influence thereafter.

What came out of the conference of July 1963 was a further-reaching restructuring of government than had been seen before. The legislature, with a term increased to five years, became a bicameral body renamed the National Assembly. It comprised a nominated Senate, with only one of eight members selected independently of the political parties, and a wholly elected eighteen-strong House of Representatives. There were thus to be no officials involved in legislation. By the time of the elections implementing these provisions, the concomitant changes to the executive arm of government had already been made. The post of Chief Secretary had been abolished, and the Governor's Executive Council replaced, in January 1964, by a cabinet of ministers. The Cabinet was drawn from the legislature on the advice of the leader of the majority party, who held the title of Premier. With the March 1965 elections this was to be, once again, George Price. But the NIP, thanks to a merger with the smaller Christian Democratic Party that had been formed by Nicholas Pollard, improved their ranking more than expected, with a 40 per cent share of votes cast. Although that translated into only two seats in the House of Representatives, it marked the beginning of the slow emergence of a substantive elected opposition.

Meanwhile, although the Governor was obliged to follow the advice of the Premier in almost all matters of day-to day internal administration, he retained residual responsibilities that were in certain circumstances crucial: external relations, defence, internal security, terms of service of public officers, and for so long as the British government's grant-in-aid continued, financial stability. This did not pass un-noticed by the more radical elements in the governing party. But in constitutional terms, British Honduras had nonetheless come a long way in the decade from 1954; it was generally accepted that this three-stage advance, driven largely by the PUP's mass mobilisation of support first on the streets then through the ballot box, had completed the political preparation for the final step to full independence at a time to be agreed. With the ending in 1966, for the second and last time, of British Treasury control of the public finances, the remaining obstacle was relations with Guatemala.

Sources

C. H. Grant, *The Making of Modern Belize*, Cambridge (1976).
Assad Shoman, *Thirteen Chapters of the History of Belize*, Belize (1994).
Assad Shoman, *Party Politics in Belize 1950-86*, Belize (1987).
O. N. Bolland, *Colonialism and Resistance in Belize*, Belize (1988).
D. A. G. Waddell, *British Honduras: a Contemporary and Historical Survey*, London (1961).

15

The Dispute with Guatemala in the Twentieth Century

Contacts and proposals in the 1920s and 1930s

Following the abortive correspondence with the Guatemalans in the late 1890s about possible railway construction, the loose ends left by the 1859 and 1863 Conventions were ignored until the 1920s. They were taken up again in correspondence which opened at the end of 1924. The eventual result was the appointment in 1929 of joint commissioners to inspect and replace the markers established in 1860 at Gracios a Dios Falls on the River Sarstoon and at Garbutt's Falls on the Belize River. The new markers were accepted by both governments in notes exchanged in August 1931.[1] Although British attempts to gain Guatemalan agreement to a joint survey of the line between the two then failed, Guatemalan officials later concurred in the results of a unilateral British survey in 1933.[2]

This agreement was followed by further correspondence in 1933, 1934 and 1935 about border cooperation. The Guatemalans took the opportunity to resurrect the question of how the British were going to implement Article 7 of the 1859 Convention, or, more specifically, the provision for establishing 'the easiest communication' between Guatemala City and the British Honduras coastline. The British rejected a suggestion that they should pay a proportion of the cost of the railway completed in 1908 from Guatemala City to Puerto Barrios.[3] These exchanges then culminated in September 1936 in three proposals by the Guatemalan government for the British government to choose from: the 'return' to Guatemala of the whole territory in exchange for a payment of £400,000; or payment by the British government of the sum of £400,000 and cession to Guatemala of a strip of land on the parallel 16 08 39, close to Punta Gorda, to provide an access to the sea; or payment by the British government of the sum of £50,000 plus 4 per cent interest since 1859, and redrawing of the southern boundary of British Honduras at the same latitude for the same purpose. When none of these ideas proved acceptable to the British side, the Guatemalan government proposed, and the British government agreed in August 1937, that the matter should be referred to international arbitration. But the two sides could not agree on who the arbiter should be, the Guatemalans proposing the US President, the British the International Court of Justice at the Hague.[4]

Inclusion of the claim in Guatemala's constitution

In the next round of correspondence (in 1940, about the terms of reference for any arbitral body), Guatemala decided to drop her eighty-year pursuit of 'compensation' for provisional agreement to the relinquishment of sovereignty, and instead to re-assert her outright claim to the whole territory on the basis that the recent impasse rendered the 1859 Convention null and void.[5] This was formalised in 1945 by inclusion of the claim in the new national constitution adopted by her Congress that year.[6] When contacts were resumed in 1946, Britain was still willing to submit the dispute to the International Court of Justice. But because the two sides were unable to agree a basis, as between equity and law, for any decision by the Court, negotiations broke down once again in 1947.[7] By the next year, public expression of the territorial claim by Guatemalan government sources was sufficiently strong for the British government to take steps for the defence of the colony, with the dispatch of a company of infantry from Jamaica and a warship from its base in Bermuda. In the event there was no move by the Guatemalans to resort to force. But the dispute continued to simmer, with, at one stage, a closing of the border; and the small British military presence in British Honduras became a permanent feature. Further rhetorical pressure was applied by the Guatemalans in 1955 when yet another constitutional text declared that the 'effective incorporation of the territory' was a 'matter of national interest'.[8]

Resumption of negotiations

Although there were diplomatic exchanges in 1948–9 arising from the events then, there were no meetings to discuss the dispute for a further fifteen years after 1947. For the British, this was partly because of the suspected Communist orientation of the Guatemalan Presidency until 1954, and partly because from 1958 a new Guatemalan President set aside pressure for legal determination of the case in favour of indirect threats of 'reincorporation' by force.[9] But with British Honduras heading by the early 1960s towards internal self-government and every indication that full independence would follow in due course, the mood in Guatemala had become increasingly hostile just when a solution became the more necessary. There had been an armed incursion by Guatemalan civilians in southern British Honduras, and references by the President of Guatemala to the creation of a 'fifth column' there.[10] When the two sides met in Puerto Rico in April 1962, the British therefore sought to defuse the tension by agreeing that the Economic Council for Latin America (ECLA) should be asked to implement a 1961 resolution to explore the possibility of closer economic cooperation between British Honduras and her neighbour with a view to her joining the Central American Cooperation Committee.[11] But beyond that there was little meeting of minds, and what had been agreed became a holding arrangement. When a scheme of internal self-government for British Honduras was announced in 1963, the Guatemalan government protested by reducing its formal relations with Britain to consular level. This did not prevent further talks in the summer of 1965, but there was no progress. The stalemate led in November of that year to the appointment of a US mediator to see what might be done.

US mediation and the ECLA report

The mediator, a US constitutional lawyer named Bethuel Webster, was appointed to look into political possibilities. He took his time to report, as did the ECLA committee tasked to consider economic cooperation. Both published their conclusions in 1968, and both reports were, in different ways, disappointing. The ECLA simply announced that British Honduras was too small and too undeveloped to benefit from membership of the Central American Common Market, and would do better to maintain existing Commonwealth preferences and to develop closer economic relations with Commonwealth Caribbean states of more comparable size.[12] Webster came up with a solution for a political relationship with neighbouring states, but it was conspicuously biased in favour of Guatemala. Under these proposals, British Honduras would become a sovereign state by 1970; but that sovereignty would be limited by the provisions that Guatemala handle relations with international bodies and that internal security and external defence be subject to consultation via a Belize–Guatemala Joint Authority.[13] The economic report was generally accepted in the colony and led to a broader enthusiasm for the Commonwealth which has persisted ever since. The Webster report, on the other hand, was widely and strongly opposed, and, to the extent that the US and UK governments were identified with it, seen as a betrayal by both.

Guatemalan threats and the international reaction

Partly because the governing People's United Party (PUP) had hesitated before denouncing the Webster proposals, a consensus within British Honduras on conditions for independence now became even more elusive. While the opposition National Independence Party (NIP) continued to oppose independence before a settlement with Guatemala, the PUP argued that British Honduras should proceed to independence as soon as possible subject only to adequate external defence arrangements. The need for such arrangements was borne out as a result of the next round of meetings in 1971–2. After initial progress towards a draft treaty of recognition and a declaration by George Price that independence could be achieved in short order, the talks stalled. This time the Guatemalan reaction was to draw up plans to occupy British Honduras by force, plans that were only forestalled by a large-scale reinforcement of the British garrison with both infantry and supporting aircraft.[14]

Because Webster seemed only to have encouraged Guatemalan intransigence, defence indeed became the key issue with both political parties. With Britain unwilling to retain responsibility in the event of independence, George Price began to search for a multilateral solution. Thus in 1972 he put forward a proposal for a joint guarantee by Britain, the US, Canada and Mexico; and at the Commonwealth Heads of Government meeting the following year there was a move for Barbados, Jamaica, Guyana and the Bahamas to join British Honduras in a Mutual Defence Scheme.[15]

For various reasons these ideas came to nothing. But Price, supported by the British government, was considerably more successful in drumming up diplomatic support. The Mutual Defence Scheme had followed strong criticism of Guatemala in the UN Security Council by the four Caribbean potential partners. From 1975, the UN General Assembly approved with increasing majorities motions every year that called for recognition of the right of Belize (as British Honduras was now called) to self-determination, independence and territorial integrity.[16] Similarly by 1977 the Commonwealth Heads of Government meeting was affirming 'full support for the legitimate aspirations of the people of Belize for early and secure independence on the basis of territorial integrity'. In 1979 the meeting of non-aligned states in Havana went further, reiterating its 'unconditional support for the Belize people's inalienable right to self-determination, independence, and territorial integrity', and condemning 'all pressure or threats to prevent the full exercise of that right'. That same year the annual UN General Assembly resolution was carried, in the absence of a Guatemalan vote, by 134 to 0, with only 8 abstentions.[17]

Further negotiations

Meanwhile there had been a resumption of talks between the parties concerned. In 1975 exchanges took place over a period of eight months. They finally broke down when Guatemala declared that there could be no settlement unless it included the cession of a substantial area of Belizean territory. It was at that point that Britain and Belize referred matters, most successfully from their point of view, to the United Nations. That in turn led to further negotiations the following year, with Britain offering a treaty providing for maritime concessions to give Guatemala guaranteed access to the Caribbean, plus British help with the funding of cross-border development. Those talks too broke down in July 1977 over Guatemalan insistence on the cession of land territory. Once again, too, Guatemala threatened to invade Belize, prompting a meeting of heads of government of six regional states that called the following month for a peaceful settlement of the dispute in accordance with the principles of territorial integrity and self-determination. That autumn discussions between British officials and Belizean Ministers confirmed that there was no willingness in Belize to contemplate even minor adjustments of the land border.[18]

A depressingly similar pattern of events followed in 1978. The British Foreign Secretary proposed to his Guatemalan counterpart a quick settlement based on a modern equivalent of the road project envisaged in 1859, plus, as before, an adjustment of the maritime boundary to provide Guatemala with guaranteed access to the Caribbean. The Guatemalan response was to restate the claim to the whole territory, although this was tempered with an expression of willingness to continue negotiations.[19] But the climate was not right for meetings in 1979, and two brief contacts in 1980 were unproductive. It was only in the autumn of that year that a further significant impetus was given to the process by a UN resolution calling on Britain to convene a constitutional conference to bring Belize to independence by the end of 1981.[20]

Independence and the Guatemalan reaction

At the end of 1980 the British government duly announced their intention of calling such a conference and their wish meanwhile to secure a negotiated settlement of the dispute with Guatemala.[21] Early the following year the two processes were initiated on parallel tracks. As a result of talks with the Guatemalans begun in February 1981, heads of agreement were concluded by ministerial representatives the following month as a basis for resolution of the territorial dispute; and as a result of a constitutional conference which opened in April, the Belize Independence Order was laid before the British Parliament in August. But whereas Belize proceeded to independence on 21 September 1981, and was welcomed into the United Nations, the Commonwealth, and the Non-Aligned Movement immediately afterwards, the heads of agreement failed to translate into a definitive treaty of settlement between Belize and Guatemala. Consequently the Guatemalan claim remained to bedevil relations between a now independent Belize and the neighbour with which she shares her longest land border.

The British thus found themselves in an uncomfortable position. Having assumed that the March 1981 heads of agreement would lead to a settlement with Guatemala within the UN timetable for Belizean independence, they found themselves expected to continue to guarantee the external defence of a territory that was now fully independent. To indicate that this should not be regarded as a permanent commitment, the British government resorted to the formula that their troops would remain 'for as long as is appropriate'.[22] Plans were laid for the garrison to leave during 1984, but when these leaked to the press the British government stated that it had 'set no specific date' for withdrawal.[23] In the event, because no significant progress was made in resolving the dispute with Guatemala, a sizable British force, centred on a battalion of infantry but including also supporting light armour and artillery and four Harrier ground-attack aircraft, remained in Belize for another ten years. The only change to defence arrangements during that period was a limited 'multilateralisation' by means of a consultative agreement with a number of other Commonwealth Caribbean states.[24]

What had unstitched the March 1981 heads of agreement between Britain and Guatemala was interpretation of what to the Guatemalans, for symbolic reasons, was the most important provision in the text. The main substantive clauses of that document provided for recognition of Belize as an independent state by Guatemala; the grant to Guatemala of 'such territorial seas as shall ensure permanent and unimpeded access to the high seas, together with rights over the seabed thereunder'; completion of a road from Punta Gorda to the Guatemalan frontier; and joint seabed and continental shelf exploitation in areas to be agreed. But there was a further provision which would enable the Guatemalans to point to some, albeit minimal, land territorial gain: 'the use and enjoyment' of the Ranguana and Sapodilla Cays at the southernmost end of the Belize barrier reef. That concession caused a strong reaction in Belize. There were demonstrations, and even strikes, and the opposition United Democratic Party (UDP) demanded a referendum.[25] All this caused Premier George Price to proceed cautiously in the talks that followed up the March accord. These took place in New York at official level in May and at ministerial level in July. Price, as had been normal since 1962, attended both, technically (because Belize was still not independent) as an observer. But the Guatemalans could not meet his insistence on a narrow interpretation of the 'use and enjoyment' provisions relating to the southern cays.[26] With the subsequent collapse of the negotiations, the process of development of the outline agreement thus failed to reach the stage of the referendum demanded by the UDP; and a further demand in July by the UDP for a referendum on independence, which they opposed, was refused.

The Guatemalan reaction to the granting of independence to Belize was to break off the consular relations to which she had reduced her formal links with Britain in 1963 and to close the frontier.[27] There was then no prospect of further talks until after the Presidential elections due in March 1982, elections that were then annulled with a military coup by a junta led by General Rios Montt. In July of that year he denounced the March 1981 heads of agreement and asserted Guatemala's non-acceptance of Belize's independence; but declared an intention to seek a solution to the dispute 'by means recognised by international law'.[28] Following expressions by all three sides of interest in a negotiated solution, talks were resumed in October 1982. But matters were complicated by a public declaration by President Rios Mont in January 1983 that, although Guatemala no longer claimed the whole of Belize, she aimed at the cession of the southern district of Toledo.[29] The position of the government of Belize, restated, also publicly, the same month, remained that while they were willing to discuss revision in Guatemala's favour of the maritime boundary together with proposals for a joint development zone on the southern land border, they would not contemplate any cession of land territory. The incompatibility of these two standpoints prevented progress in talks held between officials in New York later the same month. But tension was eased by an assurance by the Guatemalan Foreign Minister that his government had no plans to resort to force.[30]

Talks resumed once again

Despite reports that the US government was considering trying to broker a deal,[31] there were no further meetings for another eighteen months. When talks were resumed in July 1984, again in New York and focusing on 'border relations',[32] they were unproductive. The next round of discussions, in February 1985, was then bedevilled by the question of the status of the participants other than Guatemala, up to then formally glossed over. The Guatemalans, because they still refused to recognise

Belizean independence, insisted they were negotiating with the British delegation; whereas the Belizeans, with British concurrence, were adamant that the United Kingdom representatives were there as observers.[33] This did not stop the talks going ahead. But that there was no meeting of minds was confirmed by a Guatemalan spokesman's public statement that acknowledgement of Belizean independence was conditional on agreement to Guatemalan access to the sea through the (Belizean) southern district of Toledo.[34] The only further moves on the Guatemalan side during 1985 was a statement in December of that year by the newly elected civilian president, Vinicio Cerezo, that he would try to reach an honourable agreement based on 'guarantees for ... an outlet to the sea'.[35]

The climate continued to improve in 1986, with a Guatemalan announcement of resumption of consular relations in August, and an affirmation by President Cerezo in October that he intended to negotiate directly with the government of Belize.[36] This was followed in December by resumption for the first time for twenty-three years of full diplomatic relations with Britain, and then a meeting in Miami between the President and the British Foreign Office Minister of State Baroness Young.[37] At the first round of talks in April 1987, however, with the Guatemalan Foreign Minister Quinones still insisting that he was negotiating with the British official sent as an observer rather than with Belize Foreign Minister Dean Barrow, no progress was made. Although it was agreed that further meetings should be held in due course,[38] exchanges remained bogged down on the question of land cession.[39]

Things looked up in May 1988 with agreement by the Guatemalan and Belizean governments to set up a Permanent Joint Commission to prepare a comprehensive draft treaty, with participation also by Britain. As a result of five meetings over the next year, informal agreement was reached that the existing land and river boundaries of Belize should stand, that the southern sea boundary should be modified to allow Guatemala access to the Caribbean, and that some joint (offshore) development projects should be undertaken in the Belizean Exclusive Economic Zone (EEZ). This was endorsed by President Cerezo and Premier George Price, again informally, at a meeting in Honduras in July 1990.[40] Although work, including treaty drafting, continued in the next few months, formalisation of that agreement was delayed by the Presidential elections in Guatemala at the end of the year.[41]

Apparent breakthrough

The 1989 understanding was developed into the text of an outline agreement soon after the inauguration of President Jorge Serrano in January

1991.[42] By August that year matters had advanced enough for the President to announce recognition of the right of the Belizean people to self-determination; and for the government of Belize, in response, to introduce into the National Assembly a Bill which postponed definition of Belizean territorial waters off the southern cays beyond three miles, giving scope for negotiation of the details of the maritime access provision in the outline agreement.[43] This diplomatic minuet continued the next month, when the British government announced a pledge of £22.5 million towards a joint project to improve road communication between the two countries;[44] when Serrano announced that in view of the guaranteed sea access offered Guatemala by the Belizean legislation, his government was willing to continue direct discussion with 'the independent state of Belize' to arrive at a definitive solution to the dispute; and six days later, when Belize and Guatemala, on 11 September 1991, announced the establishment of diplomatic relations.[45]

All this was of course a highly significant breakthrough for Belize after so many years of antagonism. But that it was not the end of the road was confirmed less than a week later at the conclusion of a visit to Guatemala City by Foreign Minister Said Musa, the first by the holder of any political office in independent Belize. A joint declaration issued by Musa and his Guatemalan counterpart Alvaro Arzu referred to the 'intention of resolving the dispute which still exists between the two states' and announced the establishment to that end of bilateral commissions to 'search for' agreements on, besides joint exploitation of the Belize EEZ, cooperation in the fields of education, tourism and trade. The reference to the continuation of the dispute reflected uncertainty in Guatemala. But there were complications in Belize too which added to that uncertainty. Although the Maritime Areas Bill was enacted in January 1992, it had been amended since its introduction to make Guatemalan rights in Belize's southern territorial waters contingent on the successful conclusion of an overall settlement to be approved in a national referendum.[46] This provision was confirmed to the international community by Musa in a statement to the UN General Assembly on 3 April 1992.[47]

Meanwhile in Guatemala conservative elements had appealed to the country's Constitutional Court for a ruling on the constitutionality of the President's decision to recognise Belize as an independent state and to appoint an ambassador there. In November 1992 the court found in the President's favour on the basis that circumstances had changed with Belizean independence; and his decisions were endorsed the same month by the National Congress.[48] Moreover when President Serrano was replaced after a constitutional crisis in June 1993 by Ramiro de Leon Carpio, the new government, despite Carpio's known doubts, publicly confirmed its recognition of Belize as an independent state and undertook to negotiate a definitive solution to the territorial dispute. This was restated in writing by a Foreign Ministry note.[49] The steady pattern of positive development prompted the British government to announce in June 1993 that the British garrison, responsible for the defence of Belize, would begin withdrawing on 1 January 1994; and then led to an agreement between Britain and Belize in September 1993 that the British would maintain both a much reduced military training presence of their own and their programme of assistance to the local force.[50]

Regression and stalemate

The initial breakthrough that had come in 1988, with the establishment of the joint commission, had been achieved on the Belize side, with the full agreement of the opposition party, by the United Democratic Party (UDP) government that had for the very first time defeated George Price's People's United Party (PUP) in 1984. But substantive agreement in 1991 on recognition and diplomatic relations had been the work of the PUP government that returned in 1989. It was UDP elements in the Assembly that then insisted on inserting reservations into the Maritime Areas Bill before it was enacted in early 1992. Guatemalan suspicions were further aroused by the tone of the UDP campaign in the early election called for tactical reasons by the PUP in June 1993, when there were accusations of a sell-out to Guatemala. With an unexpected UDP victory coinciding with the eruption of severe political unrest in Guatemala, it was perhaps inevitable that relations between the two countries would lose the stability that seemed so recently to have been achieved. This was put to the test in February 1994, when a group of trespassing Guatemalan squatters were ordered to leave what the Belizean authorities regarded as their territory.[51] The upshot was not long delayed. A strong letter the following month from the Guatemalan Foreign Minister Gladys de Vielman to the UN Secretary General rejected the Belizean territorial sea claim on which the proposed maritime concessions were based, and referred also to an undefined land area as occupied by Belize.[52]

This regression led to a long stand-off, with joint commission meetings replaced by occasional 'technical talks'. From Guatemala meanwhile there were mixed signals. While the Vice President at one stage, following allegations of a Belizean incursion, said he did not rule out armed conflict,[53] the Foreign Minister the same month assured the UN General Assembly that his government believed in peaceful resolution of disputes. There were moments of optimism in Belize, as when in November 1997

Guatemalan officials asserted that neither in bilateral negotiations nor in any reference to an international court would their government be seeking land cession in its claim for the compensation provided for in the 1859 agreement. But two years later, in October 1999, the dispute reverted to a much earlier phase and reopened much more fundamental principles. In a letter, again to the UN Secretary General, the Guatemalan government made clear, no longer resting its case on the 1859 Convention, that it sought, instead of the compensation envisaged there, the cession of all land not ceded to Britain in her eighteenth-century treaties with Spain, that is to say all land south of the River Sibun. The same letter reverted also to the case that, because the claim was of an 'eminently juridical nature', it should be referred to either international arbitration or the International Court of Justice.[54]

Guatemalan incursions and OAS 'facilitation'

That the fundamental nature and robust terms of this new position should reverberate in events on the ground was as likely as before. Border incidents duly followed, this time involving members of the Guatemalan Armed Forces. Four times during the first half of 2000 there were armed incursions. The prospect of escalation then prompted the Organisation of American States (OAS) to act. At the suggestion of the Belizean government, the OAS appointed in May of that year, with Guatemalan agreement, two 'facilitators' to 'assist the governments of Guatemala and Belize to find formulae for a peaceful and definitive resolution of the territorial differendum between the two countries'. Working under the sponsorship of the OAS Secretary General (who acted as 'witness of honour'), the persons nominated were Paul Reichler, an eminent US constitutional lawyer, and Sir Sridath (Sonny) Ramphal, former Secretary General to the Commonwealth. The former was endorsed by the Guatemalan government, the latter by the government of Belize.[55]

The facilitators' proposals and their reception

The task of the facilitators was complex, and, like the US mediator of the 1960s, they took their time to consider the arguments, made in robust terms, of each side. They may have been influenced by a legal opinion from a panel of four eminent international jurists commissioned by the Belizean side, which concluded that 'even if the 1859 Convention could lawfully have been terminated by Guatemala, this would not have re-established any Guatemalan claim to the territory of Belize'.[56] The facilitators' report was finally presented in August 2002. The recommendations were very close to the position Belize had maintained since first offering a settlement based on restriction of her territorial sea claim. The land boundary was to be as provisionally agreed in 1859: the mid-channel line of the River Sarstoon in the south as far as Gracios a Dios Falls; from there northwards to Garbutt's Falls on the Belize River; and from there due north to the Mexican border. The only change on the ground was a proposed move about 200 metres eastwards of the marker placed (by the Mexicans and Guatemalans in 1938) at that last point of intersection, Aguas Turbias, so that the line from Garbutt's Falls bore due north more accurately.[57] As to a maritime arrangement, the facilitators simply prescribed a width, four miles, for the much-discussed access channel for Guatemala. This would lie two miles either side of the boundary between Belizean and Honduran territorial waters. The only substantial new proposal was that Belize and Honduras should negotiate with Guatemala, a 'geographically disadvantaged state' in terms of the UN Law of the Sea Convention, a reduction in their Exclusive Economic Zones. This was in order to provide Guatemala with a 2000 square mile EEZ of her own, in which, however, seabed resources should be developed jointly. Finally the facilitators recommended the establishment of a Development Trust Fund, administered by the Inter-American Development Bank, for subscription by the international community including international financial institutions and 'to be devoted to development purposes in both countries'.[58]

The Belizean government has actively supported these proposals, and such opposition as there has been in Belize has not been sustained. But while the Guatemalan government has yet to make its public position clear, the press in Guatemala came out strongly against them. Criticism of his contribution to the facilitation process (and of his neglect of other affairs) then led to the resignation of the Guatemalan Foreign Minister at the end of 2002. The next step envisaged by the facilitators is for this package of proposals to be put to the peoples of the two countries in referenda. In present circumstances it must be uncertain when those will take place. With elections due in both countries, it was unlikely to be in 2003. But assuming that referenda are in due course held, and if the results are positive, the two governments will proceed, again under OAS supervision, to the negotiation of detailed treaty texts. Meanwhile official contacts are limited to the subject of confidence-building measures to manage practical arrangements for communities that straddle the border and other cross-border cooperation. These were agreed in a 'transitional agreement' in early 2003.

Notes

1. Gordon Ireland, *Boundaries, Possessions, and Conflicts in Central and North America and the Caribbean*, Cambridge, Mass. (1941), 126.
2. Narda Dobson, *A History of Belize*, London (1973), 235.
3. ibid.
4. Ireland, 127.
5. Sir E. Lauterpacht *et al.*, *Legal Opinion on Guatemala's Territorial Claim to Belize*, Belize (2002), 52–4.
6. FCO Background Brief, Belize and the British Presence (December 1993), 2.
7. FCO Memorandum on Belize for the House of Commons Select Committee on Foreign Affairs, 27 October 1980.
8. ibid.
9. D. A. G. Waddell, *British Honduras: a Historical and Contemporary Survey*, London (1961), 130.
10. C. H. Grant, *The Making of Modern Belize*, Cambridge (1976), 240–1.
11. ibid., 239–40.
12. ibid., 232 and 314–5.
13. ibid., 258.
14. Assad Shoman, *Thirteen Chapters of the History of Belize*, Belize (1994), 221.
15. Grant, 321–2.
16. FCO Background Briefs, Belize: the Need for Independence (July 1980), 1 and Belize and the Dispute with Guatemala (February 1983), 3.
17. UNGA A/C4/34/L14 of 31 October 1979.
18. FCO Background Brief, Belize and the Dispute with Guatemala (February 1983), Appendix A.
19. FCO Background Brief, Belize: the Need for Independence (July 1980), 1–2.
20. FCO Background Brief, Belize and the Dispute with Guatemala (February 1983), 3. The resolution, UNGA 35/20 of 11 November 1980, also reaffirmed, by a majority of 139 to 1 (Guatemala) with only 8 abstentions, Belize's right to self-determination, independence, and territorial integrity.
21. Reply dated 2 December 1980 by Sir Ian Gilmour, Lord Privy Seal, to a written Parliamentary Question.
22. See for example the London *Times* (21 September 1982).
23. *Financial Times* (8 October 1983).
24. FCO Background Brief, Belize and the British Presence (December 1993), 3.
25. London *Guardian* (10 April 1981) and *Daily Telegraph* (11 April 1981).
26. FCO Background Brief, Belize and the Dispute with Guatemala (February 1983), Appendix A.
27. ibid, appendix a.
28. ibid, 1.
29. London *Times* (14 January 1983).
30. London *Guardian* (27 January 1983).
31. London *Times* (4 October 1983).
32. Belize Government Press Release 10 July 1984.
33. Summary of World Broadcasts, BBC Monitoring, 24 and 28 January 1985.
34. Summary of World Broadcasts, BBC Monitoring, 26 February 1985.
35. London *Daily Telegraph* (19 December 1985).
36. London *Times* (2 August 1986) and London *Independent* (16 October 1986).
37. London *Times* (30 December 1986).
38. Belize Government Press Release 5 May 1987.
39. Latin American Regional Report, Caribbean, RC 87–05 of 18 June 1987.
40. Government of Belize, Belize-Guatemala Relations (www.belize-guatemala.gov.bz/, 30 October 2002), 6; and *Financial Times* (11 July 1990).

41. FCO Background Brief, Belize and the British Presence, December 1993, 3.
42. Hansard , 17 March 1991, reporting a Parliamentary statement by Foreign Office Minister of State Nicholas Ridley.
43. Belize Government Press Releases 16 and 19 August 1991
44 FCO Background Brief, Belize and the British Presence, December 1993, 1.
45. London *Daily Telegraph* (12 September 1991).
46. FCO Background Brief, Belize and the British Presence, December 1993, 4.
47. UNGA A/47/173/S23837 of 29 April 1992.
48. London *Independent* (12 November 1992), *Central American Report* (13 November 1992) and *Financial Times* (27 November 1992).
49. Summary of World Broadcasts, BBC Monitoring, 30 June 1993. Two months later however President Carpio appeared to qualify his assertion by stating that recognition was 'for the time being' – see SWB 10 August 1993.
50. FCO Background Brief, Belize and the British Presence, December 1993, 4.
51. Belize High Commission London aide memoire 21 March 1994.
52. UNGA A/49/94.
53. Summary of World Broadcasts, BBC Monitoring, 14 September 1995.
54. Government of Belize, *Belize-Guatemala Relations*, (October 2002), 3, 7, and 11.
55. *Belize-Guatemala Territorial Differendum: Proposals from the Facilitators*, (OAS September 2002), 1.
56. Lauterpacht *et al.*, 67.
57. Government of Belize, *Ending the Claim: What the Facilitators Propose* (September 2002), 3.
58. *Belize-Guatemala Territorial Differendum*, 13.

16

The Nation State at the beginning of the Twenty-first Century

By the time the 2002 proposals for a settlement with Guatemala were put forward by the facilitators, Belize had been self-governing for thirty-eight years and fully independent for twenty-one. Over that period there had been a considerable evolution in the country's political and economic life. The political force opposed to the People's United Party had matured from a divided faction into a fully fledged and cohesive alternative party with two terms of office behind it. Economic diversification, achieved substantively in the 1960s with the establishment of serious sugar and citrus export industries, had evolved considerably with further growth of citrus, re-establishment of a major export trade in bananas (this time to Europe), development of a significant lobster fishery and aquaculture, and the opening up of the country to tourism.

Political life

In the 1965 general election that followed self-government, the opposition National Independence Party (NIP), the product of a merger between two earlier movements, for the first time won two seats in the National Assembly. Its narrow focus on the dispute with Guatemala, however, diminished its appeal to younger members. That, combined with the rise of two left-wing movements which coalesced into the Revolutionary Action Movement (RAM), prompted a challenge to Philip Goldson's leadership of the NIP by Dean Lindo, a younger Creole lawyer. He believed that the party needed a broader platform, with more attention towards social and economic affairs. When he was defeated in his bid to oust Goldson, Lindo formed a rival right-wing party, the People's Democratic Movement (PDM). The PDM did fight the next election, in 1969, in alliance with the NIP, but when the only seat won by this combined opposition went to the NIP, the alliance came to an end.[1] The two parties came together again, with further support from the newly formed (and business-based) Liberal Party, to contest the 1974 election. When that alliance then succeeded in securing six out of the eighteen seats in the House of Representatives (and 38 per cent of the vote), they formalised their unification, re-styling themselves the United Democratic Party, and elected Lindo as their leader.[2] This was the party that went on to win 47 per cent of the vote in the 1979 election and, under the leadership of Manuel Esquivel, to win the election itself, and to form a government for the first time, in 1984.[3]

Radical politics, meanwhile, which had emerged with the formation of the United Black Association for Development (UBAD) and the People's Action Committee (PAC) in early 1969 and their subsequent merger as RAM, had subsided after a life of not much more than a year. Their platform, formulated by graduates returning from overseas, had been opposition to 'North Atlantic' cultural and economic domination. RAM's influence had been largely, though not entirely, limited to Belize City. They chose to boycott the 1969 elections. Failure to prosper thereafter was partly because the political and cultural agendas could not be made to mesh as well as hoped, partly because the two of the three leaders who were more interested in electoral politics, Said Musa and Assad Shoman, resigned and in due course joined the People's United Party (PUP).[4] With the decision of the third leader, Evan Hyde, to avoid involvement in elections after an unsuccessful attempt in 1974, the political life of Belize settled into a two-party affair, with three further changes of government (in 1989, 1993 and 1998) after the 1984 election. The emergence of independent candidates in the 2003 election suggests that the two-party pattern could possibly change in the future. Meanwhile the tradition of a vigorous local press, including the radical newspaper *Amandala*, continues.

The substance of the political structure adopted in 1964 remains in place, although the British Governor has been replaced by a Belizean Governor General, who acts for the Queen as Queen of Belize; and the House of Representatives has expanded to twenty-nine seats and the senate to twelve. The government, too, has grown, with no less than twenty departments headed by ministers. Resident foreign government representation has also increased steadily, with Britain, the United States, Mexico, Taiwan, Cuba, all the Central American countries, and Columbia and Venezuela maintaining embassies. These represent all of Belize's neighbours plus her two major trading partners and a significant source of investment.

The economy in the 1970s and 80s

In the same thirty-year period the economy also continued to grow and to diversify. Timber exports on anything like the traditional scale came to an end in the 1970s, and the Belize Estate and Produce Company's land was eventually sold to a local businessman (who has focused on conservation), Coca Cola (who donated their share to an environmental organisation), and a US company (who have continued hardwood logging to meet local demand). Despite the demise of mahogany exports, overall economic growth in the 1970s averaged about 5 per cent.[5] This was largely due to the buoyant prices fetched on the international market by the sugar industry, which, with production increased by 1978 to 110,000 tons,[6] remained the largest single component of gross domestic product. Further diversification was achieved from 1975 when, following substantial investment in banana plantations by Fyffes and acquisition of a European Economic Community preferential quota, banana exports at last once again achieved commercial quantities;[7] and, on a smaller scale, in 1977, with the widening of the remit of the Development Finance Corporation to facilitate the beginnings of a light industry sector.[8] Other new sources of foreign exchange earnings were tourism and marine products, principally lobster. There was a setback in the early 1980s when sugar prices fell sharply, leading to the closure of the Corozal mill in 1985.[9] Banana exports, which had reached 14,000 tons by 1980,[10] also slumped by 30 per cent just at the time that the estates were being sold to indigenous growers. Fortunately these disappointments, to which was then added a slump in rice production, were partly offset by strong growth at the same time in the tourism and citrus sectors. The number of tourists reached a new record of 62,000 in 1981,[11] and with, buoyant prices in the US market, citrus acreage had doubled from 30,000 to 60,000 towards the end of the decade.[12] Export earnings from the lobster fishery also continued to grow. Trade had been facilitated too by the move in 1980 of the Belize City port to a new site, with more modern cargo handling arrangements, on the outskirts of the town.

Because the sugar industry still loomed larger than anything else in the productive economy, the fall in its earnings precipitated a net increase in the long-standing imbalance in Belize's external trade. Debt service was only kept at a low level through greater resort to concessional finance from both bilateral donors (the UK, US and Canadian governments) and multilateral institutions (the IMF, World Bank and International Development Agency).[13] This in turn meant acceptance of a degree of 'structural adjustment' as a *quid pro quo*, in particular cuts in government spending, an end to subsidisation of grain farmers through the Central Marketing Board, and a programme of privatisation of utilities, which were bought largely by overseas interests.[14] These measures, together with a tightening of fiscal and monetary policy, stabilised the economy towards the end of the 1980s; that stabilisation was then underpinned by a firming of sugar prices and, with a continuation of technical assistance and marketing by Fyffes, a doubling of banana production from the 1981 level.[15]

The economy 1990–2002

In the 1990s, both the banana and, to a lesser extent, the citrus industries began to benefit from the completion of a new deep-water port in the south of the country, at Big Creek, in 1991; and a successful shrimp farming industry was also established in the southern half of the country. For the service sector, tourist numbers continued to grow as facilities were developed to cater for 'eco-tourism' in the interior, and, from the end of the decade, cruise ships. Meanwhile timber, in the form of sawn pine, continued to decline as an export commodity, occupying a lowly seventh place behind garments and papaya in 1999.

By 1990 the land area under banana cultivation had increased to 5000 acres and production to 33,000 tons.[16] The figure for acreage remained constant throughout the decade. By comparison with the West Indian islands, individual units were already large.[17] A doubling of yield per acre, achieved by disease control and better irrigation, then took production to a record of 74,000 tons by 1997. This was 19,000 tons more than the preferential quota allocated to Belize for the European Union (EU) market, and there was difficulty in selling the surplus. The following year a World Trade Organisation ruling brought changes to that quota regime, offered by the EU to a number of former British and French colonies under the Lome Convention.[18] Prolonged negotiations led to a reduced share for Belize of 40,000 tons,[19] though the buyer, Fyffes, is now able to add unused quota from elsewhere in the Caribbean.[20] With substantial hurricane damage in late 2001, 2002 exports hovered at 39,000 tons, still, despite reduced prices, accounting for 12 per cent of export earnings. The industry is now preparing for the challenge of the complete abolition of the EU quota in 2006, although former beneficiaries like Belize will continue to enjoy tariff-free access. One result is likely to be a changed relationship with Fyffes, hitherto also the sole shipper of Belize's bananas.

The fortunes of the citrus industry fell in the early 1990s, as cheaper suppliers elsewhere, particularly Brazil, expanded production and created a market over-supply. Losses mounted, and at the end of the decade the two processing companies (one locally owned and one foreign-owned), plus a substantial acreage, were bought by the Commonwealth Development Corporation (CDC), which embarked on a programme of rationalisation, rehabilitation and strengthened marketing.[21] Production grew to record levels in the four main products by 2000 and 2001, as trees planted earlier came to full maturity. But prices fell further in the second of those years, and a continuation of that trend began to affect production in 2002.[22] Partly because of a change of corporate strategy, partly because of continuing losses, CDC then disengaged from the industry, handing over the consolidated company's assets and debt to the Citrus Growers Association. Despite these difficulties, however, citrus accounted for 22 per cent of export earnings in 2002, remaining ahead of sugar having overtaken it in 2000. For although sugar production has maintained the levels re-established in the 1990s, earnings from the industry have fallen by over 20 per cent since the peak year of 1996.[23] The reason for this is that although the EU preferential quota remains secure and prices there firm, the US quota was cut in the late 1990s,[24] and the ever-volatile open market price fell in 2002.[25] In the meantime Tate and Lyle, who reduced their shareholding in the processing company to 10 per cent in an employee buy-out in 1985, have merged with another multinational, Booker McConnell to become Booker Tate. Discussion by Belize Sugar Industries, Booker Tate and Belize Electricity of the viability of a secondary product, bagass, as an energy source remains inconclusive.

Fortunately for Belize, the recent problems of the agricultural sector have been offset by two developments. First, a shrimp farming export industry was successfully launched in 1995, which with a tripling of production between 1997 and 1999,[26] rapidly overtook the lobster fishery in earnings. Second, and, more importantly, there has been a spectacular growth in tourism. Steady development from the early 1990s of inland tourist activity began to complement the consolidation of San Pedro as a beach resort. This resulted in the number of overnight tourists visiting the country reaching 200,000 by 2000, a threefold increase in twenty years. But the industry has recently been transformed much more quickly by a decision to allow cruise ships to land passengers in Belize. From a start in 1998 of 15,000 such day-visitors, the number has surged to no less than 300,000 in 2002 to add to those who came to stay in hotels and guest-houses.[27] For further diversification of the economy, the government has in the last few years stepped up Belize's effort to attract inward investment. A 100 per cent foreign ownership of businesses is allowed, and a range of tax exemptions is offered for new enterprises and for businesses in the Commercial Free Zone in the north (which employs about 6000 people) and the Export Processing Zones there and elsewhere.[28] There has been some success in attracting small and medium-scale light industrial investment, particularly from Taiwan, but not as yet enough to make a substantial difference to the performance of the economy.[29] Development of an offshore commercial registration sector, based on 1990 legislation and covering non-resident companies, banking, insurance, shipping and aircraft, has likewise proceeded slowly, with substantial growth only in the company register.[30]

Society

The picture for the economy as the twenty-first century unrolls is thus mixed, as it has always been. In the meantime the society has continued to grow, again as in the past but at a considerably faster rate. The last census showed that, with the steady flow over the last thirty years of refugees and economic migrants from neighbouring countries, the population had exactly doubled from 120,000 in 1970 to 240,000 in 2000, with an accelerating pattern of growth showing a net increase in the 1990s almost double that in the previous decade. Moreover a combination of creole emigration and mestizo immigration has led to a fundamental change in the ethnic structure of the country: for the 2000 census also shows that as the 1980 percentage of 40 per cent for the former had declined by 15 per cent, so the 1980 share of 33 per cent for the latter had *increased* by the same amount. As a result the creole population has shrunk from being the largest single community to only very slightly more than half the size of the mestizo population, and a quarter of the total. One result of this shift, reflecting heavy immigration, is that over a quarter of the population reported that they were not fluent in the official language, English, and another fifth that they did not speak it at all. The census also shows the continuation of a historic trend away from employment in agriculture and forestry, which now account for only a quarter of the employed population, down from 30 per cent in 1991; and of the consolidation of the dominant place of the Roman Catholic Church in the country's religious life.[31]

This strong population growth has been underpinned to an extent by infrastructure development funded by government, international development agencies, and, to a lesser degree, overseas investors. The southern and Hummingbird highways have been paved; Belmopan, after years of faltering growth, is developing fast; the port is undergoing further modernisation; the telephone network, and, with the successful launch of a major hydro-electric scheme, the electricity grid, have been expanded; Belize City has a badly needed new hospital; there have been a number of major housing schemes; and the capacity of the education system at all levels has been enlarged to cater for the greatly increased number of the country's children.

The future

The future for them certainly holds challenges. The population continues to grow rapidly and relentlessly. The pernicious effects of drug trafficking and consumption have begun to make themselves felt. External debt, as a percentage of Gross Domestic Product, has increased by more than half in the last five years despite the sale of further government assets including the port; and, despite the achievement at last of self-sufficiency in beef, pork, chicken, rice and corn, the trade deficit has doubled over the same period.[32] This has caused the IMF to warn, while applauding the government's plans for corrective measures, that unless those measures are strictly adhered to, the high debt and trade deficit levels, and the low level of reserves, together pose a serious threat to the overall balance of payments.[33] Moreover, of the three more important established export industries, the competitiveness of Belizean sugar remains hobbled by the lack of alongside loading facilities for bulk-carrier ships; the future of citrus can only be secured with greater value addition, which also calls for substantial investment; and it remains to be seen whether the banana growers can, as they hope, make their way without the EU preferential quota. The compensation for these problems offered by mass tourism will need careful management.

But as the brief survey in this book has attempted to show, there has always been something precarious about Belize. It has survived so many ups and downs in the last three hundred years that it is generally assumed that it will continue to do so in the future. The pride that Belizeans, both at home and overseas, take in their country, the political stability (and the functioning democracy) it has maintained since fully representative government was established forty years ago, and the social stability of a genuinely multi-racial society, should all help ensure that such an assumption is well based.

Notes

1. C. H. Grant, *The Making of Modern Belize*, Cambridge (1976), 269–71.
2. ibid., 275.
3. Assad Shoman, *Thirteen Chapters of the History of Belize*, Belize (1994), 184. The UDP won 21 out of 28 seats in the House of Representatives, and 53 per cent of the vote on a 75 per cent turnout.
4. Grant, 271–4 and Shoman, 205–8.
5. FCO Background Brief, Belize and the Dispute with Guatemala, February 1983, 5.
6. Belize Sugar Industries Ltd., *A Brief History of Sugar in Belize*, Belize (1989).
7. Letter dated 20 January 2003 from Paul Barrett, Brand Manager, Fyffes.
8. FCO Background Brief, Belize and the Dispute with Guatemala, February 1983, 5.

9. Belize Sugar Industries op. cit.
10. Barrett letter op. cit..
11. FCO Background Brief, Belize and the Dispute with Guatemala, February 1983, 5.
12. Interview with the Chief Executive of Citrus Products of Belize, 12 February 2003.
13. FCO Background Brief, Belize and the Dispute with Guatemala, February 1983, 6.
14. Shoman, 242–3.
15. Barrett letter op. cit.
16. Belize Ministry of Finance, Preliminary Analysis of the Impact of the 1998 WTO Ruling on the Banana Industry of Belize; and Letter dated 26 February 2003 from Paul Barrett, Brand Manager, Fyffes.
17. By 2003 the industry had been consolidated into 21 farms owned by only 9 growers – interview with Chief Executive, Banana Growers' Association, 4 March 2003.
18. Central Bank of Belize, Annual Report for 1999, 34; and Ministry of Finance in Impact of the WTO Ruling.
19. Central Bank of Belize, Annual Report for 2001, 44.
20. Interview with Chief Executive, Banana Growers' Association, op. cit.
21. Central Bank of Belize, Annual Report for 1999, 10.
22. Table of major economic indicators attached to the Prime Minister's budget speech of 17 January 2003.
23. ibid.
24. Central Bank of Belize, Annual Report for 2000, 35.
25. Belize Sugar Industries Ltd., 2002 Annual Report, 4.
26. Central Bank of Belize, Annual Report for 1999, 12.
27. Table of major economic indicators, op. cit.
28. See Belize Trade and Investment Development Service, Investment Guide 2000.
29. See IMF Staff Report for the 2002 Article 4 Consultation, Table 6.
30. Interview with Director, Belize Financial Intelligence Unit, 6 March 2003.
31. Belize Central Statistical Office, Population Census 2000.
32. Table of Economic Indicators op. cit. If government guaranteed, as opposed to public sector incurred, debt is included, the 2002 figure of 58 per cent becomes 80 per cent – see IMF Staff Report op. cit., Table 8.
33. IMF Staff Report op. cit., executive summary and para. 39.

Index

Abolition Act (1833), 61
Agriculture, 72–3, 139–40, 146, 148
See also Banana industry; Citrus
    industry;
  Sugar industry
Altun Ha, 5
American War of Independence
  (1776–83), 25–7
Anglican church, 46–7
Anglo-Guatemalan Convention
  (1859), 71, 83
Apprenticeship, slaves, 61–2
Armstrong, Reverend, 60
Army *See* Belize Light Infantry
    Volunteer Corps;
  British Honduras Defence Force;
  Territorial Force
Arthur, Lieutenant Colonel
    George, 40–41, 43–4, 45, 49,
    59, 60, 67–8, 75, 76, 77, 78
Astronomy, Maya, 7
Austin, Lieutenant Governor John,
  85

Bacalar, 12
Banana industry, 111, 113, 127, 130,
  133, 144, 181, 182, 184
Bank, 114
Barrow, Colonel Thomas, 32, 41,
  49–50
Bassett, Brigadier, 41
Battle of St George's Cay *See*
  St George's
  Cay, Battle of
Bay Islands, 100

Bay of Honduras settlement, 22, 23,
  24–5, 26, 27–8, 32, 99–100
Belize, origin of name, 15
Belize Billboard, 158
Belize City Port, 181, 184
Belize Estate and Produce
  Company (BEC), 109, 112
Belize Light Infantry Volunteer
  Corps, 120
See also Territorial Force
Belize–Peten railway project, 122
Belize River settlement *See* Bay of
  Honduras settlement
Belize Town, 37 *See also* Bay of
  Honduras settlement
Belize Town Board, 153
Belmopan, 148, 184
Betson, Clifford, 157
Black Caribs *See* Garifuna
Black nationalism, 135
Black River, 23
Blackbeard (pirate), 18
'Blacks' *See* 'Free Coloureds and
  Blacks'
Blood, Sir Hilary, 162
Bonacca *See* Bay Islands
Border disputes *See* Guatemala,
  relations with;
  Mexico, relations with
British Honduras Company
  See Belize Estate
  and Produce Company
British Honduras Defence Force, 135
British Honduras Police, 120 *See
  also* Constabulary

British Honduras Workers' and
    Tradesmen's Union, 154–5
British settlement, 13–19
    Spanish threat to, 21–31
British sovereignty, 88–96, 124
British West Indies Regiment, 129
'Burnaby's Code', 24–5, 30
Business investment, 183

Caracol, 4
Caribs *See* Garifuna
Caste War (1847–55), 90–91
CDC *See* Colonial Development
    Corporation (CDC);
        Commonwealth
    Development Corporation
        (CDC)
Censuses, 37, 183–4
Cerros, 4
Chichuanha Indians *See* Icaiche
    Indians
Chicle industry, 127, 132, 142
Citrus industry, 133, 142, 149, 181,
    182, 184
City states, Maya, 5, 7
Clayton–Bulwer Treaty (1850), 100,
    104
Climate, xi *See also* Hurricanes
Cockburn, Lieutenant Colonel
    Francis, 69, 76, 77–9
Coffee, 112, 123
Colonial Development Act (1929),
    132
Colonial Development and Welfare
    Fund, 135–6, 139, 140
Colonial Development
    Corporation (CDC), 142–4
Colonial Secretaries *See* Newton, F.J.
Colonial status, 83–5
Columbus, Christopher, 10
Commonwealth Development
    Corporation (CDC), 182
Constabulary, 92 *See also* British
    Honduras
    Police

Constitution, 75–85, 117–19, 156,
    159–60
Convention of London (1786), 27
Corozal sugar mill, 142–4, 149, 181
Cortes, Hernan, 11
Courtenay, W.H., 159
Courts, 43, 75– 7, 117
Creoles, 183–4
Crown land, 111 *See also* Land
    tenure
Cultural identity, xi, 1

Dairy industry, 144
Dallas–Clarendon Treaty (1856),
    100
Dampier, William, 16
Democracy, 29–30, 153–64
Despard, Captain Edward Marcus,
    28, 29–31, 66
Devaluation, 157
Development plans, post-World
    War II, 145–9
District Commissioners, 119
Downie, Jack, 146
Dyes, 18

Economy
    nineteenth century, 108–15,
        121–5,
    early twentieth century, 127–8
    World War 1, 129
    post-World War 1, 130–34
    World War 11, 134–6
    post-World War 11, 139–50,
        156–7, 179, 180–83
Education, 46, 120, 184
Elections, 158–9, 179–80
Emancipation, slaves, 61–2
Emigrants, 109–10, 111–12
Employment
    early nineteenth century, 38–9
    post-World War I, 130, 136
    See also Apprenticeship, slaves
English settlement *See* British
    settlement

Evans, Sir Geoffrey, 140
Executive Council, 80–81, 118, 159–60, 162
Exports *See* Trade

Facilitators, Guatemalan dispute, 175–6
Fancourt, Colonel Charles, 70, 81
Finances *See* Public finances
First World War *See* World War I
Fisheries, 181, 183
Food production, 148–9 *See also* Agriculture;
  Banana industry; Citrus industry; Fisheries
Foodstuffs, imports, 145
Foreign relations, 180 *See also* Guatemala,
  relations with; Mexico, relations with
Forestry, 130, 146, 148
Franchise, 153 *See also* Elections
'Free Coloureds and Blacks,' 45–6
French Revolutionary War (1792–1802), 32–3, 48–50
Fuller, Herbert, 159
Fyffes bananas, 123, 181, 182

Garifuna, 46
General Workers' Union, 156, 157
Geographical position, xi
Goldson, Philip, 158, 161, 179
Goldsworthy, Sir Roger, 117
Gomez, Antonio Soberanis *See* Soberanis
  Gomez, Antonio
Government, 27–33, 40–42, 134, 163–4, 180
  See also Self-government;
  Maya, 5
Governors, 159–60, 164, 180
  Goldsworthy, Sir Roger, 117
  Moloney, Sir Alfred, 113–14, 118
  Wilson, Sir David, 113, 114, 118
Grand Court, 76

Grapefruit *See* Citrus industry
Guatemala, relations with, 98–106, 161, 162–3, 165–76

Harbour, 114, 115
Health *See* Public health
Honduras Independence Party, 161
Honduras Land Titles Act (1858), 71
Hospitals, 120–21, 184
Hunter, Colonel Peter, 31–2
Hurricanes, 131–2, 147–8

Icaiche Indians, 91–2, 93
Immigration, 90, 183–4
Imports *See* Trade
Independence *See* Self-government
Indians
  Icaiche (Chichuanha), 91–2, 93
  Mosquito, 59, 100
  Santa Cruz, 90, 91–2, 94–5, 124
Industries
  bananas, 111, 113, 127, 130, 133, 144, 181, 182, 184
  chicle, 127, 132, 142
  citrus, 133, 142, 149, 181, 182, 184
  logwood, 15–18, 21, 22, 23, 24, 26, 47–8, 108–9, 110, 121
  mahogany, 19, 26, 27, 47–8, 66, 71, 108, 110, 113, 121, 123, 127, 129–30, 141, 180
  sugar, 109–13, 133, 140, 142–4, 149–50, 180–81, 182–3, 184
Infrastructure, 113–15, 132, 139, 140–41, 145, 184 *See also* Railways; Roads
Investment, twentieth century, 183

Jamaica, relations with, 117
Jewish refugees, 134
Judicial system, 75–7 *See also* Magistrates

Labour movement, 153–5
Labourers' and Unemployed Association (LUA), 154

Lamanai, 4–5
Land tenure, 62–3, 65–73
Law and order See British
    Honduras Police;
    'Burnaby's Code'; Constabulary
Laws in Force Act (1855), 71
Legislation See Location system,
    land tenure;
    Public Meetings
Legislative Assembly, 82–3, 85,
    159–60, 162
Legislative Council, 117, 118, 121,
    155–6, 159
Legislative Meetings See Public
    Meetings
Legislature See National Assembly
Lindo, Dean, 179
Local government, 119
Location system, land tenure, 65–7
Logwood trade, 15–18, 21, 22, 23,
    24, 26, 47–8, 108–9, 110, 121
See also Mahogany trade; Pine
    industry
Longden, James, 85
LUA See Labourers' and
    Unemployed
    Association (LUA)
Lubaantun, 4
Lumber industry See Timber trade

McDonald, Colonel Alexander, 69,
    70, 79–80
Magistrates, 42–5, 62, 78–9
Mahogany trade, 19, 26, 27, 47–8,
    66, 71,108, 110, 113, 121, 123,
    127, 129–30, 141, 180
Maya, 1–9, 11–12
Mennonites, 144
Mestizos, 183–4
Mexico, relations with, 88–96, 124
Militia See British Honduras
    Defence Force
Moloney, Sir Alfred, 113–14
Montejo, Francisco de, 11–13
Mosquito Indians, 59, 100

Musa, Said, 173, 180
Mutual Defence Scheme, 168

Napoleonic War (1804–15), 48–50
National Assembly, 163
National characteristics, xiii
National Independence Party
    (NIP), 161, 162–3, 164, 179
National Party (NP), 159
Nationalism See Black nationalism
Newspapers See Press
Newton, F.J., 119
NIP See National Independence
    Party (NIP)
Non-conformists, 47

Open Forum, 156
Oranges See Citrus industry
Organisation of American States
    (OAS), 175
Organisation of Central American
    States (ODECA), 161

People's Committee, 157–8
People's Democratic Movement
    (PDM), 179
People's United Party (PUP),
    158–61, 162–3, 174, 179
Pine industry, 141, 182
Pirates See Blackbeard (pirate)
Planning See Development plans,
    post-World War II
Police See British Honduras Police
Political parties
    Honduras Independence Party,
        161
    National Independence Party
        (NIP), 161, 162–3, 168, 179
    National Party (NP), 159
    People's Action Committee See
        Revolitical (Revolutionary)
        Action Movement (RAM)
    People's Committee, 157–8
    People's Democratic Movement
        (PDM), 179

People's United Party (PUP), 158–60, 161, 162–3, 168, 174, 179
  Revolitical (Revolutionary) Action Movement (RAM), 161, 179, 180
  United Democratic Party (UDP), 174, 179–80
Pollard, Nicholas, 157
Population
  Maya, 4, 8
  slaves, 53–44
  eighteenth century, 18, 24, 27, 29
  nineteenth century, 37–8, 90, 109
  twentieth century, 118, 183
  early twenty-first century, xii–xiii, 184
Port *See* Belize City Port
Pottery, Maya, 7
Premiers, 164
Press, 180
Price, George, 157, 158, 161, 164, 168, 170–71
Public finances, 155–6
Public health, 120–21
Public Meetings, 41–2, 65–6, 77–81
PUP *See* People's United Party (PUP)
Pyramids, Maya, 4–5

Railways, 105–6, 114, 122
RAM *See* Revolitical (Revolutionary) Action Movement (RAM)
Ramphal, Sir Sridath (Sonny), 175–6
Refugees, 134, 183
Reichler, Paul, 175–6
Religion, 46–7
Revolitical (Revolutionary) Action Movement (RAM), 161, 179, 180
Roads, 101–3, 119, 132, 140–41, 184
Roman Catholicism, 47
Ruatan *See* Bay Islands

St George's Cay, Battle of, 32–3

Santa Cruz Indians, 90, 91–2, 94–5, 124
Sculpture, Maya, 5
Second World War *See* World War II
Self-government, 162–4, 168, 169–71, 180
Seven Years War (1756–63), 23
Slaves and slavery, 21, 37, 38, 45, 53–63
  abolition, 61–3
  legal position, 58–60
  manumission, 60–61
  revolts, 57–8
  treatment, 55–7
Soberanis Gomez, Antonio, 154, 156
Social structure, early nineteenth century, 37–9
Softwood trade *See* Logwood trade
Sovereignty *See* British sovereignty; Self-government
Spanish
  rivalry with English (later British), 21–7, 28, 32–3, 89
  settlement, 10–13
Strikes *See* Labourers' and Unemployed Association (LUA)
Sugar industry, 109–13, 130, 133, 140, 142–4, 149–50, 180, 182–3, 184
Superintendents, 27–33, 40–42, 44, 68–9, 70–71, 77
Supreme Court, 43, 75, 76, 117

Tate and Lyle sugar, 149–50, 183
Teach, William *See* Blackbeard (pirate)
Telegraph, 114
Temples, Maya *See* Pyramids, Maya
Territorial disputes *See* Guatemala, relations with; Mexico, relations with
Territorial Force, 128–9

Timber trade, 130, 141, 180 *See also*
  Logwood trade; Mahogany trade;
  Pine industry
Toltecs, 8
Topography, xi–xii
Tourism, 181, 182, 183
Trade, 15, 48–9, 122–4, 135, 144–5
  bananas, 111–3, 123, 127, 130,
    133, 181, 184
  chicle, 132, 142
  citrus, 133, 142, 181, 182, 184
  logwood, 15–18, 21, 22, 23, 24,
    26, 47–8, 108–9, 110, 121
  sugar, 109, 133, 180, 184
  timber, 130, 141–2, 144–5, 180
  World War I, impact of, 128–9
Trade unions *See* British Honduras
  Workers' and Tradesmen's
  Union;
  Labourers' and Unemployed
    Association (LUA)
Transport *See* Railways; Roads
Turton, R.S., 157

Unemployment *See* Labourers' and
  Unemployed Association
  (LUA)
United Black Association for
  Development (UBAD) *See*
  Revolitical (Revolutionary)
  Action Movement (RAM)

United Democratic Party (UDP), 174

Volunteers *See* Belize Light
  Infantry Volunteer Corps;
  Territorial Force

Wars
  War of Spanish Succession
    (1701–13), 21–2
  War of Austrian Succession
    (1740–48), 22
  Seven Years War (1756–63), 23
  American War of Independence
    (1776–83), 25–7
  French Revolutionary War
    (1792–1802), 32–3, 48–50
  Napoleonic War (1804–15),
    48–50
  Caste War (1847–55), 90–91
  World War I, 128–9
  World War II, 134–6
Webster, Bethuel, 167
White, Robert, 26–8, 44
Wilson, Sir David, 113, 114, 118,
  121–2
Wireless transmission station, 128
Wodehouse, Philip, 82
World War I, 128–9
World War II, 134–6

Xunantunich, 4